Stories of God in My Life

A Memoir of Missionary Work
from Bangladesh to Zambia

Copyright © 2015, 2021 by Marjorie Bennett

All rights reserved. This book or any portion thereof may not be reproduced or used in any manner whatsoever without the express written permission of the publisher except for the use of brief quotations in a book review.

"Stories of God in My Life" Printed in the United States

Cover and book design by Meghan McDonald

Photo of Marj Bennett taken by Luke Reynolds

ISBN: 978-1-952714-15-3

Additional copies can be ordered through www.amazon.com

Mountain Page Press
www.MountainPagePress.com

Dedication

Troy Bennett

This book is dedicated to Troy C. Bennett,
my husband and friend
who understood me better than anyone else,
who shared my hopes and dreams
for each person we met,
and loved the places we have lived.
Long before I knew my need of him, God
knew I needed him to share the love,
laughter, and adventures he gave to us.
Together we will sing the songs of Zion!
"Not to us, O Lord, not to us,
But to thy name be the glory
For thy great love and faithfulness."

Table of Contents

Acknowledgments vii
Dates and Places xi
A Note to Readers xix
Early Life in Ohio 1
The Bonus Marches of the 1930s 11
Early Life in Virginia 15
Meredith College 53
Marriage 65
Troy's Story 71
Seminary — Fayetteville/Wake Forest 85
On the *President Cleveland* 97
First Term 105
Memories of Steve's Childhood 137
First Furlough 141
On the *Hellenic Sailor* 149
Second Term 159
Bengali Weddings 173
Second Furlough 181
Third Term – Faridpur/Comilla 189
Memories of Christmas in Bangladesh 205
Third Furlough 211
Fourth Term – the War 217

Fourth Term – After the War	227
Fourth Term – Beirut and Saudi Arabia	237
Fourth Furlough	245
Fifth Term – Magura	251
Fifth Term – Zambia	265
Fifth Furlough	279
Were You Ever Afraid?	283
Leave of Absence – Kinston, NC	289
Sixth Term – Tanzania	297
Sixth Furlough – (3 Months)	305
Seventh Term – Tanzania	311
Seventh Term – South Africa	315
Barefoot in Central Park	327
Seventh Furlough	331
Retirement	339
Her Name is Tad	357
Conclusion	361
Mother's Story	365
Daddy's Story	383
Nancy's Story	389
Lou's Memories	397
Assorted Treasures	403

Acknowledgments

"...there now flows a constant stream of tenderness, a stream in which all petty desires seem to have been extinguished. All that matters now is to be kind to each other with all the goodness that is in us."

– by Madeline L'Engle, Walking on Water, as quoted by Joyce Rupp in *The Cup of Our Life*

Now I need to express thanks to the many who have encouraged me to write this book. I'm not sure this is what you had in mind, but it is what came out of mine. Unfortunately, or maybe fortunately, I didn't keep a diary so I don't have that to jog my memory. But I have saved lots of stuff and, of course, I have the pictures and slides which remind me of many experiences along the way. The children and I have stirred each other's memories to remember things we had forgotten. As I have written, everybody will not agree with me on all of these incidents, but this is my version. I have told them that their stories belong in their books when they write them. The older grandchildren may say or think, "That's not the way I heard it...from her." Well, that's the way memory works.

But I must say that I could not have gotten it done by myself. There is no way I could name all the people who have contributed to this story of God working in my life and that makes me sad. I would be sadder if I didn't know that they know and God knows who they are and how precious to me they are. Just in the past few years Sue Chapman has become an invaluable help and friend for which I can only praise God. Becky lives one hour's drive from me which is much closer than the other two, and thankfully she has been able to give some time by setting some of her own interests aside. She has read and re-read, corrected and shifted around, and still has kept it in my voice. Jesse Perry, her husband, has been great in encouraging her in her part of the work. Debbie is farther away, but has been such a big help when I try to remember the last years when she was still at home. Debbie has an incredible memory for the details. Then Steve who comes quite often and reads the things I ask him to and gives good feedback. Some interesting little tidbits that I never knew about, he added for a fresh touch. He also keeps my car going and my finances in order. This is valuable assistance.

And then there is Sam Uhl, my editor, the real thing! We showed her the narrative and piles of pictures and she assured us that this could come together as a book worth publishing. And now she has worked with us to do just that. What more could I ask? As her editing business calls itself The Cheerful Word, she personifies it, and I like that!

There are many others, friends and relatives; you will see as you read. I have approached this task as a gift to those who come after me and anyone else who may want to read it. Therefore I have not found it necessary to tell everything. I want them to enjoy or at least be interested in these stories. I have had an incredibly happy, often funny, sometimes sad, always interesting life. I am grateful to God for letting me be one of his messengers of good will. I have loved the people of Bangladesh, the Middle East, and Africa and this has opened my heart to love all men, women, and children by God's grace. I am the richest woman I know in the things that matter.

Dates and Places

Early Life – Ohio (1928 – 1936)
- Marjorie Ann Trippeer was born, Chagrin Falls, Ohio, August 8, 1928
- Move to Willoughby, Ohio, 1930
- Move to Roanoke, VA; Bill & Margie went to Memphis, summer 1936
- Visit to Memphis with Mary Jean, 1938

Early Life – Virginia (1936 – 1947)
- Graduated from Jefferson Senior High School, Roanoke, VA, 1946
- Started college at Roanoke College, Salem, VA, fall 1946

Meredith College (1947 – 1951)
- Transferred to Meredith College, Raleigh, NC, fall 1947
- Graduated from Meredith College, 1950
- Move to Bluefield, WV, 1950 -51

Marriage (1951 – 52)
- Troy & Marjorie married, Roanoke, VA, September 1, 1951
- Move to upstairs 407 14th Street with Mama & Papa Bennett, Winston-Salem, NC, 1951-52

Seminary (1952 – 1956)
- Troy in Southeastern Seminary, 1952 - 56
- Move to Wake Forest, NC, upstairs apartment, 1952

- Move to Fayetteville, NC, Immanuel Baptist Church–lived over Langfords', 1952
- Move to McKimmon Drive, Fayetteville, NC
- Move to parsonage on Camellia Drive, Fayetteville, NC
- Move back to Wake Forest, NC, on Pine Street, 1955
- Steve Bennett born, Fayetteville, NC, December 14, 1952
- Granddaddy Trippeer died, Harrisonburg, VA, January 1, 1955
- Becky Bennett born, Fayetteville, NC, February 25, 1955
- Appointment by Foreign Mission Board, Southern Baptist Convention, Richmond, VA, June 1956

On the *President Cleveland* (1956)
- Left USA on *President Cleveland* from San Francisco, CA, mid-December 1956
- Spent 1 month in Hong Kong, visited Bangkok, Thailand, and Rangoon, Burma

First Term (1957 – 1960)
- Arrived Dacca, East Pakistan, then lived in Faridpur, big house, February 1957
- Move to Dacca, East Pakistan, Elephant Road house, fall 1957
- Vacation with Barefoots in Darjeeling, India, 1958
- Debbie Bennett born, Dacca, East Pakistan, August 20, 1958
- Move to Road 4, big house, Dacca, East Pakistan
- Vacation in Mussoorie, India, August 1959

First Furlough (1960 - 61)
- Move to Wake Forest, NC; traveled through Hong Kong, Seattle, WA and Chicago, IL; summer 1960

On the *Hellenic Sailor* (1961)
- Travel on the *Hellenic Sailor* from New Orleans, LA through Crete, Greece; the Suez Canal; Bombay, India; Cochin, India; Rangoon, Burma; to Chittagong, East Pakistan

Second Term (1961 – 65)
- Move back to Dacca, East Pakistan, Road 24 house; summer 1961
- Move to Comilla, East Pakistan, big house, summer 1962
- Vacation with Pecks in Shillong, India, 1963
- Vacation with Pecks in Mussoorie, India, 1964
- Steve lived with Johnsons for seventh grade, Dacca, East Pakistan, 1964-65

Second Furlough (1965 - 66)
- Move to Winston-Salem, NC; traveled through Calcutta, India; Beirut, Lebanon; Athens, Greece; Rome, Italy; New York, NY for World's Fair, and Miami, FL for Baptist World Alliance, summer 1965

Third Term (1966 – 70)
- Move to Faridpur, East Pakistan, little house, summer 1966
- Steve to Bangkok, Thailand for high school, summer 1966

- Papa Bennett died, June 1967
- Vacation in Nepal, fall 1967
- Grandma Trippeer died, May 1968
- Vacation in Pattaya, Thailand, summer 1968
- Move to Comilla, East Pakistan, little house - then big house, summer 1969
- Becky & Steve left for high school in Bangkok, Thailand, August 1969
- Steve graduated Bangkok, Thailand, June 1970

Third Furlough (1970 – 71)
- Move to Kings Mountain, NC; traveled through Karachi, Pakistan; Zurich, Switzerland; Copenhagen, Denmark; Frankfurt, Germany; summer 1970
- Trippeer family reunion, Callaway Gardens, GA
- Steve started at Mars Hill College, Mars Hill, NC

Fourth Term (1971 – 75)
- Move to Dacca, East Pakistan, Road 4 house; traveled through Los Angeles, CA; Tokyo, Japan; Hong Kong; Bangkok, Thailand; summer 1971
- Becky returned to Bangkok, Thailand, August 1971
- The War, then Bangladesh independence December 3-16, 1971
- Becky in Vietnam for Christmas 1971
- Steve & Becky home for summer 1972
- Vacation in India: Mussoorie, New Delhi, Agra and the Taj Mahal
- Debbie & Becky to Bangkok, Thailand; Steve returned to college in US, Joi and Areb
- Becky graduated high school June 1973

- Vacation in Bangkok, Thailand; Penang, Malaysia; Chiang Mai, Thailand
- Debbie returned to Bangkok, Thailand; Becky started at Meredith College, Raleigh, NC
- Grandma Bennett died, Winston-Salem, NC, November 1973
- Move to Beirut, Lebanon for work in Saudi Arabia; Becky home for summer
- Vacation in Kashmir, India and travel through Tehran, Iran on the way
- Steve graduated from Mars Hill and met us in Beirut, Lebanon and stayed 2-3 months, summer 1974
- Becky returned to college in US, August 1974

Fourth Furlough (1975 -76)
- Move to Kings Mountain, NC; traveled through Jordan, England, island of Jersey, Scotland, and Cape Cod, MA
- Debbie graduated high school, Kings Mountain, NC, June 1976
- Becky took semester off to live in Kings Mountain, NC with us, spring 1976
- Steve in Korea with Peace Corps, 1975-78

Fifth Term (1976 – 79)
- Move to Magura, Bangladesh; traveled through Korea to see Steve, summer 1976
- Debbie started college at Wake Forest University, Winston-Salem, NC
- Debbie home in Magura, Bangladesh; traveled through Korea to see Steve, summer 1977

- Short trip to Raleigh, NC for Christmas, November-December 1977
- Left Bangladesh and moved to Lusaka, Zambia; traveled through Bangalore, India to see Pecks, February 1978
- Becky graduated from Meredith College, Raleigh, NC, May 1978
- Steve returned to NC from Korea

Fifth Furlough (1979 – 80)
- Move to Buies Creek, NC
- Debbie graduated from Wake Forest University, Winston-Salem, NC, May 1980

Leave of Absence (1980 – 84)
- Move to Kinston, NC, 1980
- Debbie in graduate school at Southern Seminary, Louisville, KY, 1982-84
- Steve in graduate school at UNC-Chapel Hill, NC, 1982- 1984
- Becky & Jesse married, Raleigh, NC, September 24, 1983

Sixth Term (1984 – 86)
- Move to Nairobi, Kenya for 6 months language study, April 1984
- Steve graduated from UNC- Chapel Hill, NC, May 1984
- Move to Dar es Salaam, Tanzania October 1984
- Debbie & Bill visited, June & July 1984
- Sue LeQuesne visited, 1984

- Debbie finished seminary, December 1984
- Debbie & Bill married, Raleigh, NC, January 4, 1986
- Meg Perry born, Raleigh, NC, February 13, 1986
- Steve & Susan married, Marion, NC, May 6, 1986

Sixth Furlough (December 1986 – February 1987)
- Move to Wake Forest, NC; visited Steve & Susan in Panama

Seventh Term (1987 – 1990)
- Move back to Dar es Salaam, Tanzania
- Brenda Ipock & Doris Powers visited; Becky, Jesse & Meg visited; Steve & Susan also visited then on their way to Bangladesh, September 1988
- Move to Ciskei, South Africa, November 1988
- Katie Perry born, Raleigh, NC, November 19, 1989

Seventh Furlough (1990 – 91)
- Move to Raleigh, Hayes Barton house; traveled through Bangladesh to see Steve & Susan & old friends, also Japan and US
- Steve & Susan move to Arlington, VA; summer 1990
- Debbie & Bill move to Atlanta, GA, September 1990

Retirement (1991- 2015)
- Move to Winston–Salem, NC, Edenwood Drive house
  Sarah Perry born, Raleigh, NC, April 14, 1994
- Anna Reynolds born, Santa Barbara, CA, November 27, 1994
- Steve & Susan separated, 1996

- Luke Reynolds born, Atlanta, GA, May 4, 1997
- Trip to Europe and Turkey
- Steve & Amelia married, Washington, D.C., October 9, 1999
- Move to Twin Lakes Community, Burlington, NC, May 2003
- Reynolds move to Rochester, NY, 2004
- Troy died Raleigh, NC, February 2, 2007
- My 80th birthday, Black Mountain, NC August 8, 2008
- Book release, Burlington, NC, summer 2015

A Note to Readers

*"Even when I am old and gray, do not forsake me,
O Lord,
Till I declare your power to the next generation.
Your might to all who are to come."*

- Psalm 71:18

I want to write my life story with one theme - how God has used different people, places, and experiences to form me, and hopefully, in some small way accomplish his purpose.

So many friends have encouraged me to write this book but I just couldn't seem to get started, until one day I thought to myself, "I'll just write as if I am talking with the grandchildren." And that set me free, and I started to write and write and write. I have had so much fun writing these memories; mostly happy, funny and interesting experiences we have had through the years. This is not an attempt to tell the history of our mission work. It is more my life story and the ways God has brought such incredible people into my life. I just want to share them with you. Some of them are really good to read to younger children but many must be saved until they are older.

Some people are so gifted in expressing powerful thoughts in just a few words. Troy used to say about some of our favorite hymns that some people can put into words what we are feeling in our hearts, and we can be very thankful for them. In this book you can see, I am not one of them. It has taken me many, many words to have my say, but I hope you will enjoy these adventures with me and my family.

Because we did do mission work in several different places and saw even more interesting people and sights in our travels to these places, I have chosen to divide this book into chapters, according to terms on the field and furloughs, from 1956 to 1990, our time with the Foreign Mission Board. I have also included my early years before going to East Pakistan, some interesting information about my family's background and Troy's, and something about our retirement years. If it seems too long to you, remember I am 86 years old now. That's a lot of years to remember. But I have been blessed more than I can say with joy and peace and thankfulness, as I have written. I hope you will experience some of this same joy and thankfulness as you read and see the pictures.

I have also learned to write down at least three things I am thankful for each night before I go to sleep. This has been such a blessing for me and seems to keep me thankful all of the time. You might want to try it!

Now for those stories I promised you...

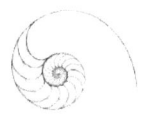

Early Life in Ohio

For me it all began in Chagrin Falls, Ohio. I was born Marjorie Ann Trippeer, on August 8, 1928; the fifth child, the second girl. I remember little of those years, but of course, am aware that five more children were born, making ten.

Let me introduce you properly to my family: First is Daddy, Benjamin Mowbray Trippeer and Mother, Leona Mary Edwards Trippeer. And the children: Benjamin Edward (Ben), born in October 1923; Mary Jean, born in November 1924; Allen Robert (Bob) born in September 1926; William Mowbray (Bill) born in August 1927; then ME (fireworks please!), born in August 1928; the twins, Donald Richard (Don) and Marian Irene, born in June 1930; Carl Arthur born in August 1931; James Herman (Jim) born in January 1933; and last, Nancy Lynn,

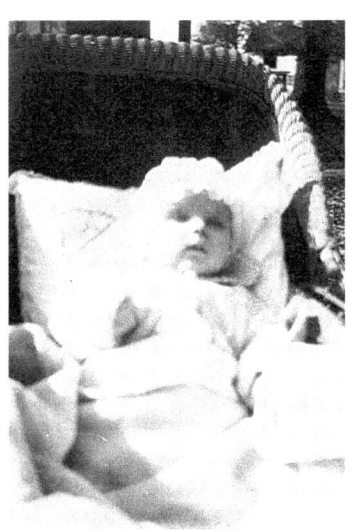

Marjorie at three months
Chagrin Falls, OH, 1928

1

Ben & Leona Trippeer with baby Ben
Chagrin Falls, OH, 1924

born in January 1934. Now that's the way to have a family so they can all grow up together! Later Mother advised us not to do it that way or to have that many children!

My father was a traveling salesman for Euclid Road Machinery Company, who was gone from home a lot. As I see it now, my mother was just what a mother of ten should be; very settled, almost always calm, and physically and emotionally strong. She did have a temper which we saw on occasion, but considering what she had to deal with, we didn't experience it that often.

Daddy was lots of fun, and whenever he was home, things were more upbeat. We did things like having picnics in the backyard, singing around the piano with him pounding out old Vaudeville tunes, playing cards, and talking around the table after dinner. I don't know that any of us children realized it at the time, but later, I became very aware that he missed out on the discipline and punishment side of parenting. Mother was not one to "wait till your Dad comes home!" as Edgar Guest says in one of his poems that we enjoyed.

I think tonight I'll tell you some things about my

family. There are lots of things to tell of course, but I'll try to think of some of the best stories. Let's see, you know that we were ten, six boys and four girls, and I was right smack dab in the middle. You can divide ten in half and have one in the middle when you have a set of twins, which we did. The younger ones that I can remember were born either next door at a neighbor's or at a midwife's house. No hospital costs at least, and that was good because our family did not have a lot of money. I'm not sure why, but when I was two years old, we moved to Willoughby, Ohio which is a small town on Lake Erie, very close to Cleveland.

One of my most vivid memories of those years was when Nancy had pneumonia. She was just a few months old and Daddy was not at home. Ben was the oldest at about twelve, and he had to carry a lot of the responsibility, and Mary Jean too. I think a lady came in to help some. There were no antibiotics then and all that Mother could do was sit by her side with a bottle of camphor to keep her breathing. She was sick for two weeks and we were really worried about her, but she was spared. Afterward, she was very small for a long time and never did get as tall as the rest of us, which isn't very tall. But she developed into a fine athlete and was really strong.

The twins were babies when we moved to Willoughby. I don't remember anything about living in Chagrin Falls. As a traveling salesman, Daddy was gone for two to three months at a time working as far south as Virginia. Willoughby was a nice little town right on Lake Erie. I do remember a company picnic, probably July

4th, at the beach. There was a huge crowd and most mothers would have panicked to have their ten children running helter-skelter in the crowd. Mother didn't panic, but when we got ready to go home, one of us was missing. Who was it? Not me. Maybe one of the boys.

Anyway, we had to wait and wait until almost dark before we could go home, tired, sunburned, and sticky with sand. Not a good ending of an otherwise lovely day. I don't think Daddy was there for that event. We could walk everywhere in town; it was that small. Once, the five big kids went to see the movie, *Alice in Wonderland*. When we came out, it was dark and I was terrified! That movie was much too realistic for me at six or seven years old. Oh, I also remember going to the air show in Cleveland. It was amazing! Those little two-seater planes flying upside down and sideways; stuntmen standing on the wings as they flew past. Really exciting, and you do realize that any kind of airplane was a marvel back then!

There was a rich man in Willoughby named Mr. Austin. He lived in a big house with a huge yard surrounded by a wrought iron fence. I don't really remember him, but I do recall one day seeing him drive down the street in his electric car. It looked kinda like the Queen's coach, you know, glass windows all around, beautiful! Nope, never got to ride in it. But, we do have one picture of our family when we were just seven children, and the picture was made in his yard, I think. We are sitting on a wicker lawn chair. I can't imagine why it was made there. Mother would send two of us there occasionally to ask for help with our bills, it was Mary

Jean and I, as I remember. I'm sure there were other times when Mother talked with him or his wife herself.

One day, we went to visit Aunt Ida, mother's aunt,

1919 Prices		1929 Prices	
Average income	$1,914.00	Average income	$2,062.00
New car	$466.00	New car	$450.00
New house	$5,626.00	New house	$7,246.00
Loaf of bread	$ .10	Loaf of bread	$ .09
Gallon of gas	$ .15	Gallon of gas	$ .12
Gallon of milk	$ .62	Gallon of milk	$ .58
No minimum wage		No minimum wage	
Life expectancy: 54.4 years		Life expectancy: 54.1 years	

back in Chagrin Falls. She had a stream through her backyard so we all went wading when a leech got hold of my big toe! I could really scream when I was young and I did!

    We moved often; I thought because we couldn't pay the rent, though Bill said it was to get more space. I can remember the last two houses we lived in. I have a picture in my mind of the house on Summit Street and the Evans family lived next door. When Jimmy was born, Mother stayed with them for the delivery. One Sunday, Daddy was trying to get us all ready for Sunday school but couldn't handle the bows on the girls' dresses. So we ran next door and either Mother or Mrs. Evans took care of that. Funny how you remember these little things.

Then we moved to Center Street into a bigger house. There was a glassed-in porch across the front that wrapped around part of the side. My most vivid memory is of Bill and me playing some game and needing some cookies. So, we agreed to ask Mother using a game—each one say a word, then the next one say a word, and it sounded like this;

Bill: "Mother"

Margie: "may"

Bill: "we"

Margie: "have"

Bill: "some"

Margie: "cookies?"

We intended it as a method to persuade. I don't remember if it worked or not, but I remember trying. I do remember one day when Bob got into some chocolate candy, only it wasn't candy, it was Ex-Lax, a laxative, and you can believe he was a sick little boy for a while.

I also remember having a birthday party in June for the twins. We were sitting at the picnic table under a tree when suddenly, CRASH; a huge limb of the apple tree fell right on our table in the middle of the good stuff to eat. That was a surprise.

One day Mother got concerned about Bob and decided to take him to a doctor. He had some strange humps on his back that were not normal. After some conversation, they finally decided it was because he was always climbing the doorjambs like a monkey. He had over-developed his back muscles.

One amusing incident about that bigger house: Daddy had been away for quite a while and came back, arriving at night. As he drove in the drive, he spotted a young man coming out of the house. What could this mean? Well, Mother had rented out one of the rooms to a young couple and the man was working at night. They helped to pay the rent, I'm sure.

I guess I have to tell the story that still proves how stubborn I can be. We walked to school of course, and it wasn't far, maybe three or four blocks. But Mother didn't want me to dawdle along the way, so she told the boys and Mary Jean to be sure I kept up with them and wasn't late. They proceeded, all FOUR of them, to push and pull me up the street. What could any self-respecting child do in such a situation? I dug in my heels and wouldn't budge. I got to school, but it wasn't easy for them.

Now I'll reveal a real secret. I LOVED school and never wanted to miss a day! Years later, I told Mother that if they had just left me alone and gone on, I would have gotten there by myself. I might have been late the first day, but never again. All she would say was, "Humph." She was probably thinking, "More of this child psychology stuff."

You may be interested to know that we sang as a group, all ten of us. Mother played the piano and we sang at churches, civic clubs, even on the radio one time. Like the Trapp family singers, only we were the

We were written up in the newspaper when we sang
Roanoke, VA, August 8, 1937

Trippeers, and not as famous. I suppose we stopped when the boys' voices started to change.

One cold, winter morning in Willoughby, Mother had been struggling to get the plumbing thawed for us to get ready for school and then all of us into snow pants, coats, hats, mittens, scarves, and galoshes and then off to school. She also had those little toddlers underfoot—by my count, five of them! That day, she got a letter from Daddy complaining about the sunburn he had gotten at Virginia Beach over the weekend. She wrote right back and told him to find a house for us in that warm sunny clime. We were not to spend another winter in Ohio!

Before we left, some very interesting pictures were

made at Aunt Ida's house. They are mostly interesting because Mother numbered us in order of birth—to help relatives know our identity, I suppose:

#1 Ben, #2 Mary Jean, #3 Bob, #4 Bill, #5 Marjorie,

#6 & 7 Marian and Donald, #8 Carl, #9 Jimmy, #10 Nancy

Mom with ten children at Aunt Ida's before our move to Virginia
Chagrin Falls, OH, 1936

The Bonus Marches of the 1930s

I've just come up with this piece of US history that I remember a little about, and I think you will be interested—it doesn't usually make the history books, I understand. Before we left Willoughby, Ohio in January 1936, I remember great excitement at our house because the Veterans' Bonus had finally been passed.

The background I'll tell you briefly. The whole matter of bonuses for soldiers was very unclear. Back in 1776 they were paid some, but in 1781 some Pennsylvanian veterans marched on Washington and demanded their pay and were expelled by the police. And after the Spanish-American War they were not paid anything. Following World War I, the returning soldiers, including my Dad, were promised a bonus. They had been paid $1 a day while they were in service and had to pay for their uniforms. This bonus was to help them get back into civilian life. The veterans were given certificates in 1924 guaranteeing them a bonus payment but it was not to be paid until 1945, twenty years later.

However, in 1929, when the Great Depression began, many, if not most of these men were put out of work due to factories and businesses closing down. Hundreds of thousands of people were out of work. They stood in food lines for hours in the larger cities. Every town and city was hard-pressed to provide for the needy. Banks were closed.

In response to this great need, some of veterans gathered in Washington, D.C. as part of a Bonus March to demand their bonus for fighting in the war. Others heard and joined them and they pitched camp right by the Anacostia River, near the 11th Street bridge. Another significant thing that happened was the forming of the American Legion of veterans which gave them a collective voice, especially as the movement spread across the country. My Daddy was very active in starting the Legion in Chagrin Falls, so of course he was active in the one in Willoughby when we moved there, and later in Roanoke. He was involved all of his life. Mother participated in the Legion Auxiliary also.

The Bonus March was largely ignored, and so their numbers rapidly grew to thousands. By the summer of 1932, there were about 43,000 marchers, 17,000 of them veterans, joined by some of their families and also the Veterans of Foreign Wars and the new American Legion. President Hoover tried to stay uninvolved, but he finally called out the troops and ordered General MacArthur to lead them into the veteran's camp with drawn bayonets and tear gas. MacArthur then set fire to the tent city and drove the Bonus Army away from the capitol. In June 1932 the US Senate voted not to pay. General Eisenhower, General Patton, and others we now honor were also involved in this crackdown on the veterans and their families.

Also in 1932, Franklin Delano Roosevelt became president, and at first took the same stance toward the veterans. There was an increasing outcry from the public as they heard about all this. President Roosevelt sent his wife, Eleanor, to see many of the locations of poverty in the country. As a result of her travels and reports, he ordered some action. One of these was the signing into law of the CCC (Civilian Conservation Corps) that built much of the infrastructure including the Blue Ridge Parkway which we enjoy today. They helped plant over 3 billion trees and built 800 parks within 10 years. Also, Roosevelt signed the GI bill, which included loans to veterans to build houses and get a college education. All my brothers except Ben, went on to attend college under the GI bill, which they would not have been able to do otherwise. The president managed to send his wife unaccompanied to see the camps and talk with the veterans. She had lunch with the veterans and listened to them sing their songs. She reminisced about her memories of seeing the troops leave for the war and also when they came home. All she could promise them was work with the newly created Civilian Conservation Corps (CCC). President Roosevelt did relax the rules for entrance into the CCC so that men unmarried and/or over 25 years old could join.

In 1935 the Senate voted to pay the veterans, but FDR vetoed it, saying they could not do it and balance the budget. Finally, in January 1936 the Congress overturned FDR's veto and voted to pay $1.9 billion to the veterans and their families. This is what my family was celebrating. We marched around the house and hollered and beat on a drum and made trumpets of our hands. Anything to make noise! I was only seven years old at the time and only remember the marching and the excitement. I expect that bonus for Daddy did help us make our move to Virginia.

Early Life in Virginia

We were on the move by the summer of 1936. Daddy was in Virginia getting the house ready. I just learned recently that he had the sleeping porch added over the kitchen before we arrived. Mother got us ready to move with help from friends. Now all is not as simple as it seems. I think Mr. Evans, a longtime friend and neighbor, taught Mother to drive. Bill says she was already driving, so I may be wrong on that memory. She bought a Buick; she needed space for eight children and herself, and obviously she would do all of the driving. Later, whenever we traveled, we sat four across the back seat and four more on their laps and two in the front.

As luck would have it, Bob had bruised his right arm badly helping Mother do the washing. He was directing clothes through the wringer. Those old washing machines had a big round tub with a dasher that swished the clothes back and forth in the soapy water. Then the clothes went through the ringer – two rollers that squeezed the soapy water out – and into the rinse water. After rinsing in a tub of clean water, they went through the wringer again. That got a lot of the water out actually. The clothes felt very much like our clothes now coming from an automatic washer. Somehow Bob's arm went through with the clothes. He had helped Mom many times and nothing like this ever happened before. Mother quickly pulled the plug but the wringer, which was supposed to pop open when an oversized item went through, wasn't cooperating. Nothing to do but run his arm back through the wringer. I would bet that's where the common phrase "been through the wringer" came from! Bob contends to this day he didn't get any preferential treatment on the car trip, except the right rear seat in back so he could prop his arm and protect it from being bumped. Also, Don always had to sit by a window because he got carsick. Some of the others of us did too but not so consistently as Don. He always did.

Mother drove through the hills of West Virginia and Virginia on those old winding, narrow roads and made it to Roanoke in good shape. I have been told later by neighbors that when they all began to pile out of the car, they thought the circus had come to town. The family moved to 828 Windsor Avenue, Roanoke, Virginia, which later changed to 2256 Windsor Avenue.

Meanwhile, Bill and I had gone to Memphis, Tennessee to spend the summer with our paternal grandparents. Why us? I don't know. It's very possible that Uncle John asked for me to come, for he had always had a soft spot in his heart for me. And Bill and I got along well together. The younger ones were too young and the older ones could be a big help at home, so here we went, off on our big adventure.

The Trippeer grandparents had moved with Uncle John nearer to Uncle Dick and Aunt Ruth. I remember parts of that trip quite vividly, like saying goodbye to Mother. Also Bill, who was always something of a skinflint, held the money. He was one year older than me. He wouldn't pay for us to get a pillow for our overnight sleep in the coach. They cost 25 cents, I think. He did allow me to get some food. We saw the Ohio Penitentiary and, silly as it seems now, I was quite scared until we got past it. We stopped in Cincinnati and were met by a lady with Travelers Aid. Since we were pretty young, Mother had sent a message ahead of us for someone from Travelers Aid to meet us and help us to our next train. She was very nice and took us through this humongous train station to her office to sit and wait till it was time for our next connection.

Our arrival in Memphis was welcome, you can imagine. Mother had dressed us in white, in some of our best clothes to make a good appearance when we arrived. People did that back then. However, by the time we got there, we had spent, I suppose at least 24 hours in those clothes, including sleeping in them. You can imagine how we looked. Not too presentable. And Granny Trippeer didn't miss that. It was the first time I had a hint of a little coolness toward Leona, our mother, though I probably wasn't supposed to hear her remark.

We had a good summer. Uncle John was wonderful!

Especially to me. He used to sing, "Margie, I'm always thinking of you, Margie...." "Margie" was a popular song sometimes heard on the radio. He had a wonderful tenor voice and his attention really won my heart. I have thought in later years, that to get that sort of personal attention when usually I was just one of ten, and in the middle at that, must have been pretty heady for that little seven year old. Two years later, when Mary Jean and I went to Memphis together, Uncle John eloped with his sweetheart Mary that summer and came back to live at Granny Trippeer's house.

I remember waking up that first morning; it was warm and sunny and things were happening on the street. When we got out there, we found African Americans selling vegetables from a truck. Apples, carrots, cabbages, watermelon, cantaloupe, you name it. They laughed and talked with all the folks. It felt like a party and we loved it! But then I opened my mouth and said something, and all the kids started to call me "damn Yankee." Made me so mad I could spit. But older heads and wiser tried to help me see their side. They said the other kids thought it was just one word, not meant as a cuss word but just a word for Yankee, and of course we were from Ohio. I had to work on my anger about them calling me that. I'll tell you, maybe that was the beginning of my cross-cultural experience.

Another special memory was when we went to the amusement park. We rode a wonderful merry-go-round. The exciting thing was that Uncle John helped me to catch the rings. They had tubes extended down over the riders as we passed under them and the idea was to grab a ring as you rode by. If you got a bronze ring, you got a prize. I seem to remember we did get the bronze ring, but I don't remember the prize.

At the end of the summer, my Grandpa Trippeer died. We were not close to our Grandpa; we hardly knew him. He worked at night and slept during the day. He had very little to say to us. Now I think he was a broken man since his business in Chagrin Falls had failed during the Depression. Of course Daddy and Mother came to the funeral, but also Aunt Dorothy Brewster who lived in California and Aunt Mary Lynn Patterson from Massachusetts. At this time Dick and Ruth, who were quite well-to-do, had no children at all and Aunt Dorothy had just one girl, Cynthia. Granny said Ruth and Leona, my mother, needed to be put into a bag and shaken up together to even out the number of children between them.

We were very glad to see Mom and Dad, you can imagine. I don't think I had thought of it as homesickness, but we had certainly missed our family. Daddy was driving the company car which was a coupe—you know, only a front seat. We rode home with Dad and Mom all stuffed into that front seat. Bill and I took turns, one sitting between them, and the

Mom, Dad, Margie, & Bill in Memphis, TN for Grandpa Trippeer's funeral, 1936

other stretched across the back behind the seat, in other words, at the window. Wasn't too bad. We had to stop one night at a motel; Dad went out and bought a watermelon and we stood around the bathtub and spit seeds into the tub. Talk about fun! On that trip was also when Daddy told us that "café" was pronounced "caf." Not knowing any better, we went on saying that for quite a while. Not sure how long it took us to get it right. No help from Mom on that one.

We arrived in Roanoke and were home. It was a big house with a square hall and living room across the front, behind them a den and dining room, and behind that, the breakfast room that could seat six, and the kitchen and back porch across the back. Also, there was a pantry off the kitchen.

Upstairs, there was one bathroom, three bedrooms, a small room used for many things, and a sleeping porch across the back above the kitchen. There was a good-sized attic which became the repository for many things; secret Christmas presents, lots of stuff we were not ready to throw away, and a big roll-top desk that was Dad's, but he never used it. I suppose there wasn't any place for it downstairs. I guess it had been his dad's. We loved to go through all of the cubby holes. What else did we get when Grandpa Trippeer died? There was the mahogany rocking chair which I now have, and the other rocking chair of oak with leather seats. Who has it? I don't know. And there was the clock, a beautiful glass-encased clock that had to be wound every week. Seems it was to go to the oldest boy. Tradition! It sat on our living-room mantle and we were very proud of it. Now young Dick Trippeer, Ben's son, has it, I suppose.

All of the boys slept in the sleeping porch. It wasn't insulated so it could get very cold in the winter. But Mother warmed bricks and wrapped them in newspaper to put at their feet. It had windows all the way around and a closed-in closet in the corner.

Our new home, 828 Windsor Ave. (later 2256) Roanoke, VA, 1936

Some people ask how we ever managed with just one bathroom. No problem that I can think of. We took turns of course, shared the tub – there was no shower. We also had a time limit; the alarm clock sat in the window sill. It worked. I've never said we didn't have arguments. Of course we did, but the good thing about having a fight with your brother or sister is, after it's all over, you're still family.

We had a long backyard, equal to two lots really. In the upper part, we had a huge old tree just perfect for climbing and a garage with an upstairs of sorts. Dad put a basketball goal on the side of the garage, and that meant that no grass grew there for years, but we all learned to play basketball. The entrance to the basement was the old kind; a slanting door over the steps going down from the outside. It wasn't a complete basement, just enough room for the furnace, the washing machine and drain setup, and a coal bin for the furnace. The unfinished part was about four feet high, just where they stopped cutting the dirt. We used that big space for our canned fruits and vegetables; we needed a big place. There was another entrance from the back porch, with steps coming down over the coal bin.

Washing was quite a chore. Of course there were lots of clothes, but we all helped. Mom ran the machine and supervised; the rest of us hung out the clothes. On windy days it was an art to get the sheets on the line hanging straight at all. And in the winter, our fingers would freeze, handling those wet things. But maybe worse than that was bringing in the frozen-stiff clothes. We had to be careful how we handled them. They could break, literally, and your favorite shirt or dress would have a tear in it. After we got them inside, we had to find a radiator to drape them over to finish drying. Heavy pants, of course, were the worst and we had plenty of them. We girls wore dresses all of the time then. And since this was in the 1930s before polyester was invented, everything we wore on the outside had to be ironed. We didn't iron t-shirts and pillowcases like my future mother-in-law did. Oh, I forgot, we had to dip those shirts in a starch solution before hanging them out to dry. Later we had to dampen all of them with water before we could iron them. This meant sprinkling water with our hands and rolling them up so the water would disperse all over the shirts. It was best to then wrap them in towels to keep them wet – not too much water and not too little. We learned by experience how much to use. Then we ironed each one. This was called WORK, and after a long stint of ironing we were really pooped. I will say that I became a very good ironer of men's shirts, maybe not as fast as Mom, but probably as good. I'll admit that we never did catch up on the ironing.

Oh, I need to tell you about the rest of the backyard. There was a sour cherry tree, just the right kind for cherry cobblers. And the rest was just open space: perfect for a garden some years, just right for a touch football game with Daddy on Sunday afternoon after a picnic. On the side of the yard there was an apple tree, just ole country apples but we loved them, especially when they were warm and you could sprinkle a little salt on it before each bite. We buried our pets including our dog Chips, under the apple tree. Beyond our yard was the alley, which belonged to everybody on the street. We used it for a shortcut to junior high school.

The Purcells lived next door and became very good friends, all of them: Pop Linkenhofer, Mrs. Purcell was a special friend of Mom's, Aunt Verdie, son Joe and his sister. Pop Linkenhofer had a wheel for sharpening knives which he did for whoever asked him. He was a good old man. On beyond them lived the Tuckers with one son, P.C., who was killed in WWII. One family that lived right across from us had a girl about my age. Nice folks. Another family had a woman working for them whose name was Merry Christmas. I'm not kidding. I thought that was the coolest thing ever.

I'm not sure what year it was, but Mother got the idea

and stirred up the neighborhood to ask the Parks and Recreation Department to make the large expanse of land and the wooded hillside that adjoined the junior high school into a city park. I'm not sure if she had people sign a petition or just got a group to go to the meetings. Mother was fully capable of speaking in front of a group like that, and she was becoming known and respected in the community. So they agreed with her and did make that land Sherwood Park with employed workers there in the summertime. At Sherwood Park we had much to entertain and instruct us: crafts, ball teams, contests, etc. They built tennis courts and laid out a baseball diamond. Swings and seesaws were put in too, and there was plenty of room for football fields. It was really great and was heavily used all year around. I suppose it still is.

One of the most fun things we did in the winter when we had sufficient snow was to sleigh ride. That Sherwood Park hill was just perfect for our purposes, even some trees to dodge. Later, when Troy told me about sleigh riding on a hilly public street in Winston-Salem, I realized how fortunate we had been. We lived close enough that we could run home and get warm, dry our clothes, and get some hot chocolate. Good! We also loved to go out to Marcia Larson's house and ride in their real sleigh pulled by a horse!

That neighborhood was perfect for playing Capture the Flag. We played on summer nights and, with the alleys and long backyards we had some very interesting searches. We also played Kick the Can after dark which was an elaborate hide and seek game. Those nighttime games could be a bit scary, but they were sure fun!

The neighbors I remember best are the ones who had a boy named Aubrey and a greyhound dog that had been a racer and still could run like the wind. He had been trained to chase a little fake rabbit on the track; later when he saw our little puppies or kittens he knew what to do with them, and he did it. He killed them. It was sad, but we couldn't blame him when we understood.

Aubrey was about Bob's age and the boys used to ride the wagon down their steep driveway and then on into the street. To make it more interesting they built a ramp on the sidewalk so they could come speeding down the drive then UP the ramp and DOWN into the street. I don't think that one lasted too long. Maybe it was the wagon that gave out. Don't remember any injuries.

Anyway, Daddy would occasionally take Mom with him on one of his trips and leave us on our own once we got bigger. On one such occasion, a Sunday night, several of our friends came home with us to hang out. That was okay, except that the little kids were pestering us and not going on to bed as they should have. Bill and I were in charge. Suddenly, we heard a scream upstairs and we went tearing up to find Jimmy behind a door which had a shoe bag hanging on it. That shoe bag was hanging on two little cup hooks, and he had hidden there, turned around and caught his eyelid on one of those cup hooks. Can you imagine? Anyway he was bleeding and crying and what were we to do?

First thing we thought of was to ask the man across the street to take us to the emergency room, which he did. I can still hear Jimmy with his head in my lap, lying across the back seat asking, "Margie, am I going to be blind?" Of course I didn't know. We couldn't see what damage had been done. Fortunately the doctor cleaned and sewed him up and the only result was that the tear glands in that eye never worked properly again. Both Bill and I did some growing up that night.

Another time when I was left in charge for a weekend, Mom and Dad brought me a record player and several records. I was speechless! I think that was one of the most momentous times in my young life. To be given something like that—and by my own Mom and Dad. I was right at the age when I would love to have a record player, but had never in my wildest imagination thought of getting one. How could I? They cost more money than I thought I would ever have. I really enjoyed that record player and was able to buy a record occasionally as I went through high school. It still brings wonder to my heart when I think of it. We didn't often get individual recognition like that, at least I didn't.

Joe Purcell, P.C. Tucker and Ben were buddies, and once they built TALL stilts, I mean tall, like up to the second story window. Really. Ben broke his arm falling from them. I remember they could see into the upstairs of the garage from those stilts. Oh, another thing, one year, maybe more, we made a kind of gun, wooden and carved like a revolver; we attached a clip clothespin to the handle and then used strips of inner tubes for the shot. Get a good stretch and it made a definite sting on impact. You knew you had been shot. The garage upstairs was good for a fortress.

Mother also used that upstairs for her chicken project. She decided to order 100 baby chicks in the spring, and kept them up there under a big light until they were big enough for the chicken coop in the backyard. When they got fully grown, she would kill one by wringing the neck. She dipped it in steaming hot water to make the feathers easier to pluck, and we would pick all the feathers off. She would singe it over a burner on our gas stove to be sure it was all clean, cut out the innards, and we had a money-making business. Occasionally we also got fried chicken for Sunday dinner, a real treat for us!

The last use for that garage upstairs that I can remember was when my brother Ben, who was in the Navy posted in Rhode Island, decided he was going to marry the girl he had met and fallen for. Mother went up to meet her family and for the wedding, and it wasn't long before Ben brought Winnie back to Roanoke to live with us. So we fixed up the garage upstairs; it wasn't bad at all. Must have been cold in the winter, but maybe she wasn't there then. I really don't remember. We did get to know her, all of us. She was as different from us as day and night—from a Rhode Island family of three children. Could she have been intimidated by the ten of us? Some of the other in-laws who are only children or from a small family tell us they were intimidated.

You may wonder about the garage downstairs; well, it wasn't much of anything. It had a roof overhead, of course, and a dirt floor. I never saw a car parked in it. What we did do there was spray our Christmas trees. It was perfect for that. Don't know where we got the idea, but we started spraying our trees silver and then decorating them with all blue and silver ornaments. Every year they were so beautiful, much prettier than anyone else's, of course.

Speaking of Christmas, that was an interesting and challenging time for us. I can't imagine how Mother and Daddy did what they did. As we kids reached our teens we did a lot of babysitting, and that helped us to have some cash. I seem to remember us getting five pairs of roller skates every year for several years. They belonged to any of us who could skate or wanted to try. We were always the first ones up Christmas morning on the block, and the first ones out on the sidewalk skating.

On Christmas morning we had to stay upstairs until everybody was dressed and ready for the day. That included Daddy, and he was the worst. We would go and try to wake him up, then rush him to get dressed. It was all in good fun. I don't remember him ever getting mad or anything. Then we would line up at the top of the stairs, youngest first and Daddy last. Mother was already down there and had turned the lights on.

A lot of the presents were clothes and useful things of course, but there was always something for fun for each of us. And the stockings! We used old hose of

Mother's. They used to be made separate for each leg where they'd attach to a garter at the top of the leg. We hung them on a string tied between the two posts of the piano. I think we always got an apple, an orange and/or tangerine, a candy cane, and other little bits and pieces. We didn't expect anything big and we didn't get anything big. We were in the middle of the Great Depression after all. But we all felt cared for and remembered, individually cared for. One Christmas when Nancy, the youngest, was about 13, she opened a box to find a very nice tan corduroy jacket. There was no indication of who had given it to her. We finally decided she had given it to herself. By that time we were older and considered it a good joke on us. She got what she wanted at least! Another Christmas when Bill was fourteen or so, he spent one dollar and bought all of his Christmas presents. I think he gave each of us kids a pencil. Maybe a bottle of cheap perfume for Mom. I told you he was a skinflint. He was.

Of course Christmas was more than the tree and presents. Our church, Raleigh Court Methodist, just three blocks down the street, had great youth activities, especially at Christmas. We went caroling, and back then it almost always snowed before Christmas. Such memories I have of walking the streets of our neighborhood and singing those beautiful songs. I can hear them now - "Silent Night, Holy Night" and "God Rest You Merry Gentlemen." Close your eyes and maybe you can feel the cold and hear the beautiful music too. "Jingle bells, jingle bells, jingle all the way" and "We wish you a Merry Christmas." The church was always decorated so nicely and the church choir sang a Christmas service, which I was part of as soon as I was old enough. I think I started singing in the adult choir when I was a young teenager. I sat by Mary Jean and she was a very good alto, so I leaned on her for a little direction. The bass and tenor soloists were wonderful, and the alto Marsha Larson too. This is when I was introduced to The Messiah; we sang parts of it every year. It was a small choir, but quite good, I think. I must confess, I don't think I thought much about Jesus at Christmas, I mean the real significance of Christmas. That would come later. I loved to sit in the balcony of that church. It was a lovely old building, and from the balcony, I could see the whole scene. I liked that.

And then there was Easter. We had eggs galore! On Saturday we decorated them, the big kids always coming up with such neat ideas for designs and the younger ones wanting to try them too. You know, like stripes, or many colors on one egg. They could be difficult to do and have them come out pretty. We all liked egg salad and it was a good thing we did, because that is what we had in our sandwiches for the next week or so. The chocolate we got didn't last nearly that long!

Now, I suppose I must tell you about Mrs. Jones, our next door neighbor on the left. Her name was Rose; a pompous lady, very proper and not friendly, at least not to us. Her husband's name was Henry; he was a little guy, about five feet tall and quite thin. They had a grandson named Jackie who used to visit in the summer. I don't know why, but he couldn't have had a good time. He never played with us or with any of the neighborhood kids. Don't know what he did. I think he may have played the violin.

Mrs. Jones was our ENTERTAINMENT. As I tell it now, we really were quite wicked, but at the time, we felt we were justified. I don't know why we were so mean; she never did anything to us. She just wasn't friendly to us or anybody. She was quite ridiculous when she dressed up in her elegant red or green or purple outfits in a suit, shoes, and a hat with a big feather waving about. This was just to go to the grocery store. And when she came home, she would honk the horn and call, "Hen-reeee" and the poor little fellow would come down and stagger up the steps with all of her packages.

Now, I suppose you can begin to imagine what Halloween was like around that neighborhood. Most of the neighbors were good, one even had candy apples and games and stuff. But of course that wasn't as much fun as fixing up Mrs. Jones' house. One year we waxed her window screens. We used paraffin wax and drew designs on the screens. It was hard to remove. You know, if we had used soap we would get the same effect but it would have been easier to clean. Easy cleaning wasn't our intent anyway.

One year I was raking leaves in our front yard and someone—who was that little devil?—dared me to pull the flowers off Mrs. Jones' hydrangea bushes. I'm afraid I couldn't resist a dare and I tore every flower off those big bushes in front of her house. Right in broad daylight with no shame at all. Well, that night or the next, Mrs. Jones came to our front door—first time ever—to speak to Mom. I was upstairs studying and could hear it all. Mrs. Rose Jones told Mom most emphatically about my destructive behavior. She said I was a delinquent and needed to be punished severely. My Mother stood there and defended me, said she knew Marjorie would never do such a thing. Upstairs I wanted to crawl into a hole somewhere and spend the night with the mice. I felt awful. But listen to this. What do you think my punishment was? Nothing. She never mentioned it to me. I later figured she was glad I had the nerve to do it. She had a bit of the devil in her too.

We usually had at least one dog. When Mary Jean got a job, she used her own money to buy a beautiful black cocker spaniel named Chips. He was everyone's pet, of course.

There was one more incident that I am a little ashamed to tell, but I think I must so you will understand how sibling pressure can push you to do things. One day several of us were sitting in the glider on the front porch and here came Mrs. Jones' precious Persian cat. It didn't bother us at all; actually I think it ignored us the way cats do. But she did stretch herself out on the wall just across from us, the wall that surrounded the front porch. She was right there in the bright sunlight, glowing so pretty and orange, and I don't know if someone dared him or if the devil made him do it, but Bob could see that he had a perfect shot and he did it. I don't know what he threw, but he had a good arm, and it went straight as an arrow right to the mark. (He should have been a baseball pitcher with an arm like that!) What do you call that sound cats make when they are hurt or angry, not exactly a roar but not meow either. Anyway, she made that awful sound, and I don't know that we ever saw her again. Not long after that our dog died, evidently poisoned, and you know what we thought. Actually, we didn't think it, we knew it, but of course couldn't do a thing about it.

But wait, this is not quite the end of the Mrs. Jones saga: Later, Daddy was on one of his trips and went through one of the towns up in the mountains, stopped at a filling station for gas, and the fellow who was filling the tank—they used to do that for all customers for free—asked him, "I see you live in Roanoke. I have an aunt who lives down there. Wonder if you might know her. Name's Rose Jones." When Daddy responded that she used to be our next-door neighbor, the fellow just muttered, "You pore feller." When Daddy came telling us about that, I think we all agreed we could let that matter rest. We laughed about it but later I felt remorse because we really were unkind to her.

There is one more thing I haven't mentioned. Mrs. Jones went to Calvary Baptist Church, so of course in my prejudiced mind I decided I never wanted anything to do with Baptists. I later realized I had some friends that I liked very much that were Baptists. Of course even later, I became a Baptist myself!

When we moved to Virginia in 1936, Daddy usually came home every weekend. It was much nicer, as we all loved it when he was there. He could be a lot of fun, teasing and finding fun things to do, but mostly the mood in the house just rose about fifty notches when he walked in. I think it was because he and Mother had such a good relationship. We knew they disagreed occasionally, but we never saw them really argue or fight; at least I don't remember it and I think I would. The nearest I ever saw to a fight was one night when we were all sitting around the dining room table after supper eating popcorn balls and talking. Dad asked Mom to toss him a popcorn ball, so she did. Trouble was, it hit him in the eye and when it did, we all burst out laughing. But it was NOT funny. Evidently, it really hurt either his eye or his pride, not sure which. Obviously we got quiet real quick when we sensed the atmosphere was heating up, but Mom and Dad were very composed. It was serious then, but I still laugh when I think of it, and he would too now. He had a great sense of humor. As I think about it, it seems to me that they didn't take themselves too seriously, had nothing to prove, and encouraged the same in us. Not bad models.

Some of their arguments were quite funny. Every once in a while they would get into an old one about whether a tomato was a fruit or a vegetable. Mother said vegetable; Daddy said fruit. Of course, when we finally pulled the dictionary out and looked it up, it is a "fruit of the vine," but Mother still insisted we use it as a vegetable and we couldn't argue with that.

Sometimes Daddy would take two of us with him on a day trip to a nearby town where he had a customer. That was really exciting and we loved to go, but of course we had to take turns, so it didn't happen too often. Usually when I went, it was with Bill and we had fun asking questions and telling stories as we rode along. We counted the cows before we came to the next cemetery. Or we looked for the Burma-Shave signs which were several small signs posted along the road as an advertisement, like: It's best for one/who hits the bottle/to let another /use the throttle/ Burma-Shave.

1936 Prices		1946 Prices	
Average income	$1,713.00	Average income	$2,500.00
New car	$780.00	New car	$1,125.00
New house	$3,925.00	New house	$5,600.00
Loaf of bread	$ .08	Loaf of bread	$ .10
Gallon of gas	$ .10	Gallon of gas	$ .15
Gallon of milk	$ .48	Gallon of milk	$ .70
No minimum wage		Minimum wage	$ .75
Life expectancy: 59.7 years		Life expectancy: 62.9 years	
		Inventions: First drive-up bank window in Chicago	

Many people thought Bill and I were twins since we were about the same size, but we weren't. The twins were Donald and Marian, and Donald was always a good bit taller than she; they didn't look anything alike either. Of course we didn't think any of us looked alike, but folks said they could tell one of those Trippeer kids anywhere. This was tested years later when I lived in Bangladesh and met a young fellow who had roomed with Bill and also visited in our home. After he knew we were related, he said he could see the resemblance. Yeah, yeah.

I'm sure Dad's presence helped Mom, and indirectly all of us kids. He was there to share some of the burdens she carried alone much of the time. There was never enough money. These were the Great Depression years and everybody was having a very hard time. I just hope you never have to go through anything like that. Not that it impacted me much. I knew Mother worried a lot; she often sent me to pay a little on the light or water bill and tell them we would try to do more next month. And very often she would send me to the end of that long block where the postman's refill box was, hoping I could get our mail early, specifically Daddy's paycheck, as creditors were breathing down her neck. We learned many ways to stretch a dollar; one of them you will appreciate. When we got holes in our shoe soles, we would cut the cardboard back of a tablet into the shape of the shoe and fitted it inside our shoes to make them last longer. That worked just fine as long as the weather was dry, but rain or snow made a mess of it in a hurry.

We had a garden and chickens; the boys mowed lawns for neighbors, and we all babysat. All the money went into the family kitty; at least I think it did. I know mine did. I once heard Daddy say that we didn't have many doctor bills, but we surely did have the grocery bills. The boys say they took six sandwiches to school for their lunch. That's almost a whole loaf. Mother got our bread at the Day Old Bakery Shop and saved some money there. Actually, she worked for the pie shop at one time, driving their truck to deliver pies. And as soon as Jim and Nancy began school, she went to work in Pugh's Department Store, manager of the boy's department, what else?

Of course we wore hand-me-downs. Occasionally, we would get a box from Daddy's sister Dorothy in California with some clothes she didn't use anymore. Fortunately, Mother didn't make me wear some of the things that looked like an older woman's apparel. I wanted some of Mary Jean's, but she was working and earning money to buy her own clothes. She would wear them until they couldn't be worn. I understand later that she did pass some things down to Marian.

Mother did one thing that I have thanked her for many times. When I was thirteen and taking Home Economics in school, she bought a sewing machine and with it came a series of lessons. She let me take those lessons so I learned to sew! You can believe I took advantage of that and have used that skill all of my adult life.

Mother was an expert at making a soup or stew stretch to feed one more. Pour in a little more water or milk and there you have another serving. At one time she worked at our church as the main cook for church meals. They liked her especially since she could slice a ham into more slices than anyone else around! We weren't the only ones scraping along like this. We were blessed, for we never felt any shame about it. Once, I got into a fistfight with another girl who was teasing me about our not being able to pay our light bill, and I just hauled off and slugged her. Don't remember what she said to make me do that, which I had never done before and have not done since. I think it was something derogatory about Mother. I don't remember how that came out. As Uncle Bob says even now, I am feisty, but I don't slug people. Well, you get the picture.

I owe a lot to Mom and Dad. As I get older, I am able to understand so much more of what they did and didn't do. I see the strength in Mother—her character, the unflinching loyalty to God, country, and family, her goodness and concern for others, especially young people in trouble. And there's something else special about her that I don't know the word for. She was able to juggle all of us depending on her and needing her in different ways, yet she never seemed to get frazzled. I don't remember ever seeing her really lose her cool. I have seen her angry plenty of times, but I never saw her lose her basic composure. She was unflappable! I don't think she ever thought of herself as a victim, bound to the house and ten kids. She was always active in church and in other community activities that gave her an outlet with adults and a channel for her wisdom and leadership skills. And she reared us that way, too, so we would have our own interests and follow our own inclinations, which of course were varied. One friend commented that it was amazing that the ten of us all being so close together in age and yet each one so different with varying interests. It's not so amazing really, considering who our mother was.

Her second child, my sister Mary Jean, was born with a brain tumor between her eyes and needed brain surgery—serious stuff!—and her youngest came down with pneumonia when she was a very small infant. Of course there were also the usual broken bones and bashed heads.

Bill contracted rheumatic fever while in the Navy and was hospitalized for a long time at the VA hospital in nearby Salem, Virginia. That started her many years of volunteer service at the Veteran's Hospital. She had six sons go off to war; what did she do? She got busy knitting caps and sweaters for servicemen and became even more active in the Legion's Auxiliary, which was important to her all her life. I know that almost everyone's mother is wonderful to her children, but I just have to think we got one of the best. Not perfect, but so right for our particular family. She could talk sports with the boys; she was very musical, played the piano and had a lovely voice; she could play a mean game of Chinese Checkers, and I could go on.

There are some folks who agreed with me, well, with all of us kids, and they supported her when she was selected Mother of the Year for Virginia in 1956. Bob nominated her and the American Legion Auxiliary supported it. Oh, Daddy would have been so proud! He had died the previous January. He always supported her in her decisions and the manner in which she was rearing

Leona Mary Edwards Trippeer
Virginia Mother of the Year, 1956

us children, handled the finances, etc. He once said of her, "I have never heard her say a mean thing about anyone." Quite a compliment from one who knew her very well.

Daddy was a proud member of the American Legion, being a veteran of WWI; he was instrumental in forming a Legion Post in Chagrin Falls before they left there. One year in Virginia, he was elected to head-up the program for the boy's drum and bugle corps. But he was hardly home at all during the week, so who went down to Wasena Park and marched those boys around and around the park week after week until they had it down pat? And who was there with them when they went to the state competition in Charlottesville, VA? And who marched down the line of boys inspecting them, white shoe polish in hand for touching up spots? You got it. My Mom. She was indomitable.

Well, there is a really funny story that we often bring up about our trip home after that big competition. Oh yeah, we won! We were the best! Only Ben was in the corps at that time and Dad had promised him that if they won, he would take him on an overnight trip to Richmond with him—from Charlottesville! And Mother would drive the rest of us home. Daddy told her how to get out of town, and off we went.

Feeling a bit doubtful at an intersection since there weren't signs for highways then, Mother stopped and asked some fellows loitering on the corner if this was the road to Roanoke. "Oh, no, ma'am, you need to take a left here and just follow that. It will take you right to

Roanoke." They were so kind, and we were so trusting and unsuspecting, we just turned left and set off. Along the way we began to wonder if we were on the right road. One of us said, "I don't remember smelling a skunk this morning." And another would say, "I don't see anything that looks familiar."

Remember, we are riding nine of us, four in the back seat with another seated on his or her lap. And this was in August, it was really hot and we had been in the sun all day. We were all tired, hungry, hot, and clueless. We finally pulled into a filling station — called filling stations because the attendant filled all your car's fluids in addition to your gasoline – and Mother asked the man the way to Roanoke. He said, "Why, ma'am, yore in Culpepper, Virginia. Roanoke's a right smart way from here." It was midnight, but there was nothing to do but turn around and drive all that long way back through Charlottesville to Roanoke. Remember, we wouldn't have had money to stop for supper and certainly not for a motel, and they were few and far between anyway. We decided those young fellows who had supposedly helped us with directions were from Lynchburg, the main rival of our drum and bugle corps, and they had lost. I don't know what time we arrived home; I was asleep. I hate to think how many children Mother had to carry to our beds before she could seek out her own. I think about how tired she must have been. That next day, I slept till noon, the latest I had ever slept in my life.

Through the years in our family all you have to do is say, "Culpepper," and we are off on a storytelling jaunt.

Of course everyone has his or her own version. This is mine.

At one time, Daddy worked for Diversey Corp. With that job, my teenage brain was secretly proud of his title of sanitation engineer to the food industry. He sold cleaning products to soft drink companies, dairies, bakeries, etc.; he traveled to do this, but not too far. The big plus to this job was when he was on vacation; he would bring a case of soft drinks to the house from one of those companies. We didn't see soft drinks much at all, so that was really special!

Oh, yeah, he worked for Superior Cement Company at one time, too. One summer he was able to get a bunch of cinder blocks to build an outdoor pit and waste incinerator in our backyard. Now that was the beginning of good times! We had a long backyard, long enough for a game of touch football when it wasn't a garden. How many times did we hear him moan and groan after trying to keep up with the kids; he had

We all loved picnics in the backyard!
Roanoke, VA, 1942

played sports when he was young but he wasn't that young anymore and there were ten of us. We laughed at his aches and pains then, but now I have more sympathy for him.

The other thing he would do after we ate was to insist we all had to run around the block. Now, I am not talking about a block with six or seven houses. Ours was a long block. Let's see, how many houses were there? At least fifteen, maybe twenty on our side, but then we had to go across the hill and up Sherwood and around the expanded end of the block that made it not the ordinary-shaped block. Needless to say, we had eaten well and we needed to work it off and we did!

Being a veteran of the Army in WWI, once in a while Daddy would get to telling some of his war stories. Nothing about killing that I remember, but one night he told us about a group of soldiers spending the night in a French farmer's barn, sleeping in the loft. He told how they took potshots at the rats running around on the ground.

Occasionally, he would sit down at the piano and bang out some old military tunes like "When Johnny Comes Marching Home Again," "My Buddy," and "Over There." Of course, all of us came running to get in on the fun. I don't know if we ever stopped to think what the neighbors might think of this racket. He would sing at the top of his voice. Daddy had a very nice baritone voice and loved to sing. When he was in the Army he was part of a vaudeville show and evidently it was pretty wild. I can only imagine with all those boys so far from home. The original hope had been for him to go to Annapolis Naval Academy, but when the war broke out that was the end of that dream.

While I'm thinking about music, I should mention Kate Smith and her rendition of "God Bless America" during WWII. Oh, that woman could sing. She was tall and large with a big voice, a contralto I think we would call it. We must have heard her sing that song at least a hundred times, maybe more. And we never tired of it. She was singing for the whole country and God gave us courage and hope through her magnificent voice!

I think one of the strongest things about our family was the bond that Mother and Daddy had. Though Daddy wasn't there all of the time, we always knew that she spoke for both of them. Had he been there, they would have agreed on our punishment or misbehavior. They both had high ideals for their family, for us to do the best we could. We would not all succeed in the same ways, but we could succeed in our own ways. And that was good enough for them.

When I think of my early years in terms of what God was doing, it's harder to recognize. We never talked about church, God, the Bible or anything religious at home, though we did always have a silent blessing before meals.

I am grateful that I had a couple of adults who took a special interest in me. Reverend Mayer, the preacher of the Methodist Church in Willoughby, Ohio was the first I remember. What comes to mind is that he noticed me; for example, he would talk with me and ask my opinion about things. Just before we moved to Virginia, he taught me to always remember to count to ten before expressing my anger; and I had a temper, too.

We're all home! Left to right: standing Bill, Ben, & Bob; seated: Margie, Dad, Nancy, Mom, & Mary Jean; front: Carl, Don, Marian, & Jim Roanoke, VA, 1942

The second person who influenced me was Mrs. Saville, the superintendent of the Intermediate Department of Sunday School at Raleigh Court Methodist Church in Roanoke, Virginia. She gave me special opportunities to lead in SS, and because she was usually at home, she encouraged me to come by her house on my way home from school. I don't remember what we talked about, but I stopped by many days and enjoyed her company and attention. Perhaps she endeared herself to me because she, too, noticed me.

I had a friend, Ruth Cadd, who was also from a large family; seven I think. Her dad would have the two of us come by his beautician training school in the afternoon after school was finished and they would shampoo, curl, and set our hair. They were practicing on us, but we thought it was great to be made all pretty. I remember my curls bouncing along as I walked, just like Shirley Temple.

As I think about it now, I realize that being the middle child of ten meant that I didn't get a lot of attention from anyone at home, except that I was the "lap baby" for almost two years, longer than the other older kids. What does it mean to be a "lap baby?" Well, it's what it sounds like. I was the baby of the family for almost two years before the twins were born. Of course, then I got pushed off Mom's lap for sure with two of them to take my place. I don't remember ever feeling neglected or left out, just not noticed as special. We were "The Trippeer kids," and proud of it. I was part of the Big Kid's group and that was special, even if I was the youngest. We got to stay up later, but I don't remember any other perks. Actually, we often thought the Little Kids got favors and benefits we didn't get, like easy hiding places for the Easter eggs. And how many times did Mother say, "Now you're older. Let him or her have a turn first." Or "Since you are older you can do this job. The little kids aren't big enough for that yet." Like hanging out clothes on cold, windy days. Or taking the garbage down to the alley after supper when it was dark and scary outside. That kind of thing.

In my teens I started attending a youth group called the Training Union at Virginia Heights Baptist Church. The church was a local church and several of our friends went there and told us about their cool evening activities. Several of us Trippeers went there at the same time. I think I was the oldest one, but Marian and Donald and Carl, I think, also went. Lou and Helen Reichensberger, who were the leaders, were childless, but they made up for it by directing their interest toward helping young people learn about God and the Christian walk. They not only led Training Union, but also opened their home to the whole crowd after church on Sunday night. They had some snacks, music, and lots of talk and games. I was one of the older young people in the group at that time so I spent more time with them planning programs and activities and talking about any problems that came up. They were very good to me, and I think understood me much better than I understood myself at that point. I was then at the stage when I had not realized that I was not a real Christian at all; I expect they knew that. But I was seeking and wanting to please God. They were two helpers on my journey.

I had attended a Methodist summer camp when I was twelve years old where I heard a missionary from Japan speak. I was deeply moved, and made a decision at that time to go to Japan as a missionary. I had read voraciously through the years and was especially interested in stories from other cultures. There was a set of books, stories about twins from twenty or thirty countries that I borrowed from the public library right near our school. I devoured them all. I considered myself a mission volunteer, and for some reason, assumed that I would go as a single lady. This may have been because I had not dated much, and my brothers had not helped my self-esteem in that area (as brothers are wont to do).

As I look back now, I see myself as having been quite shallow, making people laugh just to gain attention, sometimes not being strictly honest and not trying as hard as I could have to do well in school. Interestingly, I did not do what I considered to be bad things, and thought of myself as quite righteous, especially compared to others who smoked, drank, flirted, and other things which I never even wanted to do. They were never a temptation to me.

In junior and senior high, I discovered that I had an interest in writing. Not creative writing, but reporting. I worked on the school newspapers and really liked that, including the logistics of putting a paper out. I love to sing and sang in choirs and glee clubs until high school when working on the newspapers took over as my first-place interest. I still love to sing and have enjoyed music all my life. I also liked sports, but there wasn't much for girls except physical education classes where we usually played volleyball.

As I attended Roanoke College in 1946-47, a coach there trained me to be a basketball referee, which I enjoyed. But, more than that, I liked playing field hockey later while I was attending Meredith College in Raleigh, North Carolina. I had never played before, but really enjoyed it. Scholastically, what was it like for me to follow four older siblings? It wasn't bad; occasionally I would be encouraged to do as well as Mary Jean or Bob. They were the two best students in the family, I think; I can't say for sure, because we didn't compare our report cards. I was a mediocre student; I probably—well surely—could have done better if I had studied more and had less fun, but Mom never gave me a hard time about it. I suppose she thought I was doing my best, and usually I was. I did like to get outside in the afternoons and I did like working on the newspaper, so those activities occupied more of my time than studying too hard. Now your Papa has a different story. He never talked about it much, but he made very good grades all through school and in college also.

It was the fall of 1947, and my freshman year at Roanoke College in Salem, Virginia. I lived at home and managed to obtain the finances to attend, thanks to my Uncle Dick, Daddy's brother. During that first year I was introduced to many things I had not known before. I still did not drink or smoke and had no desire to. I think I can fairly say that I was truly double-minded, I clung to the thought of myself as a mission volunteer and was really intrigued with journalism, but at the same time, I loved to be part of the crowd, even tried to be the life of the party. Especially with girls, I could be quite witty and I teased a lot, just having fun.

Reflecting on that year, I think God was using my self-righteousness and vague commitment to missions as a sort of protective fence around me. I was always wrestling in my mind with what was the right thing to do. Because of this, I never did get hooked on some of the habits that could have changed my life course.

In April of that year, I was double-dating with a friend. We went to the youth revival at First Baptist Church being led by a team of students from the University of Richmond. I was completely caught up in the excitement and sincerity of their testimonies of God actually making a difference in their lives. My experience as a Christian was not like that at all. My attempts to even know what God wanted me to be or do had come up empty. And they were sharing how God had led them to speak to a friend who was hurting, and God had helped them to do it. And one shared how he had such a hard time forgiving a friend, but as he read the Bible and prayed about it and talked with trusted Christian friends, he was able to forgive the person completely. That was not my experience. I could see that I was missing something very important and I wanted to know what it was.

I don't think I had ever heard anything like this before. I had been to revivals every year at Grandin Court Methodist Church, and every year I went down to the front to rededicate my life, but to my knowledge no one ever sat down with me and tried to figure out just what I was dealing with and committing to.

So, all this time I was thinking I was a Christian, and a good one; and suddenly it dawned on me that there is something more that I didn't know about; something important. I made an appointment with one of the students to talk with him one Sunday afternoon. I told him about myself and my desire to be a missionary and the lack of understanding I got at home. In other words, I presented myself as a misunderstood Christian young person. I don't know how much he sensed of my blindness and duplicity, but whatever he said, and what I felt, that night I began my long walk to God.

It took some time to realize that I wasn't a Christian at all, for I had no awareness of God or his presence. That summer was a time of intense Bible study, especially with one group of young people who were very helpful. On Sunday nights, I started going to Grandin Court Baptist Church where many friends were very helpful. I met several young people who were Christian, and Baptist, and that helped me changed my lifestyle.

One of the results I noticed was within me: before, I had been making myself remember God and his pathway; now I was aware of God all the time without any effort on my part. I really wanted to do what would please him. I just had to learn what that was, and of course, that has been a task for a lifetime.

This was my first year in college, but I knew that I needed to make a change to some place where I would get the help I needed to grow as a Christian. My friend, Gin Bowman, who was also at Roanoke College that year, was transferring the next year to Meredith College, a Baptist women's college. I had never heard of Meredith before, but what I did hear convinced me that it would be a good place for me.

A word from a wise man of long ago:

"If a man (or woman) does not keep pace with his companions, perhaps it is because he hears a different drummer. Let him step to the music he hears, however measured or far away."– Henry David Thoreau

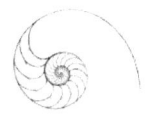

Meredith College

Gin and her sister, Charlotte, both encouraged me, so I talked with Mr. Martin, the bursar, and he said to come on down and we could work out a plan for financing. Such faith he had in me! The truly amazing thing is that Mother and Daddy didn't object at all; they seemed to trust that I knew what I was doing. So, I went to Meredith and Mr. Martin was as good as his word; he helped me to find jobs, such as working in the kitchen and dining hall, acting as a receptionist in the parlor for boys who came for their dates, picking up shoes for repair from the other students, and as a cashier in the Bee Hive snack shop.

I pitched in and worked hard at my jobs and in my classes. It was exhilarating for me to be in an all-women's college. I loved it! Miss Lou in the dining hall was always a good counselor, Dr. Mary Lynch Johnson, an English professor, was a valuable friend with her encouragement and advice, and also Dr. Leslie Syron in the Sociology Department. She helped to steer me toward social work itself and that is what I would need later. The latter two both urged me on in my desire to

Georgia Hinton, my best friend
Meredith College, Raleigh, NC, 1950

serve as a missionary.

But, I suppose the one I was closest to, and loved the most, was Georgia Hinton. She was a worker in the kitchen and I worked with her every day washing glasses and talking up a storm. Both she and her husband worked in the kitchen at Meredith; both were always cheerful and so loving toward me—exactly what I needed at that time.

She helped me to maintain my perspective. When you are in school all of the time, you can forget how folks outside in the working world live and think. It was good to talk with Georgia; she would always cheer me up! We were able to maintain our friendship after college, and later, our daughter, Becky, who lived in Raleigh, was Georgia's friend also. Nice!

Sometimes I missed my family and our camaraderie around the dinner table and I really missed the mountains that surround Roanoke Valley. Sometimes Gin and I would look off in the distance at evening time, squint our eyes and imagine that the bluish smoky haze on the horizon was mountains.

I didn't need any encouragement by then toward mission work. When I gave my life to God, for me it was understood that I would be a foreign missionary. Before, I had never even thought of what God might want me to do. But, now I had no doors closing indicating that I shouldn't do this, so that was my plan. I would prepare and go as a single lady missionary. My initial thought was that I'd go to Japan because of the war. But later, I became intrigued with Tibet as an unreached place.

One day in my junior year, Gin and I hurried down to the veranda connecting the main building and the dorm at Meredith College. Waiting for us was JC Mitchell, Gin's present interest, who had asked her and me to go with him and some other preacher boys to Clayton, NC for a weekend revival. It was winter break, a long weekend, and we had opted not to go home. We already knew some of the fellows from the Miracle Book Club, but we hadn't met Troy yet. When we first saw each other, he said, "You must be Trip" and of course my reply was, "And you must be Troy." We had heard about each other from mutual friends. I should say here that everybody in my family was called Trip by their own circle of friends. Why Trip? What was my last name? That's right. Trippeer, so Trip.

That was an interesting weekend. Gin and I stayed with one family and the fellows at other places. I remember she and I had talked into the wee hours and needed to go to the bathroom before we went to sleep, but that meant a walk down the path in the dark and very cold night. We shivered and giggled all the way.

In the first service, I got my introduction to the way these youth revival teams work. JC was leader of the service and was to do the offertory prayer. He announced that Gin and I would sing a duet, "I'm a Child of the King," during the offering. I had never heard the song. Remember, I had been a Methodist until very recently. During the prayer, we slipped over to the piano and I whispered to the pianist to play through the whole song as an introduction; I would know at least what it sounded like. Fortunately, Gin and I could sing duets pretty well, so it went okay.

On Sunday at dinner at the Whisnant's house, we were all together and the fellows were full of themselves. At that time I thought Leonard Rollins was the coolest one around, and he was in rare form. I don't remember which one it was who made pitter-patter sounds on the table at one point in the conversation to indicate that others also had to go down the path to the outhouse. The Whisnants, Eph and Sadie, were to become wonderful friends to me. Sadie was on the Meredith board and whenever she came for a meeting, she never failed to look me up and we would have a good talk. She was very encouraging of my hopes of being a missionary. She had grown up in China and she and Eph went back for a short time, but had to leave due to ill health. I came to really love her.

Sometime after that first weekend, Gin had a date

with Troy and I went along with Bob Auffarth. We went to see some play at Wake Forest, *The Taming of the Shrew*, I think, and whenever something funny happened, Bob would poke me in the ribs to be sure I got the joke. Now, Bob was a football player, quite robust in build, and at intermission we had to move our seats around so he could poke the other side of me. I was getting bruised.

Troy & "Trip" in courting days
Wake Forest, NC, 1949

Later one Sunday afternoon, Troy called Gin to go out for a walk in the country that used to be just the other side of Meredith College. They insisted I go along. Later, we laughed and said he went out with her but came back with me. Not literally, but that was the beginning of our friendship.

I was a very young Christian at that time, and he was so much more knowledgeable than I, though I didn't think of it at that time. We were a good match for each other; I challenged him and he challenged me. Our main contacts that year, my junior year, were Friday nights at Mrs. Celia Middleton's Miracle Book Club. What a blessing that was, real serious Bible study and fellowship with other earnest Christian young people.

We came from Wake Forest College, NC State, and Meredith. She was a wonderful Bible teacher and a very understanding and devout person. Great role model for me, at least. That was when Troy and I got to know each other better. He was one of the few who had a car and he brought students from Wake Forest and then came over and got us at Meredith. He was smart and nice and knew his Bible a lot better than I; also he was a lot of fun.

I was secretary and that was perfect for me because I thought I had to pay such close attention and try to get every point down. I probably took more intensive notes than I needed, but I was a young Christian and thirsty to learn all I could. My only other experience of Bible study had been with a group of young people in Roanoke the summer after I made my commitment to Christ.

I had taken "Old Testament 101" the previous year under Dr. McLain at Meredith; he was a good teacher but his attempt to jolt some of the girls out of their "Baptist straitjackets" was hard for me to hear. I resisted a lot and he knew it. Of course in later years I have found myself saying some of the things he was saying. At that time I was not in a straitjacket, but was a floundering new Christian trying to understand the basics. My ignorance and sincerity must have been evident to all in that group at least. When I was in the Baptist group, it quickly became apparent that I didn't know the language. To tell the truth, I never have liked using such expressions as "saved" and "come to the Lord," but at least now I do know what they mean. Now I can try to say the same thing in a more common way.

I had such good friends at Meredith: Buck and Crim and Lavern and Yarb and, of course, Gin and Charlotte. They had real names, but this is the way I remember them, and I loved them dearly. We had good times. There was also Sue and Winnie Fitzgerald, Maggie and Jed and so many others.

How can we measure how much these very fine people influenced our lives? It seems I am constantly appreciating more and more the value of a Liberal Arts education, a broader look at the world and everybody in it, including myself. The value of a women's college, I know now, is hard to beat. It was just right for me. I had six brothers and didn't need to know about boys. I thought I already knew it all, but the environment of women working and trying to accomplish big things was just my cup of tea!

During that next summer I worked in Oklahoma City

Gin Bowman, my other best friend
Meredith College,
Raleigh, NC, 1950

My graduation portrait
Meredith College,
Raleigh, NC, 1950

with the Home Mission Board, and was surprised and pleased that Troy carried on a regular correspondence. When we returned to school, our relationship continued much the same. We didn't really date that I remember.

The summer work was good as I, with my partner Liz Thompson, walked the streets of Oklahoma City looking for Native American Indians and inviting them to come to our church activities. We lived in the upstairs of the Indian Center, a downtown storefront. It was great and I learned a lot about meeting and befriending new people. The local people kept telling me I would see their mountains when we went to Falls Creek, the Baptist campground. Well, we went and I was looking for mountains when they pointed out two or three hills to me. I ran up one of them in fifteen minutes. Coming from North Carolina, they were hardly mountains, but it was all in good fun! The missionaries we lived and worked with, Mr. and Mrs. John Isaacs, were fine people. I learned so much about mission work in the US, especially among Native American Indians. I stopped off in Cherokee, NC when I came home on the Greyhound bus. Cherokee, NC was more a Native American Indian town whereas the Native American Indians in Oklahoma City were scattered and of different tribes. Also, the Cherokees were marketing their skills, commercializing their culture. And they still do. I have been there one more time later and they have all sorts of things for sale that represent their culture.

After college, I needed to work to pay off my college

debt. Uncle Dick had loaned me the money for my first year at Roanoke College in Salem when I lived at home. When I wrote and told him my plans for the future, he forgave me that debt. Mr. Zeno Martin at Meredith had been wonderful; I think he believed in me more than I did in myself. I'm sure he pulled some strings for me, as I only owed $500 when I graduated. Of course, I had been quite frugal and had worked a good many hours. Even so, that wasn't much, though it seemed huge at the time. When I got my first job, I sent $50 every month until it was paid off. I don't remember what I was being paid, but my budget was really tight. When I got married, I had $85 to put in the pot and I was proud that I had that.

That summer, I worked at a café in Roanoke and earned some money, but I was looking for something more promising. Being at home did allow me to work on the city-wide youth revival, which a group of us brought to Roanoke. And that experience, speaking in many churches and encouraging their support, brought me into contact with many of the Baptist churches in the Roanoke area.

Finally in the fall, I was offered a job at First Baptist Church in Bluefield, West Virginia as secretary/director of the mission to the neighborhood children. This was an education for me as I learned to use a mimeograph machine to print the Sunday bulletins. Also, there was another thing called a hectograph. If you wrote, typed, or drew a design on a piece of paper using a special purple ink and then pressed it into a very shallow pan filled with some sort of gelatinous substance, it would transfer, and then you could make copies. I don't remember how many copies it made before it got too faint to see. That was the hectograph. And a mimeograph machine was another messy way to make copies. But with that one, I had to type the bulletin onto a special kind of paper without a ribbon so as to cut through the special paper to make letters. Then I would put it on the machine and put ink in — but not too much — and spread it around. Finally, I could run papers through one at a time by turning the big cylinder, and they would receive the printed words. When it dried, I had to do the other side, same way. Long before computers or even electric typewriters. Your grandmother is a very accomplished woman in the old ways!

I don't think I did a very good job as director of the children's mission. FBC was in a downtown area that had "gone down," and very few in the neighborhood attended the church. But, there were a lot of children in the neighborhood and on the streets. This was an effort to reach out to them with activities and love. There was one little boy who really caught my heart. His name was Charles Ray Hurt; he was four or five years old. He and his mother and older brother lived in one room in a very old building. However, his mother and brother worked somewhere and often there was no one at home when Charles returned from the streets in the evening. When I became aware of how alone he was, I did get involved, and Florence Moore, who was minister of music at the church was in it with me. We couldn't do much for him but one night we got him for a sleepover. We all stayed at Flo's house. When we put him in the bathtub, we had to change the water three times. We could hardly believe how dirty he was — ground-in dirt that made his skin darker than it was. He was a spunky little fellow and I have thought of him many times through the years. I can only hope and pray that he has had others to show him love and concern. He would be in his sixties now. Imagine that!

"At times our own light goes out and is rekindled by a spark from another person. Each of us has cause to think with deep gratitude of those who have lighted the flame within us."

– by Albert Schweitzer

Marriage

Psalm 141:3
"Set a guard over my mouth, O Lord;
Keep watch over the door of my lips."

Troy was still at Wake Forest that year while I was working in Bluefield. At Christmastime, he told me he felt God wanted him to go to the mission field, and he was changing his major to pre-med. He would need to take summer school to catch up on some science subjects.

In the spring, he had a weekend revival somewhere in West Virginia and came to see me. That was when we realized we were getting very serious. I'm not sure just when we decided to get married. Things were moving pretty fast about that time. Of course, his decision to go into missions made a huge difference, for I had said I wasn't planning to marry anybody. Somehow I had gotten it into my head that I would be a single missionary. But now I had gotten involved with Troy and needed to be sure that marriage to him was the right thing to do. I didn't have any doubts about loving him.

I loved him and admired him. But should I take that next step? As happens so often in life, I truly wanted to please God with my life and this was a critical decision. But I didn't have any dreams or visions to guide me, so I did what seemed right and I've never regretted that decision.

Mrs. Susie Jeffries, sister of Mrs. Middleton back in Raleigh, was in the same church in Bluefield and had a bookstore that I often visited. First, because I love books, but also to talk with her and get her perspective on matters I was thinking about. She was a huge help to me during this time. Several of the folks there were such good friends to me. One night they gave a wedding shower for me, told everyone to bring canned goods, since they thought I had enough other stuff. But as I unwrapped the canned goods, they would snatch them out of my hands and rip the labels off. Which meant that I went away with several boxes of unmarked cans of food and a handful of labels. Fortunately for us, Troy had worked in his Papa's grocery store for several years and could often guess what was in the can by shaking it and listening. True, sometimes we did have tomatoes instead of peaches, beans instead of corn, but no problem. We had fun with that one!

And then it was time to go back to Roanoke and get ready for the wedding. As you may imagine, I was not one of those brides who got all hyped up about the wedding, but of course I wanted it to be nice. I asked my sister Marian if I could borrow her bridesmaid's dress from a wedding she had been in recently. It was pink and I have always thought I looked better in pink

Marj with sister Marian, my maid of honor
Roanoke, VA, 1951

than in white. I'm not sure where I got the veil, just a short one. Marian was my only attendant and she wore a green dress from the same wedding, so we matched.

Troy didn't get there until noon on the day of the wedding. He had been preaching revival services in Norfolk, I think. Anyway, the night before—the last night of the revival—they had a shower for him and loaded him down with gifts. His car was filled up with them. A nice lady had asked him if he had pearls for me, to which he replied, "No." She insisted he had to have them, so she gave him a string of pearls for me, and I have worn them many times through the years and thought of that nice lady. I never knew her name.

We didn't really have a rehearsal, just a sort of run-through in our living room. Mother and the others had prepared a great luncheon for everyone, a picnic I think, and then it was time to get dressed. As I think back now, I think I was in a daze. Was this really happening to me? But I kept going and got to the church on time. Troy's friend was to sing and he worked things

Troy & Marj
Grandin Court Baptist Church
Roanoke, VA , September 1, 1951

out with the organist of the church when he got there. She later said that she had never had so much fun at a wedding. The reception afterward was really nice. I expect Mother and Daddy both collapsed when we left town. But during the wedding they were cool, real cool.

Troy's old friend, Wilson Stewart, got really aggravated with Marian and her boyfriend at the time, who took us to our car. He didn't get to decorate it at all. We got away and went to Galax, VA to a hotel which my Daddy had recommended. One problem; it was Saturday night and we were right across from some kind of honky-tonk. They were really happy over there! Daddy had been there on weeknights, not weekends. The next day we headed to Fontana Dam, which was our destination for the week.

Fontana Dam was a great place to go and we enjoyed it. One funny thing happened. The very first morning, we heard a woman's voice calling, "Troy. Troy." He went out to see who in the world she could be. You'll never guess; one of his old girlfriends from Winston-Salem! She had gotten married the same day. I forget what kind of help they needed, but it was no problem.

How did she know he was there? I don't know. We surely kidded him about that, especially his friends back in Winston-Salem who knew them both.

Then, we settled in with Troy's parents. We lived upstairs at Papa and Mama Bennett's house at 407 West 14th Street in Winston-Salem. June also had a room up there. We had a bedroom/study, a kitchen/eating area and access to the shared bathroom. Troy was in medical school and I worked as a secretary in the pathology department at Baptist Hospital. We usually went together in the morning, but seldom came home at the same time. Two things really helped me with this job. First, I had taken typing in high school and second, I had three years of Latin. For all of those medical terms, this was very helpful. My job was to listen to the Dictaphone into which the doctors had spoken reports on pathological studies and I typed what they had dictated. It wasn't hard at all. I enjoyed it.

As a young bride living upstairs in his parents' home, we were downstairs a good bit, especially in the summer evenings when we would help with canning. Mama had a really neat peach peeler that I loved to operate. After we finished, we would go out on the front porch and sit in the swing and cool off. Nice! We had bought an electric stove and it wasn't long until Mama had one put in her kitchen to replace the old Majestic, a big woodstove with a chimney and water heater that really heated up the kitchen.

Fitting into the family was an interesting challenge. Mary and Mallie were in Winston-Salem with their

1950 Prices:		Gallon of gas	$ .18
Average income	$3,216.00	Gallon of milk	$ .84
New car	$1,511.00	Minimum wage	$ .75
New house	$8,450.00	Life expectancy	68.3 years
Loaf of bread	$ .14	Invention:	credit cards

families so that was good. RO and Muriel came in often with their four girls. We didn't see much of Phyllis and William who lived in California. I remember one day RO talked with me about something, but his tone was very condescending, as if he were talking with a teenager. I kept my cool, but later as I thought about it, I realized that in my family I had been one of the Big Kids, but in this family I had married the next-to-youngest. Later I was to hear Mary and Phyllis refer to June as Baby Sister. There were times when I bristled for Troy when RO would talk down to him, but usually it wasn't a problem. Troy never mentioned it; he had great respect for RO, so I tried to honor that. When you marry, you may run into something like this.

In the spring, Troy decided he couldn't do med school and preach too, and he really wanted to preach. He had taken a job as pastor of a very small church there in town. So he chose to drop out of med school. His professors tried to talk him out of it, but he was determined at the time. He regretted it a time or two later on, but not that much. He would have been a good doctor, though. His Papa said, "It's about time he settled down to preach."

Troy's Story

In this chapter, "Papa Bennett" is Troy's Papa.

Let's see, what can I remember that Troy told me about his early years? First, he was born Troy Carson Bennett on April 12, 1929 in Hanes, NC. I'm pretty sure his was a home delivery by Dr. Slate, who delivered all of Mama Bennett's babies at home. Dr. Slate came from Winston-Salem when called by Nurse Perkins. Nurse Perkins was a resident nurse in Hanes with her office right beside Papa Bennett's General Mercantile Store. There were seven children: RO (or Rome), Phyllis, Mary, Mallie, William, Troy, and June, whose twin brother died at birth, born over a span of 17 years to Romy Olive and Beulah Mae Miller Bennett.

Papa Bennett came from Stokes County and Mama's family were from Eastern North Carolina. I only know that her father worked for the mills. They liked to laugh about Romy going to court her in a railway sidecar, an open car they pumped by hand. And he brought Mama back that way too. Troy's Papa was the manager and part-owner of the Hanes Mercantile Store in Hanes town. At that time Hanes was a small mill village in the country but is now a suburb of Winston-Salem. He was also the local postmaster, the banker and the pharmacist. Obviously he was a very important part of the community and highly respected by the mill workers. In the early days, Papa Bennett wasn't in the church at all, but I suppose Mama helped him to see the light because he certainly did and was very active from that time until the end.

I am indebted to June Bennett Rikard, Troy's younger sister, for much of this information. She told me that Papa Bennett would call on payday to learn how much cash he would need to cash the millworkers' checks, then get the cash from the bank in Winston-Salem, bring it back to the store and lock one of the older daughters in a special cage with the money and her job was to cash the workers' paychecks. The problem he had with Mr. Hanes in 1936 occurred when Mr. Hanes learned that Papa Bennett was extending credit to these people. Of course the country was still in the throes of the Great Depression and people simply didn't have the money to pay. Papa was not willing to see any of his neighbors and friends go hungry. I understand this perfectly because we were in the same boat, though in Roanoke. If you read about that time, you'll learn many, many people were struggling with hunger. It was no disgrace; too many people were in the same boat.

Some interesting notes from their family life that you'll be glad to hear. When RO was four years old, he had a problem with his leg and foot; his foot was drawing up, actually doubling under, and he was becoming lame. Dr. Slate had no idea what it was, nor could the doctors at Baptist Hospital in Winston-Salem help—this was before the big polio epidemics in the 1930s and 40s. They told Papa Bennett to take him to Gastonia to a Shriner's Hospital there, which he did, several times. I remember Troy talking about it, so it must have been over a period of several years as Troy wasn't born until RO was 10 years old or so.

In the 40s, I think she said '44, as she was recovering from some ailment, June was anxious to join her friends skating in the street. It was the middle of the summer and that just looked like too much fun to miss. Finally the day came when she could get off the front porch steps, put on her skates and go for it. As she sailed down the street, you can imagine how free she felt, released from captivity. But as she reached the corner of 14th and Patterson Street, she had a flashing, blinding headache that threw her to the ground. She couldn't walk and was just lying there crying until Troy came running and carried her home, not far, about four or five houses away. She remembers this vividly because it was her big brother caring for her; he didn't seem to remember that part at all. Sorry, June! Anyway, she had polio, which especially affected her left arm and side; the leg somewhat, but the arm was the worst. There were so many children sick those summers; I have no idea how many were crippled or died, but I can tell you parents were terrified. Swimming pools were closed; children didn't go to public parks or anywhere. I don't remember if we went to

Sunday school and church then or not. We stayed close to home, really close.

But here was June with a full-blown case of polio and Papa and Mama Bennett with a little experience with RO. They had done physical therapy on him for months after his bout, and if I remember correctly, he always wore a special shoe on that leg since it was shorter than the other. This was a rather common occurrence. But back to June:

The doctor suggested they send her to a polio hospital in Hickory, but the parents decided that was not the best thing to do. Rather, Mama Bennett and June stayed at the house, Troy was farmed out with family friends; he was seven years older, Papa Bennett stayed with relatives; the older children had married and moved on. Of course, they could not come into the house for any reason at all. A lady up the street ran a boarding house where many of the in-town mill workers ate, so she prepared a big tray of food every morning and brought it to the house and set it just outside the back door so Mama could get it. Her schedule was grueling: every two hours, day and night, she had to put hot compresses on June's side and arm. She kept a hot plate with a deep pan of water and the wet towels right in the downstairs bedroom so she could get to them as needed.

This went on for four weeks and then June had to stay in bed another two weeks before getting up and moving around. As I have said, her leg was not so much affected so she was able to walk, but lifting and bending that left arm was another matter. At first, they took her into the bathroom which was right off the bedroom and, putting her into a tub of hot water, they would stretch her arm about quarter inch more each day. Finally, they didn't need to put her into the tub anymore, so they would lay her out on the dining room table sprinkled with Johnson's Baby Powder and Papa would work her arm, bending the elbow and raising her arm away from her side. Boy, that must have been painful for all concerned. As June remembers, this therapy went on for the entire next school year. Fortunately, she lived close to the school and was able to come home easily for the noontime ritual.

    I have learned through the years that it really is true; parents do suffer deeply when they see their loved ones in pain. Anybody does. Actually, June was a very lucky girl. She didn't get the bulbar type of polio, which affected the lungs and caused many to be unable to breathe and unless they were in an iron lung, they were totally paralyzed. She had Mama and Papa to care for her. In fact, June heard one of the doctors say to them that if she had gone to Hickory, she couldn't possibly have gotten the kind of care she needed, the care which her own parents gave her. She has had some residual difficulties through the years, but she has been able to handle them well. Now, that's the saga about the polio epidemic and you just hope you never live to see anything like it. Thank you, Dr. Salk, who later developed the polio vaccine!

    I suppose you would be interested to hear some of the things Troy said about his ancestors. There was

Grandpa Alexander King who, as I understand, left his wife and a houseful of children and went west. Something about an Indian lady, but I don't know about that. Actually, I don't know if any of this is true. You know Troy was good at embellishing his stories. At one point, Grandpa King lived in Atlanta when Aunt Phyllis was living there. It is said that when he came back to Stokes County, his wife said he could stay, but that he would have to sleep on the front porch, not in the house. I never heard where he ate his meals. He, or somebody, is buried in a tiny little cemetery near King, NC that was cut down in size by a new road. I saw this myself. She is buried in the big new cemetery down the road a piece. Now that's the way to handle a fellow who runs around too much. Who says women got their power through the Women's Movement? You might like to know that he and two other men were the ones who picked the location for the county seat of Stokes County and named it Danbury. History records that they were all drunk at the time.

But, there was also Doctor William Swain King, his son, who was a highly respected citizen of the community. His wife was Lethia Ann Cook King. Dr. King was an educated man and was particularly entranced with classical literature. He was so fascinated that he named his eight daughters names from those works: Malvena Sofrona, Lura Delra, Morella Carolee, Quentora McQueen, Rosella Amilene, Mollora Beldene, Judd Muller and Louvella Vandora.

I'm not sure how many children they had at the time, but in 1870 or 1871 he took his family to Utah to join the Mormons there. He only stayed six months and two days before becoming disillusioned with the Mormon faith and brought his family back to Stokes County where he worked for over 30 years. He was especially known for his treatment of typhoid fever. He would be Troy's great grandfather.

Troy's grandfather was Pinkney Bennett, married to Malvena Sofrona, known as Frone King. They had 13 children, but she died of childbed fever when the youngest, Troy Carson, was born. He also died, and it was this baby's tombstone that Troy saw years later as a little kid in King, NC. It kinda scared him since he had the exact same name. Pink Bennett died two years after his wife and so the house and over the 400+ acre farm was sold for $4,102 and the younger children were homed out with relatives and friends. The older ones were already married. But Romy, known as Rome or to us as Papa Bennett, struck out on his own. He joined his brother in a grocery store and later moved into Winston-Salem to another store.

Papa Bennett had wanted to be a doctor and did actually start at Yadkin College, but after a short time, dropped out. With the death of his parents and the concern for the younger children, he felt responsible to work and provide for them what he could. He felt a special responsibility for the youngest, Nell. He made sure she got through high school.

Speaking of Aunt Nell, I met her and she was a bird. She had dark hair and sparkling dark eyes. She was feisty too. She told us a really good, true story about her husband who had a habit of kicking when he was asleep. Probably Restless Leg Syndrome, which had not been heard of then. Anyway, when he kicked, he often kicked her out of bed. One night she realized he was getting ready to do it again, so she just up and jumped out of bed to watch what would happen. He kicked himself out of bed and was mad as a hornet at her! Well, we of course laughed with her. Not sure he ever did though.

I don't know much about the Hanes town time, but Troy did recount how he would go to Papa's store and beg for candy. One day Papa Bennett had had enough of it and he took little Troy behind the post office section of the store, got his yardstick and switched him good. One of those memories that stays, especially because he was so embarrassed to have customers witness the scene.

Troy Bennett, just a little fellow
Hanestown, NC, circa 1933

RO had a dog. Troy always wanted one, but didn't get one until he was a college student. After that, we had dogs most of the time. RO also did some boxing at that time and had a ring set up in the garage, I think. This was the follow-up to his bout with polio which resulted in one leg shorter than the other. He did a lot of things to build himself up physically.

We have a picture of Troy as a little shaver, maybe five or six years old; his hair was almost white but his eyebrows were quite dark. Pretty cute!

In 1936, the family moved into Winston-Salem and Papa Bennett opened a grocery store on Northwest Boulevard which he operated for many years, until WWII when the rationing got to be too much for him. Mama and Papa lived at 407 West 14th Street just off Patterson Avenue until they had to move in with June and Bob for their care. Later, one of our family's favorite lines from the store experience was what a little boy said when he forgot to bring the ration stamps to get his groceries, "I lost a walk." We often lost a walk and had to go back for whatever we had forgotten.

Their new location was ideal for school and church. They were less than a half block from Northwest Elementary School and about three blocks from North Winston Baptist Church in which they all became very involved. When the children went on to Hanes High School, it was still within walking distance. At the elementary school they had tennis courts and a swimming pool so Troy took full advantage of those. He became quite

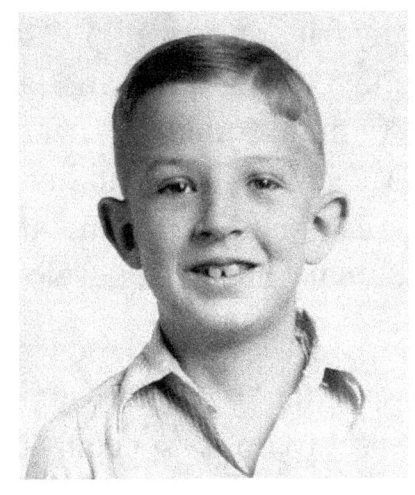

Troy growing up; pretty cute school picture!
Hanestown, NC, 1935

good in tennis and in many other sports as well. He was quite late to be diagnosed with astigmatism, but after he got glasses, he could take part in baseball and other sports when he needed to see. He was a natural athlete and loved all sports, so this was one of his interests through the years.

He had a friend while in elementary school, Ty Park, who was Chinese and he and Troy became fast friends. One thing Troy appreciated about Ty was his ability to draw cartoon characters. Learning this skill gave him many hours of pleasure, and later, when he had his own children, one of the favorite evening activities was for each of us to write one large number and Troy would convert it into a picture. He was really very clever at this and we always loved doing it. Evidently Ty moved on because there was no mention of him in later years.

Troy had many friends, some whom I have made my friends as well. Wilson and DW Stewart were his longtime buddies and later, along with their wives, we maintained this friendship after retirement. Also, Marian Phillips and her twin brother Hunter were very good friends. Marian later went to Nigeria as a missionary until she developed cancer.

After we retired, he was reminded that he was the president of the Reunion Class of 1947. He didn't really want to do it especially after his old friend Jim Holder expressed no interest at all. But as time went on, he did do it and Jim was one of the most supportive. This was the time when I got to know some of them better and they got to know me. They even let me be secretary for the group, meaning I did all the contacting. But it was fun and we had some really good times bringing together all the class members still able to come. No old girlfriends surfaced; I already knew about all of them, I think. Actually, I got to be good friends with two of them. I had learned about them when we applied to the Foreign Mission Board and one of our assignments was to write our life history in detail: year by year, family details, school, dating, of course our religious experience, call to missions, etc. and so on.

During his junior year in high school, a revival came to Winston-Salem and Troy became very involved in it. As a result, he was seriously challenged about his own relationship with God. He had been baptized when he was younger and joined the church. However, in his case, that had not resulted in any real change in his life. During that revival he was challenged by the preaching, but especially by talks with Alec "Mutt" Bahnson, a local fellow who had had a critical experience with God while in the war. Troy's life was then transformed and on a different path.

He and Hunter Phillips were to be co-captains of the football team their senior year. They resigned from the team to give their time to preaching youth revivals. This really shook things up; both of them felt deeply that they wanted to serve God in this way, and both were very effective in this work.

June told me about that time which must have been very exciting for Troy and the fellows he was hanging out with: Wilson Stewart, Hunter Phillips, and others. June said they would come to the house and sit in the living-room and plan, sing, pray—doing what new exuberant Christians do. She, who was supposed to be in bed, would sneak down the stairs and peek through the banisters. Must have been quite exhilarating for her too. All those fellows in her house and she just a young teenager. They formed a Youth for Christ group in town; I think I remember they met at First Baptist Church with Dr. Ralph Herring's encouragement. Most of these fellows were students at Hanes Senior High School; Troy graduated from Hanes in 1947.

In later years whenever the children asked for a story about his childhood, he would usually tell them about the scrapes they got into when he was younger: when they stretched a rope across busy Patterson Avenue to cause cars to stop and then dropped the rope and ran. The police found them and took them downtown. I do know his Papa had to go to the police station at least once to get him out. I can picture Papa Bennett saying, "Pushed the button a bit too hard that time, son."

Hunter Phillips & Troy: newspaper clipping when they left football to preach
Winston-Salem, NC, 1945

Troy went to Wake Forest College in Wake Forest, NC just north of Raleigh. He had always been a very good student and continued this record with a planned major of Philosophy and Psychology. Again, he made some very strong friendships which have lasted through the years. And, as I described earlier, he and I met during those college years.

Troy graduated in 1951 and by then we were planning to get married. He had been accepted at Bowman Gray Baptist Medical School in Winston-Salem.

After Troy and I married in 1951, we went to Troy's home church, North Winston Baptist. That was where I felt the need to establish my identity, especially after one Sunday when a woman asked Mama in my presence, "Is this Troy's?" Sounded to me like I was a dog or maybe a book or a backpack, whatever; that didn't last too long. They certainly know who I am now! After all, I wrote all of the letters for the next 35 to 40 years.

Well, that is short shrift with his life, but I just can't remember all the details of stories, like driving into the back of a mule on a dark road, driving a car without a heater in the dead of winter, and going coon hunting, which he did once after we married. No, we didn't eat it. Oh yes, they had a minstrel performance at Hanes High and he, DW, and Wilson Stewart got the African American janitor to sing bass with them. Troy loved to sing, "Dem bones, dem bones, dem dry bones, they gonna rise again," and, "One black, two black, hot shining shoe black, chocolate to the bone....Get out and waaaalk."

Seminary — Fayetteville Wake Forest

So, for Troy to train for the ministry he went to seminary in Wake Forest, NC. We moved there in the summer of 1952, and by that time I was pregnant with Steve. A little later, when Troy accepted the pastorate at Immanuel Baptist in Fayetteville, they made arrangements for us to move there. At first we lived in the upstairs apartment at the Langfords' house, and then later moved to McKimmon Road. Eventually, the church bought a house on Camellia Drive for a parsonage, so we moved there. These moves were just the beginning!

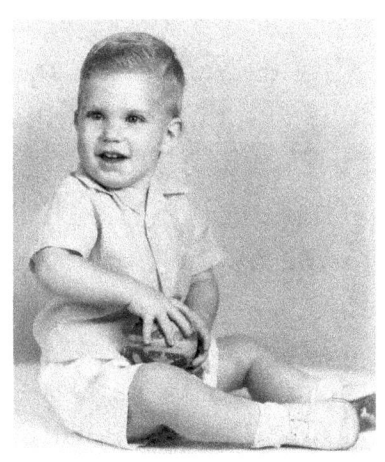

Steve, one year old
Fayetteville, NC, 1953

Somebody asked about the births of our babies. Any excitement there? Well, of course there was excitement. Our first child entered this world on Sunday morning, December 14, 1952 at Highsmith Hospital in Fayetteville, NC. That morning I told Troy I thought I was having labor pains. Madge Langford who lived downstairs confirmed my thoughts and Troy took me to the hospital; then he left for church, but I heard later that at the end of the service he announced that he wouldn't tarry because I had gone to the hospital. First child on the way! Troy kept saying, "Unto us a child is born." He didn't say a son is given until later. Back then we didn't know ahead of time. Soon, Stephen Lanning Bennett made his appearance without much trouble.

Bones McKinney, one of Troy's seminary schoolmates, had asked him when Steve was born, "Boy or girl?" When Troy replied that it was a boy, he said, "That's good. After this it doesn't matter what you have." When Troy told me that, I told him he could tell Bones he didn't know anything; I had a lot I wanted to teach my girls. And I did!

At the time, we were living in that upstairs apartment in Hoyle and Madge Langford's house. It was quite adequate for us except that it was upstairs and thus had slanted ceilings, in the kitchen especially. Troy kept banging his head on the ceiling. His head already had lots of scars from various injuries from hitting his head. He was a bit taller than most men.

One night I went to the bathroom and when I flushed the commode, it exploded. Really! You never heard such a racket, which was compounded by the wild barking of our dog Sheba, a young boxer we had acquired. Another story there. Anyway, the commode situation was explained later by Hoyle, who had talked with the plumber who had worked on the system the day before. Seems he had hooked up the hot water to the wrong pipe. It wasn't really an explosion, but it sounded like one in the middle of the night and the dog barking just turned the volume up more.

About that dog, when we lived in Winston-Salem over Mama and Papa, Troy was offered a boxer mix that had been used for experiments at the hospital. She was such a nice dog they didn't want to put her down. So we said yes, and promptly Troy arranged for her to go to Morganton where Uncle RO lived to have a visit with a pureblood boxer that RO knew about. The desired outcome happened. She had six or seven puppies and we kept one – Sheba, who actually had very good lines and markings for a boxer. Of course she got bigger and bigger, especially in the two-room apartment in Wake Forest, but I walked her every day and she was okay. When we lived upstairs at the Langford's, she was in a good place because they also had a boxer. Then we moved into the little house over the fence on McKimmon Drive. Sheba was still getting bigger and bigger but was a really good dog — young and energetic. One time we left her with the Langford's dog in the enclosure while we went out of town. Guess what she did? She just jumped right on that other dog's back and over the six-foot fence!

She was great with Steve. He would sit in his playpen and take a lick of an ice cube wrapped in a wash cloth and then give Sheba a lick. Good friends. But the mailman was terrified of her, and others wouldn't come to our door if they saw her looking out the window. So, we had to get rid of her, which was probably just as well as we couldn't take her overseas with us. After that, we had small dogs; dachshunds are not quite so intimidating.

We had a lot of good friends there at Immanuel Baptist Church. It was right in the neighborhood with Honeycutt Housing, which was US Army housing, so we were surrounded by lots of military families whom we could help. But there were also older, more settled folks who had been there for some time. We learned a lot from them.

Rossie Barnhill lived just up the street from us; she was my confidant and friend. Steve and I went up to her house many an afternoon just to see Miss Rossie. Other days I took him to the Jewish synagogue's playground. We loved that sliding board. He was a cute little guy and we had lots of fun! We knew so many good people at that church, including the Langfords, Bill and Edra Cain, Jim and Kathleen Nance, Paul and Carleen Teague, Johnnie and Emma Rice, and lots more. Such good people. So patient with us just learning how to lead a church. Churches that do this with young pastors play a very valuable role. There was also the Huggett family right across the street from us who had three children; the youngest was Steve's age. We enjoyed many good times with them and they eventually came into the church, too.

One interesting thing happened when the people of

Fayetteville were getting ready to celebrate some anniversary of Fayetteville. The men were encouraged to grow beards. Troy tried to grow one, but his hair is quite fine and thin, and his beard was too. Add to that his habit of stroking his chin when he was thinking and you'd think he rubbed it off. Finally, Paul Teague, a barber and church member, told him, "That beard has to go!" Well, it really did have to go. It didn't look good at all, he was quite mortified at first to have to shave it, but he got over it.

One time my Mom and Dad came for a few days visit. While they were with us, the subject of roaches in the house came up. Dad said he could fix that. That's what his job was at the time, keeping bakeries, dairies, and soft drink companies clean. So on the morning of their departure, we put up everything loose on the kitchen counters, closed the doors and he started his sprayer. When the designated time was up, he turned it off, took his sprayer, closed the doors again and told us to let it stand for an hour or so, and they left. He told us we would need to wipe everything down when it was finished. He wasn't kidding! When we opened the doors and looked in our kitchen, everything was dripping with a very heavy coating of oily spray. What a mess! We had to wipe and wipe and wipe. Maybe you can imagine what Troy had to say about my Dad going off and leaving us with such a mess! In one way it was funny, but we worked a long time to clean up that gunk! It did, however, get rid of the roaches and other critters.

Christmas 1954, we spent with my folks who had

moved to Harrisonburg, Virginia to be nearer Daddy's work. While we were there he had a heart attack—not his first one—and so was in the hospital when we left to go home. I have to admit that I just didn't think he would die. I couldn't imagine the world without Daddy in it, but on January 1, 1955, Mother called and told me to sit down. She knew I was pregnant with Becky. Then she told me Daddy had died.

We took Steve to Mama and Papa Bennett's in Winston-Salem and drove back to Harrisonburg that night. Dad was buried in Harrisonburg, but his body was later moved to Evergreen Cemetery in Roanoke. All of the children got there except Jim, who was in Germany, and Ben. Jim had recently received a letter of commendation from his commanding officer — Daddy was really proud. We were all glad he had a chance to express this to Jim, since it had always seemed to us that Daddy was especially hard on Jimmy for some reason; he probably thought Mother spoiled him. Don't know. Anyway, it was a hard blow, to lose Daddy at age 55, but one blessing I get from it is that all of my memories are of him as healthy and vibrant and full of life and fun. We loved our Dad!

My favorite picture of my parents:
Ben & Leona
Roanoke, VA, circa 1953

Nancy was attending Madison College right in

Harrisonburg. However, when Dad died, she dropped out of school, and she and Mom moved back to Roanoke. But the old house was way too big for them, so they sold it and bought a much smaller one on Suburban Avenue. Mother returned to her work with children who had to be out of school due to illness or accident. At one point she worked at the detention home. On game nights she would take a batch of fudge to the detention home and do a little innocent gambling on the outcome of one game or another.

Troy continued in seminary in Wake Forest, NC but I stayed in Fayetteville and played with Steve and tried to keep track of things at the church. Steve was a healthy baby, which means he was a good baby. We did have some trouble finding the right milk for his sensitive stomach, but finally got that worked out. Troy was gone most of the time, but I had a great time just playing with Steve. We also kept another little girl about the same age as Steve for a few weeks as her mother was having some problems with postpartum depression. Her name was Cathy and she was another easy baby, so I just had fun taking care of babies.

One more incident I should tell you about. One day two-year-old Steve fell and hit his forehead on the front step. He needed two or three stitches. We were planning to make a trip to Canada the next day to visit Jack and Eleanor Murray, friends of Troy who had a cabin up there. He had been there many times; he actually helped to build the place. It was a lovely cabin facing the lake, and only accessible by boat across the lake.

So, we took Steve with a bandage on his forehead. As we were coming back, his stitches started to itch and were standing out the way they do. Troy just took some fingernail clippers and cut those stitches and pulled them out. Well, I wasn't so sure about that since I had no experience with such things, but he seemed to know what he was doing and Steve didn't complain, so we rode on home. We stopped at Niagara Falls for one night. Oh, I thought I had never seen anything so beautiful as the lake up in Canada and the forests surrounding them, and now Niagara Falls. This small town girl was seeing the world!

Becky was next of course, and she was also born in Fayetteville at Highsmith Hospital. That morning was pretty funny. Troy was off in school when my labor started. I called and told him and since he wasn't coming home till later that day, I arranged a ride to the hospital with our friend across the street, Howard Huggett. He rode with his friend since they worked together. So, there I was in the back seat on the way to the hospital, doing my thing. They kept worrying about me—why wasn't I moaning and groaning like their wives did? Well, I just wasn't, but I was definitely in the birthing process and needed to get there.

Becky, one year old
Wake Forest, NC, 1956

When we arrived, they had us sit down in the hallway while the receptionist took down my information. She called Howard up, thinking he was the father. Every question she asked him, he had to turn and ask me. Finally, I persuaded her to let me come and answer the questions. Then, as we were going up on the elevator, Howard said he wanted to come too, to be sure everything was okay. His friend also wanted to come because his wife had delivered just a few days before and was up on that floor still. The nurse muttered as we went up in the elevator, "I'm sure glad I don't live on Camellia Drive." It all worked out okay, Troy arrived not too long after that. Of course, back then, they didn't let the fathers in the delivery room, but he did come in the little labor room where I was waiting to go into delivery. But good gracious, this child had red hair, really red! Later we learned that we both had red hair in our families, back in our lineage somewhere. So now we had Rebecca Ann Bennett, born February 25, 1955.

When the church in Fayetteville got to the place where they could afford a full-time pastor, Troy said it was time for us to be moving on, which we did. We moved to Wake Forest and lived in an apartment in an old house for his last year of school. I was also able to take some classes that I really enjoyed. I studied Old Testament under Dr. Leo Greene and Religious Education taught by a man whose name I don't remember. Boy, have I ever used what I learned that year. I have taught Old Testament classes more times than I can count, and I still love to teach it. And, of course,

Troy, Wilson Stewart & Hunter Phillips: from elementary school through seminary together Wake Forest, NC, 1956

the Religious Education course was also helpful as I worked with various churches.

All this time we had been in correspondence with the Foreign Mission Board and during this last year we started doing more writing; life histories, getting references, that sort of thing. The Personnel Committee felt the need to know as much as they could about us before sending us off so far away. In June 1956, after Troy graduated, we were appointed by the Foreign Mission Board of the Southern Baptist Convention. Nowadays, people have to have two or three years' experience before signing on with the Foreign Mission Board, but Troy already had a lot of experience since he had been pastoring or supply preaching for years, all through college and then in seminary at Immanuel and others.

Left to right: my mother, Leona with Papa & Mama Bennett at Troy's graduation Wake Forest, NC, 1956

We went to Richmond, VA for our orientation in the late summer of 1956. There, we learned what to expect from the Board as far as financial support, shipping our household things, all that administrative stuff. It was a pretty exciting time, I can tell you. We were booked to sail from San Francisco in mid-December on the *President Cleveland*. Our trip was scheduled to leave right before Christmas, but we were raring to go.

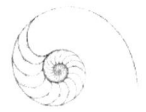

On the *President Cleveland*

The *President Cleveland* (15,359 grt, 609 ft. long), built in 1947. Sailed briefly as *Oriental President* for Orient Overseas Line before scrapped in 1974.

The *President Cleveland*
San Francisco, CA, December, 1956

The family was booked to take the Christmas Voyage of 1956 on the *President Cleveland*, an ocean liner going from San Francisco to Hong Kong. Before embarking on our charter voyage, we spent a few days in San Francisco to celebrate Steve's birthday by going to the zoo, which was tremendous fun. From Hong Kong, we were to fly through Bangkok, Thailand and Rangoon, Burma into Dacca, East Pakistan for our first mission assignment.

Before leaving California, we visited a Santa Claus

who was situated in an open corner of a department store. It was very interesting as both Steve and Becky were a little intimidated by the jolly man in the red suit. We had never stressed the Santa Claus part as we talked about Christmas; we did play along a bit, but mostly treated him as part of a game. When they finally asked us about him, we just told them that's what it was—a game. It's a good thing we did, because in years to come, sometimes part of their Christmas didn't arrive until a week or two after Christmas day and they knew it came in the mail. That's a most amazing time that I'll tell you about later.

One serendipity for us was that the ship first stopped in Los Angeles, and we were able to see our friend Marian Phillips who was in Golden Gate Seminary there. That was a treat for all of us as she was a favorite family friend. She had been a friend of Troy's since primary school.

Our next stop, or port of call, was Honolulu, and everybody was up on deck to watch the hula dancers. Dr. Abernathy had encouraged us and the Glasses, who were going to Singapore, to be sure to see this show. When I went to get Becky up from her nap, she had developed a high fever. Fortunately, there was a hospital on that ship and we cooled her down quickly. Just months earlier, when she stayed with Emma and Johnnie Rice, she had a similar incident so we were somewhat prepared in how to respond.

Traveling on the *President Cleveland* was really very nice. We had a cabin with four bunks and we signed up on a schedule sheet for a bath because there was just one bathroom with a tub to be shared in our hall, but that was okay. There was a playroom for the children, shuffleboard, and a pool and card games for the adults. We were assigned a time when we could go to eat. There were lots of nice people to talk with on the ship.

Troy, Steve & Becky on the deck
We're at sea! 1956

On Christmas day, the seas were really rough; the waves were tossing even that huge ship. There were four preachers on board, and Dr. Abernathy, who had traveled with the President Lines before, was asked to schedule services, which he did. The other preacher was a Navy chaplain who insisted he wanted to do the Christmas day service. That would have been fine, except that he got deathly sick on that very rough day and had to make several dashes to the rail. Well, there you go; even the Navy men can get seasick. I had heard of people turning green with seasickness, but that day we saw it. Ernest Glass was literally green, but he insisted on coming to the table to eat. He didn't last through the meal, but his wife Marjorie and the children thrived despite the rocking waves, even their small baby. We were secretly glad when he left the table; it made us a bit sick to look at him.

As I look back, this is the time I remember feeling most homesick. Here we were, going to do the work I had dreamed of for years, but this day, this time, just wasn't Christmas. We had had a nice Christmas in the States before we left. There was a beautiful Christmas tree and lots of pretty decorations on the ship of course, and a big dinner, but it wasn't Christmas. No caroling with friends, none of the things that made Christmas real for me. But it was the celebration of Jesus' birth and I sensed God very close as I walked on the deck by myself; we were a long way from home and going even farther. As I look back, I can see that it was then that I really turned my face toward whatever God had in store for us. I had made my choice. I was committed to loving and serving people as God's ambassador, whatever the price. We had left home and chosen a new life.

I was later to realize that every time we moved, I had a personal struggle. I always had a hard time the first few weeks and months, not because I didn't like the place we had gone to, or questioned whether we should have moved, but just missing what we had left behind. I had to learn over and over again to let it go. We would remain friends with all of those wonderful folks we knew along the way of course, and we tried to stay in touch with them, but as soon as we landed in a new place we found ourselves making many new friends and learning new landmarks, tastes, and languages. We were to do this several times during the years to come, but of course I didn't know that—a young mother with her family sailing along on this luxury liner over the deep blue sea on Christmas Eve. "Sailing, sailing over the bounding main...." I never felt the distance from home again that way. Well, maybe when my mother died in 1968, and one other time I'll tell you about later. We didn't have telephones to call home, and we certainly didn't have the computer with Skype and all that cool stuff that we have now in 2015. Letters took six to eight weeks to be delivered. Telegrams were for emergencies.

We made a brief port call in the Philippines and got to meet some of our fellow missionaries and went to the local zoo. That was good but very brief and then we went on to Hong Kong. We spent a month in Hong Kong for Troy to learn the ropes about the mission treasurer's job from Jim Belote. What a blessing that month was! It was wintertime and cold, but the hospitality was very warm. The missionaries in Hong Kong took us shopping, told us stories about their time on the field and funny mistakes in their language; they were wonderful with our children and just made us feel part of their mission family. I'm sure this is what they intended, since we didn't know when we would have other missionaries from our mission board in East Pakistan. We even attended one of their mission meetings. It was very helpful for us to get the feel of things.

We lived in a hotel, learned to use chopsticks, rode the ferry over to the Kowloon side of Hong Kong, and went up in the cable car to the Peak to see Hong Kong by night. That was really beautiful—and just a bit scary to be truthful! Troy went out one day with one of the men and saw the other side of Hong Kong; the desperate poverty, shacks all over the side of a hill, so much need. We went to church in a school nearby. When the Chinese came in, they threw all of the windows open and kept their coats on. So we did too. It was cold! I think that was the first time I had seen houses surrounded by eight-foot-high walls with pieces of broken glass in the cement all along the top. It was put there to stop thieves.

We were awed by the beautiful handmade work we saw; the embroidered silk and the intricately carved rosewood furniture tempted us, but we managed to resist. We have been back through Hong Kong several times since and I still marvel at the beauty of their work, the exquisitely decorated tablecloths, which I did later buy and still have now. We didn't get any of that furniture though. "Lay not up for yourselves treasures on earth...."

Hong Kong is built around a harbor with part of the city on the mainland and part on an island. Kowloon is on the mainland and was separated from the "new territories" which were part of China. Hong Kong was rented to the British for 99 years as I remember. The island was called Hong Kong Island. We went to a restaurant on a boat at the Hong Kong side of the harbor. We saw the live fish swimming in big tanks, then picked the fish we wanted to eat for dinner and they prepared it. Now that is fresh.

Oh, I haven't mentioned the food. It was so good, so much variety, such delicious combinations and some very new and different tastes. It's not quite the same as Chinese food in the US. As we waited for our dinner, we saw some little houseboats nearby with families living on them, the little children tied with a rope around their middles to prevent them falling into the water. Looked smart to me.

On a rooftop in Hong Kong
Becky had to go, so...
Hong Kong, 1957

Since it was winter, we saw something else which you would find amusing. They had the little children—not toilet trained—in long pants with an open seam at the right place. They just held them out over the gutter beside the sidewalk and as they walked along, they let it go. Not so sanitary, but convenient. Papa went to get a haircut one day and agreed to have the fellow shave him as well. But they finally realized that he couldn't get Troy's chin as smooth as the Chinese. Actually, he was quite chapped for a few days from such a close shave. We were learning all the time.

We got to know one Christian fellow who had a tailor shop to which we returned several times through the years. He named his baby boy after Troy. It was a good introduction to mission work and we have always been so grateful to all of those missionaries and the Chinese people who welcomed us so graciously.

We then flew on to Bangkok, Thailand where we spent several days with the Judson Lennons, fellow missionaries and North Carolinians. Troy had lived in Judson's mother's house while at Wake Forest College. The main things I remember about this time are the heat, which felt wonderful after the winter weather we had experienced in the US and Hong Kong. Something else which I have never had again was a coconut pudding made by the Lennons' cook. She steamed the coconut right in the shell (I think). I know we ate it out of the shell. I had lots of experiences with coconuts in Bangladesh, but never that delightful dish again. When coconuts are green, they have water inside which is good to relieve thirst on a long hot hike, but otherwise somewhat bland. If you put some sugar in it and maybe something else to thicken it and steam it in the shell—who knows? Maybe it would make that delicious pudding I remember. We headed on to Rangoon for an overnight stop and then to Dacca, East Pakistan.

First Term

"Lord, I cannot do this by nature— Make me able to do it by grace...."
– The Imitation of Christ, Book xix, 122

Here we are! Coolies carried our luggage
on their heads
Dacca, East Pakistan, Feb. 7, 1957

Dacca, East Pakistan was all so new, so different, so noisy, and full of strange smells. It was crowded, lots of pushing and shoving, shouting of the taxi drivers and coolies but our new friends knew what to do, especially Roy Cloud and Rod Brown. It was 1957 and we were to stay with Roy and Esther Cloud for a few days in Dacca before Troy went to Chittagong, the port, to

Traveling on the rivers, Troy saw & felt the many challenges ahead
East Pakistan, 1957

clear our goods. The children and I would go with Rod Brown by taxi, steamer, train, and rickshaw to our new home in Faridpur. There, the Browns, Australian Baptist missionaries, lived upstairs and we were to be downstairs.

Traveling on the steamer to get to Faridpur was a special pleasure because we had to travel overnight, which gave us the opportunity of seeing the river in the moonlight, when there was moonlight. Sitting up on the deck we could hear the murmur of voices of many people, and the rattle of pots and pans for a while, but then everything would be quiet and we could just soak in the stillness of the river and its mysterious treasures. I was thinking of others who had traveled this way before us, and also of others on the steamer with us. There were crowds down in the hold, in Third Class, not so comfortable as we were. We could hear a faint baby's cry; sometimes a burst of laughter, and then all was quiet again. We were so privileged to have the means to travel like this. Dear God, help us to be generous, not only with material things but also with our love and joy and caring.

One interesting contrast we observed was that when

we were in Hong Kong we were cautioned to watch our bags and not let the coolies get too far from us; to keep our eyes on our stuff. But here in East Pakistan with people so poor, there was no concern about that. We could be confident the fellows would take our bags where they needed to go. Isn't that a wonder?

I should back up and give just a little history. William Carey and his associates had come from England into Calcutta, India and the surrounding areas beginning in 1793. Australian Baptists had followed several years later; I really don't know how long they had been in the area, but they had spread over what was now known as East Pakistan. By this time it seems they had overextended, or maybe just wanted to concentrate in the northern part, which was more responsive to the message. So they invited Southern Baptists to take over the southern/central region, including Faridpur, Comilla, Rajbari and Gopalganj. New Zealand Baptists were working in the southeastern area also, in Chandpur and Brahmanbaria. The only reason I am telling you this is so you will know that we were not really pioneer missionaries as some folks back in the US like to think. We were pioneers for Southern Baptists, but the others got there way ahead of us and had done some good solid work, established schools, an industrial training school, and medical clinics as well as churches. Obviously, the need was great.

In fact, when we arrived in Faridpur, Jane Brown was there and she had a rather active clinic going. The previous Australian wife who had been there was a doctor, and thus had done a lot of good. The local people assumed the women missionaries were all doctors. So Jane, who was not a doctor, said she used mostly Vicks VapoRub, which felt effective and sometimes helped. Of course, she also had iodine, aspirin, rubbing alcohol and such that she could use. Actually, I did end up doing a good bit of that myself, using just the good hygiene and first aid I knew, which was more than most Bengalis had been exposed to. Occasionally, we had to send someone to a doctor, but they didn't want to go that way; the treatment was questionable and they had to pay. We had brought a good supply of medicine, thanks to a friend of Troy's who was in the medical field, so we were well supplied. In East Pakistan the number of Christians was very small. We used the figure of less than one-third of one percent; the great majority was Muslim and a small minority was Hindus. In most towns the Christians tried to live in the same neighborhood, very much as internationals do today in the US. In Faridpur on the Christian Compound there was a church, the Industrial School, and a primary school. I am not sure how they procured all of the land but it was probably through the Australian Baptist Mission. I know our mission was buying some property from them. It was a large piece of property for we also have to count in the big missionary house and at least twenty to thirty other small family homes with small gardens. There were a few who lived elsewhere in town, but not many. The Compound was well located, not far from the main part of town and very close to the train station. There were two very large tanks—ponds—that were used for washing just about everything: clothes, animals, humans, dishes. Now some homes also had a tube well near the house and used that water for some of these purposes. Most of them did have a small garden and maybe a few chickens and a goat or two, sometimes a cow. This probably contributed to the strength of the community, living so close together.

They had several natural leaders, men and women. The pastor was elected each year from the men of the community. But the women who had gotten some education to be midwives and teachers were highly respected in this community.

Interestingly, one afternoon I was at a neighbor's house and a man was there who was complaining about the shortage of nurses in the country. He said there were seven doctors for every nurse. I asked how he could explain that. He said that they had depended on the Christian community to provide nurses, but in recent years they had failed to do so. And why would that be?

I told him I knew why. It was because the nurses were not treated respectfully by the men patients or by the male doctors. So their parents just didn't want them to go into that profession. The Muslims wouldn't want their Muslim girls to be nurses and dealing with men and older boys. No comment. As schoolteachers, the women, both Christian and Muslim, had more respect from the students and their parents.

Let's think about the houses we lived in. We first went to Faridpur, Steve was four and Becky almost two. We lived in the first floor of an old, old British Raj style house; verandas down the entire front, with

Steve & Becky with Ranju Debnath at our new home
in Faridpur, East Pakistan, 1957

three rooms through the middle, high ceilings, cement floors, no windows, but lots of French doors, overhead fans in every room except the kitchen and bath. The house had been built by the Australian mission many years before. The back veranda had been closed in to make a downstairs kitchen, bathroom, entryway, stairway and another bathroom. Upstairs was similar. We later closed in the two end spaces of the front veranda downstairs to make a bedroom and a study.

Now, about the kitchen and bathrooms (we had two baths): Originally, the bathroom and kitchen had been outside in separate buildings. The kitchen had a table or two, a cabinet with wire netting (screen wire to you) so that we could keep food away from flies and other critters. That was it. Oh, there was a spigot and a sink. Papa was the best one ever to get things set up for me to be able to "Do the necessary things like cooking." The local people do all of their kitchen work on the floor or ground, so this was different. However, it is true that Australians had been living in that house for years, from the beginning of the work in fact, so we didn't really shock anyone with our different ways there.

As I said, the ceilings were high, maybe twenty feet, and we didn't have windows; we had French style doors. This didn't bother the birds; they came in the vents and built their nests in them too. I didn't mind them but I did mind the frogs that came in through the open drain holes in the outside walls of the bathrooms. They came into the kitchen, too, and I'm not sure where else, but the frogs knew where they were and liked to come in and hide under our furniture, especially bookcases and beds. Every night before we went to bed, Troy and I got our two yardsticks and went hunting frogs. We always, always found several, and chased them out of the house. The children were separated from our bedroom by a large living/dining room—yeah, with bookcases and frogs!—so I was trying to avoid stepping on one of them in the middle of the dark night. I did not want to step on a frog with my bare feet. I don't think I ever worried that they would come right back in. Of course we were also getting used to kerosene lanterns and sleeping under mosquito netting. That was an adjustment, though for the children I think it was a comfort, a feeling of safety in their little cocoons. By the way, I never stepped on a frog in the dark.

Bathrooms were interesting. In the first place, one had an outside door. Hmm, why would that be? To bring in hot water in those old recycled kerosene tins which had been heated on an open fire by one of the servants. We also needed outside access to take clothes outside to hang on lines or maybe just spread on the bushes. We had a bathtub in that bathroom where the washing of clothes was done by hand by a woman servant. There was a basin and spigot and a commode with its water tank up high overhead. You had to pull a chain to flush it.

In the other bathroom we had an old timey wash basin except ours wasn't pretty like you see with a pitcher in some of the very old houses, a spigot and the same kind of commode with a chain. Then there was a low wall about three inches high with a drain in the outside wall and a spigot about a foot off the floor on the wall inside this enclosure. This was our shower. That water was usually cold — it came from the roof, I'll explain later — but, we got those kerosene tins of hot water also. To shower, we poured water over ourselves, first to soap, then again to rinse. It works. Millions of people in the world do it this way today. One day, I saw our servant/helper cleaning this very bathroom. He intended to clean the commode, but what he did was take the basin we washed our hands in and threw water at the commode from across the room. We just laughed to ourselves, of course. What else can you do? Obviously, he thought this work was beneath him. His name was Mubarak; he was a young village fellow who knew nothing of our ways. I wonder what he tells his grandchildren about us now.

Do you remember me saying that we got our water from the roof? That was because we had someone pump it up there every day into another supply tank because we needed the gravity for it to fall. The city supply just filled a tank on the ground. We were grateful for that, as many women and children had to carry theirs from a pump on the side of the street.

One of the first things we discovered was that the Australian mission furnished their missionaries' houses in pretty much the same manner in each house. They were made at the same place, I guess; the Mission Industrial School at Faridpur. So, we were blessed with this same furniture and didn't have to go out and arrange and wait to have some made. We received a wonderful letter from Jane Brown — our upstairs neighbor-to-be-and basically, she told us to pretend we were coming to the end of the world and prepare for that. When our stuff did arrive, we had the kerosene stove we had ordered and a kerosene refrigerator from Sweden which would come two months later. Before that, we ate with the Browns upstairs, bless them! And, until we got the kerosene fridge working — it continued to be a challenge! — we ordered ice from Rajbari, about thirty minutes by train from us. When it arrived, it was covered with sawdust, but we washed it off and it cooled things in a picnic cooler for a while. We had to boil the milk twice a day to keep it from going sour.

We had electricity from 2:00 to 4:00 in the afternoons, at least in hot weather, and then for two to three hours in the evening; that is when the electric company was working. When it wasn't, we used kerosene lanterns; you know the kind you see in *Little House on the Prairie*. It was hot! Of course, there was no air conditioning, but we did have overhead fans in all of the rooms when we had electricity. During the short time we lived there we decided to screen the house, verandas and all. The Australians thought we were nuts and would burn up, but you know Americans, we just went on and did it. Well, we didn't burn up and it did keep the mosquitoes out and I think later the Australians did the same to their houses. Actually, that first summer was hot — don't ask me how hot. I don't know. One night we were sitting out on the front veranda trying to catch some breeze when I told Troy, "Now I know why God made nighttime. What a relief after a bright, hot day!" And, of course, it is true. We couldn't bear the bright light all of the time, even if it weren't so very hot. Thank you, Lord, for dark cool nights.

July 4th was a hoot. We were to have a picnic at our house for the others, that is, the Browns and their two girls and Laurie Skinner, a single Australian who also

The Debnath family, left to right: Mrs Debnath (Shiulirma),
their children & Mr. Arun Debnath
Faridpur, East Pakistan, 1957

lived on the compound. The picnic went very well and then I brought out the cake. Now, this was one of my first attempts to bake a cake in a kerosene oven, which was a feat in itself, but I decided we needed an American flag. We didn't have one, so I made one on top of the cake. All the Americans, the Bennetts and Jane Brown, pledged allegiance to our flag. I know Jane had a hard time saying it because she was laughing so hard. But, I noticed no one had any trouble eating it.

We had a huge walled in garden — yard — for the children to play in. Steve was lucky to have Ranju, a boy about his age and size, to play with. He often came, especially when his mother, Shiulirma, came to help me learn Bengali. Shiulir-ma (her name means mother of Shiuli), was a well-educated woman, a fine Christian, and I felt very fortunate to have her to help me learn my way around. She became one of my best friends in Bangladesh. Troy had little time for language study since he had mission business to tend to, and much of that had to be done in Dacca. This, of course, entailed traveling by train, steamer, taxi, and/or rickshaw. Travel anywhere took a good bit of time.

Going to the store in Faridpur was very different from what I had ever known before. The first time I started out with Rod and Jane Brown, Rod told me I could go out by myself if I had Steve with me. A girl was no good, but a boy of any size was considered protection. Imagine that, little Steve just four years old, my protector.

One afternoon, two young men came to the door and

wanted to talk. I told them Troy wasn't at home, but they were welcome to come in, which they did. We talked a while; they were very friendly and were no problem. Then Rod Brown came home and realized they were in my house and he was furious! He came in and told them to get out. They should know better than to take advantage of a woman that was home alone. Had Mubarak, our helper, been there, it probably would have been okay, but he wasn't, and it wasn't okay. Another lesson learned. They were coming fast and furious now!

Another day, I lay down with Becky to take a nap. I usually read to the kids and, of course, I was as sleepy as I wished they were. That day I dozed off and when I awoke, she wasn't there. I went looking and guess where I found her? Outside the gate to our yard — how did that happen!? — sitting in the cab of a big truck with two Bengali men just talking and having the most fun. They were fascinated with this little red-headed girl — it was quite red then — and thought she was cute as a button. Well, what could I do? I claimed my child back. No problem; they were happy and I was very happy! I did ask Batash, a really nice, smart Christian young man who was working in the office, about it. He was quite apologetic that he hadn't noticed her in the truck, for if he had, he would have intervened. All's well that ends well, but it was another lesson for me. Come to think of it, where she was would be a lot better than her falling into the big tank right outside our wall. She was just two years old at the time.

Troy and I took the children one afternoon across

the street to the police lines where we had heard there was to be a football — in the US they call it soccer — match. There was a big crowd gathered round, but it didn't take long to realize that the crowd was entirely male except for you know who, Becky and me. I found an excuse to leave and that was another good lesson learned. About those police lines, they were right across from our house and even though we had a deep front yard, that didn't stop us from hearing the band every morning at 6 am marching out with the bagpipes and drums, sending a cacophony of music across the neighborhood. If it hadn't been so funny, it might have been irritating, but it was funny, and much more effective than an alarm clock!

Our helper Mubarak went to the market for me and then helped in the kitchen and around the house. Also, Eadali (E-a-da-lee) worked the garden for both families and washed the floors and brought in the hot water, which he heated at the old outside kitchen. He was anxious to please, but I don't know if I ever understood him or he understood me. And Gohair was something else! He was an old man who had worked for the missionaries for years in the past. I mean an old man. Now of course old there was not like it is now here. He may not have been in his 70s yet; I really don't know, but he was old. I think he had had a hard life and not the best nutrition, for he was bent over and so thin; I don't think he had any teeth. He couldn't work anymore, but came around every few days with eggs and wanted to talk a while. I couldn't understand much of what he said either, but I learned gradually. Part of the problem was some people's country accent, but a lot of it was their many years of using pahn, leaves with a narcotic effect. It made them sound as if they had a mouthful of saliva every time they talked.

Pahn is a leaf which people chew and is very popular in that part of the world. It turns their mouths red and their spittle is very red. You can see it almost anywhere that people spit. There is also a betel nut which is chopped up and chewed, but that may be more expensive. As you can imagine, for country folk on the street it was no problem to just spit it anywhere. It ruins their teeth though. And of course is unsightly on the streets, the walls, etc. But, for the high and mighty, it is a little more difficult to do it in an acceptable way. If you have ever heard of snuff, a tobacco product that is chewed and was used a lot by people in America and Europe in the early days, then you can compare it with pahn except that pahn is fire engine red. And I think tastes hot. I never tried it. I could have, but never had the desire and thankfully no one ever pushed me to do it. They had pretty brass dishes for the pahn leaves and for the stems which they dipped into the white stuff (some sort of lime mixture I think). I understand it was to cool their palates. Very elegant!

Toward the end of the summer two exciting things happened. First, we heard that not one, but two couples had been appointed to come to work with us; Trueman and Jane Moore and Frank and Wynone Gillham. They would arrive in the fall. The second bit of good news was the arrival of Dr. Winston Pierce and Fon Scofield. Dr. Pierce was on the Foreign Mission

Board, and he was also from North Carolina, so he was homefolk. Fon was the photographer for the FMB. Well, that was exciting, I can tell you. It would be hot for them, but they had been hot before.

We gave them the best hospitality we could muster. I don't remember where they slept, but sleep they did. Dr. Pierce was a gentleman of the old school, the type you don't see too often these days. You know, the kind of gentleman who makes a grand gesture of treating a lady like a lady. Honestly, we didn't see them much back then either. Now, we had been away from the US for almost a year, learning a lot of new ways plus a new language, and of course new people, and it was hot, hot, hot. Hot is not my best temperature. I thrive on cool, so the Heavenly Father had to help me through a lot of hot days. Anyway, when they came to that little country town to see us and treated us so nicely, well it was pretty overwhelming. I felt like a bedraggled water lily, always sweaty, hair wet and stringy, not very pretty, and that man bent over so gallantly and kissed the back of my hand. I almost burst into tears. It was such a nice gesture. I hadn't realized how low I felt, I suppose. I needed a bit of a boost. Thank you, Dr. Pierce.

And that crazy Fon Scofield could say the funniest things. He kept us laughing, and that was good for our souls too. One day, he was sitting at the table and he waved his glass in the air and called to Mubarak, "Agua." Mubarak brought some water. Fon said, "It works every time. Anywhere you go in the world, all you have to say is 'agua' and they know you want water." I couldn't help adding, "It helps if you show him your empty glass." He was fun. Agua is water in Latin and maybe some other languages too.

Anyway, as a result of their visit and our talks with them, it was decided that we should move to Dacca, the capital, in order to facilitate language study and orientation for the Moores and Gillhams who were to arrive soon, and also to ease Troy's handling of the treasurer's work. Well, that was to be a challenge. Many times, Troy made decisions and just told me about them later, as we both had our hands full. But, the gist of it was that for some reason we were to move our stuff, such as it was, by boat. The rivers were still plenty high so that was good, because when they were low, the boats could not get close to the docks for unloading, and of course the train didn't go all the way from Faridpur to Dacca, so there would have to be transshipping and all that could be very tricky. We packed our things up again.

The type of country boats used to move our household from Faridpur to Dacca, East Pakistan, 1957

Fortunately, we hadn't bought any furniture since we had used that of the Australian Mission. But, we did have the barrels we could repack with our things that we had brought from the States. It was enough. Then we went back to Dacca and this time we stayed with Henry and Cassie Ross. I remember I caught a bad cold and had a sore throat and the Ross' cook prepared hot ginger tea for me. Oh, that was good and boy, it did help! I have used it many times since. I was learning all the time.

We moved into a house on Elephant Road. It was owned by Begum Dillon (Bay-goom Dee-lohn) who lived next door. We had a living room, dining room, three bedrooms, a kitchen, two baths, a covered front veranda, and one side not covered. There was a good yard for the children to play in and a house for the servants in the back. At that time we had a cook, a bearer (a kind of butler who helped with many things), a part-time sweeper, a mali (gardener) and later added an ayah (nursemaid) after Debbie was born. I know that sounds like a lot and it was. Lots of days, I didn't want all those people around, but they were very particular about what work they would do. The cook only cooked, shopped, and cleaned up the kitchen with the help of the bearer. The bearer also dusted, made beds if needed, and served the table if asked. He was also responsible for the two children when I was out. Actually, he was not too satisfactory at watching after Steve and Becky, so we had to work on that. When Debbie came, we made other arrangements. The sweeper came in and swept the floors and it was his job to clean the bathrooms. No one would do the job of another servant; it just wasn't done. The ayah was exclusively for the care of the small children; she would wash clothes if needed, but I used the washing machine I had brought from the US. She hung the clothes out. I didn't let her use the machine; I was afraid she might hurt herself. They had no experience with machinery. When I told the cook how to use the pressure cooker I went into great detail with stories of beans blowing all over the kitchen as I waved my arms wildly. I also stressed to him about the hot steam that would come gushing out. They had great respect for the pressure cooker, and that was the idea. I used it. I just didn't want any of them being injured using these things they were not accustomed to.

Keep in mind, these people spoke very little English, so I was forced to learn Bengali in a hurry which was good, of course, but it also meant some misunderstandings. Like the bearer who heard the instructions and then went out to the kitchen and asked the cook, "What did she say?" Of course, learning the language is a matter of more than learning some words; we also have to try to lose our accents and to sound like them and be able to hear and understand them. These were, to some extent, illiterate people, so they didn't even speak the same Bengali as we were learning in some instances. For the most part, they spoke what we called "grammy Bengali" which means village Bengali; in other words, it was like going from New York City to the Deep South. Big difference! But that was all part of the adjustment we needed to make. It was hard some days, but also exhilarating to be faced with new challenges virtually every day, some more pleasant than others.

One note: That sweeper, Sharohn (sha-rohn) worked with the Baptist Mission the entire time we were in the country and became a most dependable helper in many ways beyond being a sweeper. He became a good and trusted Christian friend. He proved to be a strong leader in his church. He is literate—he speaks five or six languages—and knew the city of Dacca in great detail. Troy depended on him for some very important business. In fact, one time, one of the missionaries from another mission asked Troy for help in getting a large check cashed. Troy said, "Sure, no problem. I'll just send Sharohn." The fellow was pretty shocked that he trusted our sweeper with that much money, but Troy assured him that this particular man was fully trustworthy. We truly love Sharohn. He is a true friend;

Sharohn playing the sitar.
He was a man of many talents!
Dacca, East Pakistan, 1957

he stayed nearby, years later, during the war. I'm not sure who was encouraging whom, but I suppose it worked both ways. We were glad to have him there and he knew his family was well cared for.

We were also delighted to find in Dacca an American Sunday School, which was meeting in one of the American family's homes. There was a good-sized group meeting before we got there and we enjoyed being part of their activities. Eventually they asked Troy to be the regular teacher and I worked with the children's classes. They also had an American school already started using the Calvert Correspondence Course from Baltimore, Maryland. This developed as various mothers who were homeschooling their children with Calvert decided to join together. Esther Cloud was a school teacher and she was instrumental in getting this important work started. The classes were small, but we had good teachers. When the children got old enough, we taught them some board and card games. Becky was still young when we started this and she would get up and run around and not pay much attention and WIN. Oooh, that would make Steve so angry!

Troy was able to line up a very good location, not only for his office, but also for the reading room we were opening to provide good reading materials, some secular and, of course, some Christian. It was located close to Dacca University and right downtown, so a lot of people passed that way and used the room. It was also close to the big new mosque, which was a very busy place.

We did our language study there. We found an amazing teacher, Shautish Chakraborty, who had been teaching many other missionaries for several years, and was the most patient person you can imagine. He had a wonderful sense of humor, which really helps when you are teaching or learning a new language, and he was a Christian, a converted Brahmin. He had also written a little book, let's see, what was it called? Conversational Bengali or something like that. It contained many of the idioms and ideas that would come up every day. Contractions and expressions, like, "Whaddya think?" in English. We worked very hard at this, reading, writing, speaking and understanding. Here are a couple of proverbs he taught us: "The man who lives closest to the station is always late for the train," and "Tend to your own spinning wheel." In other words, mind your own business.

Bengali is based on the Sanskrit language and is written under the line instead of on top. Also, it has a good many more sounds than our alphabet, especially those that are distinguished by a breath as you speak, like wen or when. So with "when" you should say "hwen." I've been told by some teachers of English that there are words in our language where we should make that distinction, but I don't remember being taught that in school, do you? Words like, "when," and "where." There you go, learn something new every day.

John 3:16

রণ ঈশ্বর এই জগতকে এতোই ভালবাসনে য.ে তনি তাঁর

একমাত্র পুত্রকে দলিনে, য.নে সেই পুত্ররে ওপর য.ে কেঁ

বিশ্বাস করে সে বনিষ্ট না হয়. বরং অনন্ত জীবন লাভ করে

Let's see, it wasn't long after we moved to Dacca that the Moores and Gillhams arrived. Troy had arranged a nice two-story house for them with a good yard for the children to play and to have a garden. Boy were we glad to see them! When the Moores came they had two children, Trudy and Willis. The Gillhams had just one son Mark. The Gillhams actually didn't stay long; for health reasons they were transferred to Japan, and later resigned. That was a downer, but still we had the Moores and each of us in our own way was glad to have their companionship. When they got there, we could form a mission, an organization of FMB missionaries in that country. We were small but we would grow. Later, Trueman asked Troy how we had made decisions when we were in Faridpur when it was just the two of us. Troy said, "Simple, we talked about it over the breakfast table and agreed what needed to be done." We didn't keep minutes though. Maybe that would have helped to make it official.

A really neat thing happened during our first four-year term. A.C. and Lefty Barefoot from North Carolina came to live in Chittagong with USAID. Troy had

First Term

known A.C. at Wake Forest College and I had known Lefty at Meredith College; she was a year ahead of me, but proved to be a very fine and understanding friend. Sooooo, of course, we went to Chittagong to visit them. They lived in the Boat House, which, from the outside did look like a boat. They had three children also, but I can't remember their names. I do remember one thing A.C. did that I was pretty amazed about. He was slicing raw, ground meat from a hunk of frozen meat and giving it to the children. They thought it was delicious. Well, here I was trying to be super careful about what we ate, and we certainly didn't eat meat raw, but then I realized they had commissary privileges and so that meat was from the US, and according to A.C., it was safe. What do you think?

Lefty was quite an athlete, so she got involved in that sort of thing in Chittagong. Once, a group of women came to Dacca to compete in some athletic contests, and Lefty told us that they were staying at the university hostel, where the beds were so short that her feet stuck out the end. She was pretty tall, it made a great picture. I don't think I have mentioned that almost all Bengalis are rather short, many men grow to around five feet, and the women are even shorter, so they make the beds short. The men who worked for us weighed less than I did. I expect some of it is poor nutrition. Americans used to be a lot smaller than they are now too. Davy Crockett was a little runt of a guy, I hear.

The Barefoots went with us on vacation in 1958 when we went to Darjeeling in north India. We had really been looking forward to this as we had heard that it was nice. This was where other missionaries had gone for language study in the past, but at this time Americans were not welcome to live in India. The trip up was by train, a small gauge, I think they call it. We chugged on up the hills going into the Himalayas. Now you know, those are real mountains. Oh, it was so beautiful! You know I love mountains, and my heart was about to burst, just looking at the peaks and breathing in that cooler air. It was wonderful! And, watching the people along the way was fascinating. To see the way they wrap themselves in clothes on top of clothes to keep warm, but had bare legs; and they carried those heavy loads from their foreheads, using a sling across their foreheads and then back to the burden on their backs. They are small people, but their legs were bulging with muscles. They seemed so happy and carefree, waving to us on the train and laughing. I can still see their faces; they had a different look from the Bengalis, a more oriental look, which we found to be true of the hill people in general.

Living in one of these hill stations, as they are called, was an experience. Furniture was simple; the kitchen was very basic. We had to heat water for anything we wanted hot. It got really cold at night, but in the daytime the air was delightful. Sometimes, when we woke up, we would be surrounded by clouds, but often they would clear away enough to see some of the peaks during the day, even Kachenjunga, the third tallest mountain in the world. We did a lot of hiking and went into town. We saw a coolie carrying a piano on his back. Really! He had a sling over his forehead and back

First Term

to hold the piano. Those men are quite small but so strong! They were amazing!

In August of 1958, we were living in Dacca, East Pakistan, so Deborah Leigh Bennett, our third child, was born at the Holy Family Hospital, which was run by Catholic sisters from America who were our good friends. That made it a very pleasant experience, to know so many of the hospital personnel. The day Debbie was coming, Troy came home from work with Trueman Moore. We only had one vehicle at the time, a white Jeep, and Troy was telling Trueman to take it on home when I informed him that we might be needing it. Oh well, that started things rolling. I hadn't mentioned the labor pains to anyone at that time. We didn't have a telephone, so I couldn't call Troy. And, anyway, I wasn't that far along. Later that evening we went to the hospital, just about ten minutes from our house. Since things were moving pretty slowly, Sister Christine used forceps to bring Debbie into the world. She later explained that she did it because she had another patient in the next room who needed her. It wasn't a problem at the time, but later I noticed that Debbie didn't seem to be able to turn her head to the right.

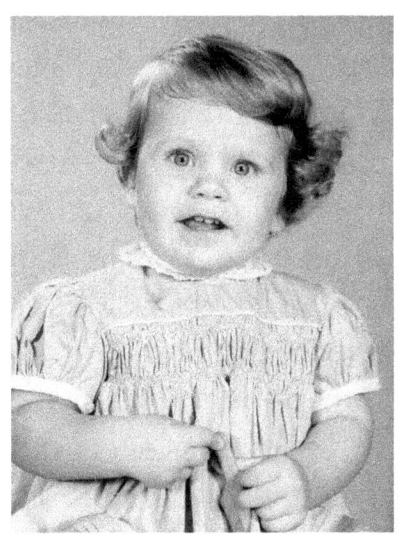

Debbie at one year
Dacca, East Pakistan, 1959

At her six-week checkup, I mentioned it to Sister

Left to right: Steve holding Cherie McKinley,
Trudy Moore holding Lee Moore,
Willis Moore, & Becky holding Debbie
Dacca, East Pakistan, 1959

Christine and she said that when we went to the States in about a year, Debbie would probably need surgery to correct her neck problem. As I remember it, she said there was a fibroid mass on the mastoid muscle in her neck that could cause her head to draw to one side and even keep her face from developing properly. If not corrected, her eye would be smaller and her mouth drawn. Well, you can imagine how that affected us. Our pretty little Debbie with that kind of deformity. What could we do? We didn't panic, we just prayed and talked with an Australian doctor who was staying in our home the next week or so. He said to let him think about it as he thought he remembered reading something about this sort of thing. When he came back two weeks later, he told us it was probably due to the forceps delivery. If we would exercise her neck, stretch those muscles every day, it should help. So, every evening that was our regimen. If Troy was at home, he held her shoulders on the table or bed. If he wasn't around, Steve straddled her and held her stable. I took her little head between my hands and gently forced her to turn to the right, a little more each day. She didn't like it, of course, but we did it for almost a year until we realized she didn't need it anymore. To this day, she doesn't want anyone messing with her neck! Right Debbie? Thank you God for that doctor who was there at the right time and place.

One funny thing happened, when Steve went to Sunday school the next Sunday after Debbie was born, he told a friend excitedly, "Guess what we have at our house! A new Jeep!" It had come with the Gillhams' shipment and was a welcome addition, but Debbie didn't make the news that day.

The next year, Jim and Betty McKinley and their daughter, Cherie came, so our little mission team was already growing. We joked that we would just grow the mission on the field by having babies. The Moores had Lee that year and Jimmy later; Debbie was born in August. Kathy McKinley was born the next year, so we were growing even from within!

In August of 1959, with the encouragement of Woodrow and Elizabeth Turner, we went again to India, but this time to Mussoorie, which is on the western side of India in the

Becky & Debbie loved the baskets!
Mussoorie, India, 1959

mountains. There is a boarding school there that we had been encouraged to think about for our children when they got older, ready for high school. Both of the Turner children were there in school at that time. To get there, we first flew to Calcutta, then got the overnight train across India to Dehradun and finally got a taxi to take us about 30 kilometers up to the town of Mussoorie. Then we had to go on foot or rickshaw to our house above the town. Debbie and Becky rode in baskets on coolies' backs and I rode in a covered rickshaw pulled by a coolie.

One time I was holding Debbie in the rickshaw and it started to rain. When it rained, they stopped to set the luggage down that they were carrying on their heads; they set them beside the road where water was running in a good little stream. When we stopped, I got the benefit of the cover on the rickshaw, but when he picked up the handles again to pull it, I was tipped way back. I had to put Debbie up on my shoulder to keep her relatively dry. When we arrived at our cottage and opened our bags, everything was soaked, but we were there. And it was cool. It was quite an experience and we couldn't complain. "I lift my eyes to the hills from whence cometh my help."

I remember the first morning in Mussoorie; it had been quite cloudy, but later in the morning one of our neighbors came out and called us, "Come, see the snows! This may be the only time you will see the peaks since this is the rainy season." But she was wrong, for we had many light, cool, sunny days up on the mountaintop when we could see the snows. We heard rumors that the Dalai Lama was in the area having escaped from Tibet earlier that year, but of course we didn't see him. Later we learned that the rumor was true. We got one of those Tibetan, beautifully colored embroidered pictures then. School was in session at the boarding school so we had some good times with some of the families there for school. I remember talking with a neighbor about some problem between India and Pakistan. It was so obvious that we were each reading our own country's version of the problem. Needless to say, we didn't settle that debate, whatever it was.

I think the most important thing we did was to celebrate Debbie's birthday; she was one year old. The neighbors had children. I remember one little girl especially, so we all celebrated together. These hill stations are truly lovely places and it's not hard to understand why foreign families spent most of the year up there and let the man of the family stay on the plains

The ferries were a little risky but we always made it safely across the rivers
East Pakistan, 1959

and do his work. Of course, one of their major reasons for staying up there was for their health. The plains are hot, and ten months of hot weather and high humidity can sap one's strength. Remember, there was no air-conditioning. We were acutely aware of the dangers to our health and so we tried to be careful. We always lay down after lunch to read, or sleep or both. We tried to drink plenty of liquids. The theme song went, "Mad dogs and Englishmen go out in the noonday sun."

In 1959, we had three families come to work with us: Frank and Jean Baugh with their three children; Harold and Betty Cummins with their two little girls; and Pat and Betty Johnson with their three older children. We were growing again! We needed more housing for these folks to do their language study and were able to rent a house on Road 4 in Dhanmandi, a part of Dacca. So we moved into the lower floor, and the Baughs moved into the second floor. The Cummins' and the Johnsons were in the White House. The McKinleys had moved to Comilla after one year of language study and the Moores were now in Faridpur.

A really funny thing happened one night when we had a young Bengali couple come over for supper. We had a good time, but before they left, the lady needed to use our bathroom. She shortly returned to the living room with a startled expression on her face. "There's a frog in that toilet!" she exclaimed. Needless to say, we all laughed, but also sympathized with her in her discomfort. I'm not sure just how Troy dealt with that intruder. We never had that happen again.

Our last Christmas of that first term was a challenge. Remember those barrels we had packed with all the things we thought we would need? Well, those barrels were about empty, and they didn't contain any toys or anything resembling toys. The shops didn't offer much that appealed to us. I found three pairs of underpants for Steve, which I wrapped separately. Our good friend, Abdul the mistri (carpenter), was making a dollhouse for Becky and a jumping horse for Debbie. But, we had no furniture for the dollhouse and no springs for the jumping horse. In other words, we had no presents for the children and they knew it. Then on Christmas Eve day, Papa came home from work

Abdul, the mistri (carpenter) became a treasured friend
Dhaka, Bangladesh (now called), 1990

Steve & Becky finally smiled for the camera when we let Debbie join them!
Christmas photo for relatives, 1959

at lunchtime and said, "Good news! Santa Claus has come." He had nine parcels from the States with all the things I had asked the Bennetts and my mom to send. Can you imagine the fun I had that night after the children were in bed, opening and wrapping the presents we had planned for them? Our Christmas tree was just a local one made from one tall stick and a few other sticks attached, then all wrapped in green tissue paper. But, we had a joyous Christmas!

    Furlough time was approaching and we were ready for it. We left the field in the summer of 1960, and flew by way of Hong Kong, Seattle, and Chicago, visiting friends and family on the way. Nothing much happened, except that Steve left his stuffed dog at my brother's house. To his dismay, he wouldn't get it back for many years. I thought he had about outgrown it, but when he did get it back he claimed it as his, and still has it somewhere.

Memories of Steve's Childhood

Steve was about six years old the year we went to Mymensingh for a meeting of Australian, New Zealand, and American Baptist missionaries. We were staying with the Carl Ryans who had a large place, enough to sleep the five of us.

In the evening, as I was preparing the children for a bath and then bed, I wasn't able to find the bathtub stopper. For some reason, I asked Steve if he had any idea where it was. As I remember, he didn't say anything but just started walking around with a thoughtful expression on his face. He went from room to room in the house, and I followed him. He wandered in and out of several rooms before going into the room where we were sleeping. Every time I see in the comics the *Family Circus* when little Jeffy is sent on an errand or to find something, he wanders in and out all over the neighborhood until he finally comes home again, I am reminded of this. Well, Steve didn't wander all over the neighborhood, but he was in pursuit of something, and nothing caused him to deviate from his meandering path. Not a word was said, but finally he went into the room where we were to sleep, opened the wardrobe door—which we were not using—and reached up and took the stopper off the shelf and gave it to me. He said nothing. He never did say anything about it; he just gave it to me as if that was the usual place to find a bathtub stopper.

We could have known right then that he would be a cool one, not too easily riled up about anything.

I remember one time when he did get riled up, and that was about Daddy. For some outlandish reason, Troy wanted to weigh an iron beam and the only scales were our bathroom scales. So, he took them out in the backyard, unbeknownst to me, but not to Steve, and with the help of some fellow lifted the beam and put it on the scales, except that they dropped it on the scales and smashed them flat! That made Steve so mad. I've never been quite sure why it mattered to Steve so much, except he was at that age where I suppose he had been checking on his weight rather regularly. Or, it may have been simply that it made him furious to see his dad, who ought to have known better, do such a dumb thing.

Here is a good tale. We used to ride in rickshaws a lot in Bangladesh. The three children and I could get into one rickshaw with Steve hunkered down on the floor. One day, as we approached our house and turned in the drive—it was a pretty rough dirt road—Steve just up and jumped out while the rickshaw was rolling. Well, we hadn't gotten over the shock of that when he decided to jump back in! Again, while the rickshaw was still rolling along. Now, that was a foolish thing to do and he knew it as soon as he did it. But, that was a bit late. The rest of us had to laugh, while he nursed his bruises and scrapes.

Another time, he was riding his bicycle around the Faridpur compound when he noticed a cow tied up ahead with the rope across the path. This presented no problem to him. In his mind, he'd just ride over the rope that was lying flat. Actually, there was a problem, because the cow decided to move just as he approached, which tightened the rope and threw Steve off the bike. Over the handlebars, I think. I'm not sure what was injured the most, his face and arms or his ego due to the embarrassment of landing on his face in public because of a cow!

What used to tickle me was when I would be fixing supper and Steve would come down and hang around the kitchen. "I thought you were reading, son." "Yeah, I was, but it got too scary." He was a funny guy.

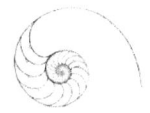

First Furlough

For our first furlough, we moved to Wake Forest, NC. A furlough is time away from the mission field for rest, meeting medical needs, studying, and speaking in churches and other groups about our work in order to stir up interest for them to pray, support, and perhaps go to serve also. Our furlough after four years on the field was to be one year. We went to Wake Forest, NC because we had family and friends nearby, and also a house was offered for our use by a professor and his family who were to be away from their jobs.

We were delighted to find that Gene and Ann Owens lived just up the street and their son, Raymond was Steve's age. Those boys had a lot of good times together. I had prayed especially for Steve to find a good friend during this year because he hadn't had a really good experience with the boys in East Pakistan. Thank you God for Raymond Owens.

Across the street lived a family which included a daughter, Cynthia, who was Becky's age. They went to kindergarten together. Becky loved it! What was that teacher's name? I think it was Mrs. Wiggins. Yeah, really! Sounds like Beatrix Potter, doesn't it? Anyway, she had a way with words that tickled Becky, and to see her playing with the other children felt good. Debbie was at home with me and we did a lot of walking around and visiting, especially with one family just across the street who had two little girls about Deb's age, so all three kids were set for friends.

Troy was gone a lot on deputation, talking about the work on the field, and he also took a course at Baptist Hospital in Winston-Salem on Pastoral Counseling, which he really enjoyed. He learned some good stuff about relating with people, and, of course, when he came home he told me all about it, the visits with patients and reporting on them afterward to the whole group. They would quiz each other about why they asked this, why they didn't ask that. The discussions could bring things to light that otherwise went unattended to, such as problems that they, the students, might have and not be aware of like fear of death, or suffering, or marital problems, or failure, or fathers, or whatever. If topics came up that they didn't want to talk about themselves or were afraid to talk about, the students hadn't pushed it with the patients. If a tender issue came up, they had moved on to another subject. Interesting! And, of course, it was useful for us too as Troy and I would discuss the cases he had and what our reactions were to various situations. I learned a lot vicariously, just like when he was in seminary. It was a good experience, but we missed him and were always ready to do something fun on Friday nights like play games or go to a good movie.

Of course on Sundays he usually went to some church to preach and talk about our work. Sometimes we went with him, but not always. We figured we, the parents, were the ones called to be missionaries. Our children lived with us and loved their life most of the time. But, I can imagine some of the stories they have told their friends, especially Steve, who tells some good ones, but not up in front of the church. Many weekends, the children and I went to Rolesville Baptist Church in a small town nearby. It was a good church and they were very welcoming of us. They never got to know Troy at all, but the children got a good introduction to a typical Baptist church in America.

When we could, we visited family, especially Papa and Mama Bennett in Winston-Salem and my mom in Roanoke, VA. One weekend, my brother Carl came to visit us with all seven of his children. We really had a time with all of those little ones rolling around in their snowsuits, all bundled up.

Mother and Nancy's new house had a big basement that allowed for out-of-towners to come and stay. Of course Marian, Carl, and Jim were all living there in their own homes and, let's see, Lou and Mary had family to stay with in town. We had family reunions there that were fun. One time they had one at Fishburn Park, had everything spread out on the tables, ready to feed the many babies and toddlers, when all of a sudden here came a drenching rain. There was nothing to do but grab kids, food, and run for the shelter. It literally rained on that picnic. They still laugh about it, but we were overseas at the time and missed out on the fun. We heard about it while we were back in the States. That's the kind of thing that isn't much fun when it happens, but later, it's a riot!

Once, when I was speaking at a church to a ladies group, we had a question and answer time at the end. One of the ladies asked why we didn't give the Bengalis forks and spoons to eat with so they didn't have to use their hands. Can you imagine trying to get 150 million people to eat with forks and spoons when fingers are so handy? (Study history and you'll see Europeans haven't been using utensils all that long.) Another lady told us her daughter said a boy at school said he lived where a jackal came and ate up a baby. I knew right off that was one of Steve's stories, and it had some truth to it. There was a beggar woman who came around in Faridpur, sleeping outside at night with her baby and a jackal did come by and take the baby away from her. We hadn't realized what an impression it had made on Steve.

I can't remember anything special about that Christmas except that we took the children to a toyshop just to look around. Wonder of wonders! Miracle of miracles! They had a good time, and we finally told them they could each choose one toy to take home that day. I think Steve chose a BB gun, Debbie found a little pull toy she liked, but Becky wanted a rabbit. Well, it wasn't the season for rabbits, of course, but I asked the saleslady if they might have a rabbit in the storeroom. She looked and came out with an orange and yellow beauty. So pretty! Becky was smitten at once. It was perfect. The funny thing was when we went back to Granma and Papa's house, Granma just couldn't understand why on earth we would buy them new toys just a few days before Christmas. But, we knew why and they were happy. They got to pick them out themselves.

We did have a dog that my mother had brought us when she first came to welcome us home. He was a cocker spaniel mix—rather wild, I'm afraid—and he never really settled down. It was probably not a good idea to have a dog for just one year like that. One thing I do remember is when we went to Raleigh, which we did for shopping, etc., we would stop at Finch's where they had good, hot family food, and they also had a Treasure Chest that the kids loved. They liked to get the candy cigarettes and smoke them. It was easy in the wintertime because their breath caused some smoke to rise. We also had a turtle that somehow got out of the dish and we couldn't find it until I swept behind the dining room door, which stayed open all the time. There he was in a dust bunny.

When we went to Winston-Salem, we usually spent time with Aunt Mary and Uncle Bill, especially in the later years. We liked to go there; Uncle Bill Knott was so much fun. He used to tease Debbie saying, "Fattie, Fattie, two by four, can't get through the kitchen door." I don't know why he said that; she wasn't fat at all, but she seemed to enjoy the teasing. Steve liked to be with the boys; Bob and Bill were both older than he but always kind (I think) and Waco was almost his age, just a few months older. In fact, many of the clothes

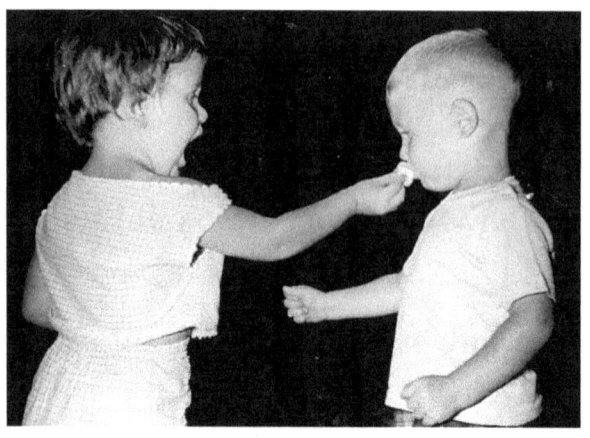

Debbie feeding her cousin, Tim Rikard, a marshmallow
Winston-Salem, NC, 1961

Steve wore were hand-me-downs from Waco, and then went on to Bec and Deb.

One day that year, I was combing my hair and noticed a gray hair. What did I do? I pulled it out. Later, another one, and then I started to realize that if I kept this up I would be balder than Troy, so I stopped doing that. Don't know why I was getting gray hairs; I wasn't old. A friend had suggested that perhaps I was getting three gray hairs for every move I made. Good grief, that could be bad news for me! I think it was because everyone always thought I looked a lot younger than Troy, and I figured we could keep it that way. He didn't seem to mind, especially since he was seven months younger than I!

I did do some speaking, of course, but mostly we wanted to see that the children had a good year in the States. I remember at a conference in Mars Hill, I talked with Dick Young, who was one of the early voices for Pastoral Counseling. I asked him, "How can we give our children a sense of security that home gives when we keep moving around so much?" His answer has come to mind many times over the years, "I guess you'll have to make your relationships so strong that wherever you are is home." Tall order. Hope we did!

During every furlough, we tried to visit some of our friends, like the Andrews family in Wilmington, and the Rices and Teagues and others in Fayetteville, where we had lived while Troy was in seminary. We had some good friends there, and most of them had children about the same age as ours, so that was nice.

On the *Hellenic Sailor*

The *Hellenic Sailor*
New Orleans, LA, 1961

C.S. Lewis, quoted from *Letters to an American Lady*, a letter dated October 30, 1958

(I first met Lewis when I was in Magura. He has become one of my favorites. No, I didn't meet him personally but I found his books and was hooked by his insights and his humor.)

"I suppose living from day to day ('take no thought for the morrow') is precisely what we have to learn—though the Old Adam in me sometimes murmurs that if God wanted me to live like the lilies of the field, I wonder He didn't give me the same lack of nerves and imagination as they enjoy! Or is that just the point, the precise purpose of this Divine paradox and audacity – called Man – to do with a mind what other organisms do without it?"

After our first furlough when we lived in Wake Forest from 1960-61, we flew to New Orleans to board the *Hellenic Sailor*, a Greek freighter. There were only four other passengers, an Indian woman traveling alone and the ship captain's wife with their two children. Troy decided that we should go into Chittagong by ship to "test the waters" that is, to see if it was helpful to go through customs with our goods as we returned to the field. Since we were the first ones to return to East Pakistan from furlough for our Foreign Mission Board, we were the test case. It turned out to be quite an adventure because the ship was a freighter. Much of their load were Jeeps for Burma and loose wheat for Bangladesh, which was actually East Pakistan at that time. For some reason, we were delayed in our departure from New Orleans, and this became a critical factor in this story.

A day or two before our departure, we flew into New Orleans and were able to go aboard the Sailor to see our accommodations. The cabins were fine; the common room/dining area had two tables and other seating arrangements which were good. When I questioned if there was any place where the children could run and play, I was shown the walkways on both sides of the cabins. They were about a yard wide and

12 to 15 feet long with a railing with two rods on the outside to prevent people from falling down to the cargo area or the ocean. That wouldn't do for Debbie, since she was not quite three years old. It didn't take me long to realize that we were going to need more supplies; we headed for the nearest Woolworths and I stocked up on Do-It-Yourself books, supplies to make sock monkeys, games, etc. We were to need every bit of it. Actually, it turned out to be not nearly as bad as I had thought.

Right before we left the US, we had to get some immunization shots, including one for cholera. As we rounded the Florida coastline, for some reason Steve had a reaction to the shot, and his arm swelled up to about double its size. The captain's treatment consisted only of alcohol compresses. He was the doctor on board and provided everything we needed. Thankfully, the swelling did go down. If it hadn't, we would have had to leave the ship and go back to the US by Coast Guard transport. Later, I got an upset stomach, and the captain told Papa his treatment for that was alcohol compresses. Actually, we learned on that voyage that his cure for anything was alcohol in one form or another. So we tried it for my stomach. Ooof! Papa wasn't always as careful as he should have been pouring that alcohol on my abdomen, and sometimes I got REALLY HOT in an inappropriate place. But, I did get over the bug. My body's self-defense kicked in to cure me, I think.

After a few days on board, the captain evidently decided we were okay and took us up to the upper deck. We had to access it through the engine room, which was a problem for the first mate, but not for the captain. Of course, we tried to be as unobtrusive as possible. Lo and behold, there was this rather wide expanse on top of everything. On a building we would call it the roof; on the ship they called it the top deck. It was great, especially since the captain had a plastic swimming pool up there for his family. At first, we only went up after the captain's family came down. The way it worked out was that the captain and his family went up there about 9:30 or 10:00 am and stayed about an hour; then we were allowed to go up and enjoy the pool, the view, and the freedom of movement for an hour before lunch. After a couple of weeks, as we became friends with his family, they invited us to come on up earlier and, of course, we were glad to oblige. My, what a difference that made for us, for the children especially.

Our other entertainment place was in the central common room. The children could run and play some, and we were able to play board games on the tables. We had originally thought this voyage would take six weeks, but as it progressed, we realized it was going to be longer. We ended up on

Troy with our children on the *Hellenic Sailor*
At sea, 1961

that ship for ten weeks, which meant Steve and Becky were late starting school. Fortunately, I had those learning books for math, reading, and writing which we worked on every day. This kept them busy, and they were not behind their classes when we finally reached Dacca. I made sock monkeys for each of the children. They were great to make and even more fun to play with. Later, they would hang from the ceiling fans when they played circus.

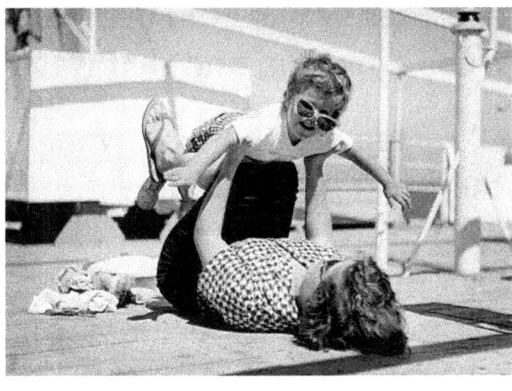

On the top deck: Debbie is a flying angel! At sea, 1961

When the captain learned that Troy played Canasta, he insisted we teach them the rules. So, Troy did the best he could remember, and we had some good times playing cards. One problem: The captain cheated, but he wouldn't be corrected; he said he was captain of the ship and his word was law. However, later when we stopped in Rangoon to unload Jeeps, an army sergeant wanted to play cards with us. When he saw how we were playing, he was very upset. "This is not right!" he insisted. But, the captain said, "On my ship, we play by the Bennett rules." Enough said.

Because of our delay in leaving, Debbie had her third birthday while we were on the *Hellenic Sailor*. The captain's wife, Cordelia, helped me make a cake, sort of. We used a pudding mix and ladyfingers which she already had, and decorated the top with M&M's. Debbie liked it, and that was the important thing.

Washing clothes was women's work according to the captain. I went down into the hold of the ship to wash the clothes, then hung them in our cabins. The captain had a bad impression of American missionaries because, on a recent voyage, a family had traveled with him, and that woman spent all her time in bed and the husband did the wash. He approved of our arrangement.

We went through the Suez Canal, and that was interesting. There was sandy desert on the east but lush prosperity on the west. When we stopped at Port Said, Egypt, we went to an old style, British-type restaurant for tea. Papa tried to take pictures of a coffee vendor on the street but was forcefully reprimanded, so he gracefully retreated. Also, we stopped in Karachi, West Pakistan and Bombay, India where we saw sculpted shrubbery cut to look like different animals. Next was Cochin, India where they had to offload dried shrimp, lots and lots and lots of dried shrimp. Did they ever smell! Then, we headed on to Colombo in Sri Lanka and up the Irrawaddy River to Rangoon, where they unloaded 100 American Jeeps. In Burma? What are we doing taking Jeeps to Burma? Evidently the US was providing Jeeps to Burma and who knew what else. You never know what form US aid is going to take. Ask me no questions, I'll tell you no lies.

As we were going up the Irrawaddy River, they had

to sound measure the depth of the water all the way to be sure we didn't get stuck. The tide was out and the water was shallow. Of course, they had to do that coming out also. All of this took time, but "malesh," not to worry, as we later learned to say in Arabic.

We got off the ship in Rangoon and went to see the Baptist church there, which had five different language groups worshipping there every Sunday. There are many different tribes in Burma, each speaking a different language. The mission work in Burma was some of the very earliest, started by Adoniram and Ann Judson. We also met one of the missionaries, who was the brother of a friend of mine from school.

Then we headed to Chittagong, the port city of East Pakistan. Just one BIG problem, because of our delay, the tide was out when we got there. It was the wrong time of the month to bring a ship in. The tide would be out for days, which meant that we could not go in. There wasn't enough depth for a ship the size of the *Hellenic Sailor* to pass. In order to diminish the draft of the ship, they had to unload all of that loose wheat for East Pakistan. Each day, we watched smaller boats come out with coolies and burlap bags for off-loading the wheat. They filled the burlap bags with wheat and loaded them into their small boats and went back to the city. It would take a long time to unload all of that wheat. Actually, it took a whole week. Every day we stood on the deck of the Sailor and watched Pakistani airplanes come and go from Chittagong to Dacca where we wanted to go, and there was nothing we could do but wait. All this time we only had electricity about two hours a day, and fuel for the generator was running low. It was very hot and humid, and without electricity that wasn't much fun. At night, they hung a kerosene lantern on each end of the ship so others would know we were there. Of course, the captain was embarrassed, so we tried to be very patient and understanding about the whole thing. During this time, the fellows in the kitchen would fill the empty wine bottles with water to use for drinking and cooking. That gave the water an interesting taste!

The East Pakistanis prefer to eat rice three times a day, but it is a small country and they are not able to grow that much rice. One of the products the US sends to poorer countries is wheat which the US has in abundance.

The customs officials would not allow us to come into Chittagong on one of those lighters (small boats). We had to come in with the ship and go through the customs inspection. Now, that was interesting too, when we finally did it. We had a cured ham, which Emma and Johnnie Rice, old friends in Fayetteville NC, had given us just before we left. Troy hung it in the closet while we traveled, and that is where it was when the customs agent came aboard. He didn't pay any attention to the ham at all. But, he did spot the new shirt, still in the wrapper, which Troy had received as a gift right before we left. He took it and said, "It is just the right size. Thank you for bringing such a nice gift for me, Bennett Sahib." This is called baksheesh, a bribe to you; we didn't have much choice. We actually thought it was funny, because for Muslims, pork is forbidden and contaminates everything around it, and of course he was a Muslim. But, he didn't have a thing to do with the ham, so his hands were clean. We enjoyed the ham, and so did a lot of our friends, and the story that went along with it.

Second Term

Let's go on to the second term. We lived in Dacca in order for Troy to do his language study. He had not had time to do this first term since he was treasurer and thus handled all of the mission business. Steve was in fourth grade at the American Community School; Mrs. Webster was his teacher. He really liked her and she was a very good teacher. Becky had Mrs. Turner as her first grade teacher and she loved her. All of the teachers were very good friends and that made it nice. Ron and

The East Pakistan Southern Baptist mission with friends
Dacca, East Pakistan, 1961

Montiel Peck came for their first term with the Assembly of God mission and they were to become very close friends. During that time, I continued my study of Bengali. It is not an easy language, but we had good teachers and, fortunately, were given time to learn. We never stopped learning up until the day we departed Bangladesh. We lived on Road 24 in the Dhanmandi area and then at the end of that first year we moved to Comilla to work with the Baptists there.

As we moved, we decided it was time to get a dog. Friends in Narayanganj bred dachshunds, and so we got one of them. That made the move even more challenging. I don't remember the details, but we got the dog as we boarded the train in Narayanganj. Troy had gone on ahead so I was with the three children traveling on the train with the dog. Let's see, her name was Winnie. I had had dogs most of my life, so was very comfortable with them, but we'd never had one with a rat's tail like Winnie's. It took a little getting used to. I had experience with cockers and with a boxer.

Again, we were to live in one of those big British

A flame tree & our home getting a new roof
Comilla, East Pakistan, 1962-65

Raj-type houses. Only in this one, we had the whole house. Downstairs, we had the three rooms across including a dining room, a living room, and a guest room with a kitchen. A study and bath were built along the back of the house; an entryway on the side. The screened front veranda had steps going upstairs on the right side. Actually, we heard they were built after the house was complete when they realized that they had been going up and down on the bamboo scaffolding and they had forgotten the stairs. They fitted them in at the end of the front veranda. They were quite steep and were divided into three segments, curving around. There was a pretty stained glass window at one landing. One day when the girls and I were coming downstairs, Winnie was following us and she kept catching my skirt and kissing the back of my legs with her cold, wet nose. I finally had enough of it and gave her a swat. Trouble was, I gave her a push that put her long dachshund nose right through the center of that pretty window. I expect she was shocked but she was not injured, I'm glad to report.

One interesting experience during that year was our trip to Shillong in Assam, India. That was a trip! We went by train to Sylhet, East Pakistan and then by taxi. We boarded the train quite late at night, so immediately got ready for bed. There were four seats, two up and two down. Then, we put a cot in the middle of the compartment since we had it to ourselves. The train was pretty noisy and jerky. Later, as we tried to sleep, we heard a very whispery, trembly, plaintive voice say, "Mama, I can't sleep." When we turned on the light, we saw little Debbie, just 5 years old, whom we had put on the cot, literally bouncing several inches up and down in the air from the cot. Talk about funny! We decided someone heavier needed to sleep there. I suppose it was Troy.

Shillong was wonderful, cool and pretty and restful. We found a wonderful bookstore—always a treasure for this family—and lots of good vegetables and fruit we didn't get in Comilla. Speaking of books, that was our introduction to the Noddy books from Great Britain, which we all enjoyed tremendously. I know they are considered socially incorrect now. Noddy was a little black fellow, I mean black; so black that he was actually unrealistic, but the stories were fun.

Ron and Montiel Peck, our new friends from Dacca, joined us there and we had some good times together. We went for picnics near the river and visited a park in which they had huge goldfish in a pond with a lovely arched bridge over the lake. Troy and Ron found a golf course and were enjoying that, so they suggested we come along and bring a picnic lunch to eat on the grounds. We did, and all went well until they suggested we take a shortcut home, just down the hill here and across that creek. Across the creek, yeah! The children of course just hopped across with a boost from Troy, who with his long legs could straddle it. Then I, who was quite agile then, followed suit, but when it came Montiel's turn, it was a different story. We all said, "Just jump as Troy swings you over." It sounded good, but it was a problematic attempt, and, of course, Troy had to make the most of it by hollering, "Oops, we're gonna fall." But, they didn't and we all had a good laugh with some measure of relief, I must confess. I had to wonder afterward if Troy was serious about falling, but luckily that didn't happen. I wish we had a picture of that!

The Pecks didn't have any children so they enjoyed sharing ours. One day we went on a picnic not too far away. We have some lovely pictures of the stream coming over the rocks. We crossed the stream and sat on the rocks to eat our picnic lunch. So nice! And so private and restful. You do realize that in Bangladesh there was no place at all that private. People were everywhere and liked to watch what we were doing.

On the way back from Shillong we came down out of the hills on a local bus that wasn't too crowded. It was okay, except that in the middle of nowhere, Becky had to go; had to go. What do you do? I didn't feel we could ask the driver to stop, and anyway, that would have been horribly embarrassing for Becky. I'm not sure what the locals would have done in such a case, but I just did the best I could think of. I had a sanitary napkin in my bag and I pulled it out and told her to do her thing there in the bus. She had a hard time doing it for she was quite a shy child. I don't know if anybody even saw and if they did, they probably didn't think anything of it. They are very earthy people; I guess they have to be. Of course, then I was stuck with this very wet pad. I threw it out the window. I figured it was biodegradable.

So, we got back to Comilla and our work there. I

haven't told you about Chana. He was our gardener. He was slow, but he was a good fellow and did a reasonably good job in the garden. One morning, I looked out to see a strange apparition in the middle of the tomatoes. When I asked what that was he said, "To keep the bhoot (ghosts) away." This was because our tomato plants were looking very good and fruit was beginning to form. We would have called it a scarecrow to keep the crows away, but he had a good idea. He made it with a long pole with a clay pot turned over on top. The pot had a most scary face painted on it in white lime paste. I may have made the mistake of saying the plants looked really good. I learned not to do that sort of thing. Bhoots! I can't remember how effective it was but we had plenty of tomatoes.

We actually lived close to many Christian families and their children would come to play. There was quite a crowd of boys who gathered in a big field next door to play soccer. There was just one problem, some days they were glad to have Steve play, other days they bullied him. That was when we learned the expression "Red monkey" which was their derogatory term for white people. We had to learn to "turn the other cheek." It was a hard lesson for a child.

Next door on one side was a West Pakistani family with three girls, Shaheen, Nasreeen, and Noreen, who became good friends with our kids and they played well together. They were Muslim. They spoke English quite well, which was good, because their mother tongue was Urdu. It was with them that Becky got a real "green apple stomach ache," only hers was from green lichis.

We learned a lot from those folks. They were, in a sense, foreigners among the Bengalis, and I think appreciated our presence there. The wife told me once that her husband would never divorce her. He couldn't afford it because of the marriage contract that had been agreed upon between the two families. They seemed to be reasonably happy. I also learned that the philodendron plant is known as the "money plant" in that part of the world. If it thrives, it means you are rich. I never quite understood if it meant you would become rich, or you were already rich. This family's money plant was a really long winding stem with not many leaves, and it went up above the door and around the whole room, draping over each of the doors. While it was long, it didn't look too healthy to me. It probably never got any fertilizer. I didn't dare ask her what that meant about their wealth status.

We also had coconut trees in our yard and once a year the mali would hoist himself up those trees and prune out the dead leaves and stuff, then cut the coconuts that were ready. There's nothing quite like fresh coconut. The Bengalis had a gadget called a kurani for shredding it that was pretty cool. It was made of metal, shaped so you could put your foot on one end to hold it steady, then the other end curved up quite like a cobra's head, and it had tiny, very sharp points that tore that coconut meat right out of the shell till it was as clean as a whistle. Sometimes we just broke the shell and cut it out in hunks. It made a really good salad mixed with pomelo.

We homeschooled in the upstairs central room. Steve

Marj using the kurani to grate coconut
Comilla, East Pakistan, circa 1963

went into fifth grade, Becky into second and Debbie started kindergarten after we moved there. We shared any activities we could, like reading *David Copperfield* and *Lorna Doone* out loud, which was good for the reader and fun for the rest of us. We also made a huge map of the United States for Steve's study of the US. We all worked on it. We made the map, quite large, with papier-mâché and painted in the mountains, rivers and valleys, etc. Interesting. We used the Calvert Correspondence Course out of Baltimore, Maryland to do this, and it was good. They supplied every single thing we might need, down to pencil erasers and rulers. I think we all enjoyed doing school that way. I know I did. I was relearning many things I had long since forgotten or almost forgotten. They had the children start writing little essays as soon as they learned cursive, and then advanced each year till finally they were writing with outlines and doing research. The history books were fun to read, and reading assignments were always appealing. Math and science? No problem. Poetry was important, and that was good too. They also encouraged creative writing, which Becky especially enjoyed and wrote some really good poems in later years. The kids had to take a test every month, which I sent to a teacher in Baltimore to grade. She was assigned to the students for the year, so we developed good relationships with them. I really feel all three of our children got a firm foundation in education and they have done well in higher education. There is something to be said for that one-on-one attention.

A friend who had been a school principal in the States talked with me before we started our homeschooling. She had also been in Burma and taught her son, but she said I should not do what she did. She was so anxious that his education not suffer that she sat by him all of the time to be sure he got everything right. Of course, he became very dependent on her and had a hard time when they came back to the US and he went into larger classes without her. So, I was lucky that I had three to teach, and I made a point to have knitting or sewing to do so I would not get impatient when they dawdled. Also, I took time to check with things in the kitchen. I had a cook, and that, of course, made a big difference. When we had recess, I tried to show the children how to do different things like high jump, broad jump, race and such; then of course, there was always the garden which they helped me with quite enthusiastically.

Our plan was to homeschool through the eighth grade and then they could go to a boarding situation like Mussoorie in India, and later we learned about Bangkok as an option. We felt that by high school, they would want to go where they could be with other young people of their age and interests. By that age in East

Pakistan, many girls who were Becky and Debbie's good friends were thinking about marriage, not more schooling.

One of the fun things we did in that big house in Comilla was to play hide-and-seek after supper. The upstairs was great for this. We turned off all the lights and then would scatter to hide while one counted. Inside the wardrobe, on top of the wardrobe, under beds, inside the bathtub, behind long curtains over those French doors, there were lots of good places to hide. It could be kinda scary up there in the dark, but it was fun.

Meanwhile, Troy was going out to surrounding villages, meeting with local church leaders, and teaching in Lay Leadership Schools. I stayed pretty busy being teacher, mom, neighbor, and church member.

One Sunday after church, a rather puzzled Steve came into the kitchen and asked, "Who was the king in the Bible named 44?" Well, that had me baffled too, but as we talked, we realized that the teacher had been talking about Potiphar. In Bengali they don't have a pure "p" or "f"

Mrs. Roy, a fine Christian & good friend
Comilla, East Pakistan, circa 1963

sound, but they do have something in between the two and that is what they use in Potiphar's name. I can just imagine Steve trying to figure out what in the world he was talking about, but of course he wasn't going to ask the instructor, especially in front of the class of children.

We decided to take our second vacation trip to go to Mussoorie again and invited the Pecks to go along with us. So we flew to Calcutta and got the train across northern India to Delhi. From there it was a taxi ride up to Mussoorie. We planned to stay about three weeks when we traveled that far. We stayed in a house with three apartments. The Pecks stayed in one of the other apartments. It was a good location, for it was literally on the side of the mountain and we had good views of the valleys to the south and north. The weather was very pleasant, so we got out every day to hike or picnic.

Once, we all—except Montiel Peck—decided to hike to Ferguson Falls. It was a pretty long hike, the last part over broken up shale. Shale can be very slippery. The falls were very small, at least when we got there. Maybe other times of the year they are more impressive. We said we had seen a lot of good places to stop to eat on our way there. But, the surprising thing for us was when Uncle Ron just walked over to the high tension tower beside the falls and started climbing around on it like a monkey. We were fairly dumbfounded until he told us that he used to make a living painting those towers. We didn't try to follow him, but sat down in that rocky place and ate our lunch. Then we started back and were constantly reminded that every hill you go down easily, you have to come back up however you can. It was a long hike and the girls and I were glad when we met some fellows on the road who had horses and, yes, we could ride them. That felt good!

One night, we all—except Steve—went to some meeting at church. As we were coming back up the hill we looked ahead and could see Steve standing in the road in front of our house. Wondering what the problem could be, we hurried on up and he told us he was glad we were home. I don't think he ever said he was afraid, but we figured he was.

Almost every night the adult Pecks and Bennetts would play cards, usually Rook. The men were consistently winning and Montiel and I were getting tired of it. They told us if we did what they did, we could give them some competition. And what was that? They used signals. Can you believe that? Well, we did, and got our heads together to figure out some signals of our own. And we won. They were amazed, but when we told them we just did what they did, they were quite shocked that we should cheat that way.

Another day, Troy went down to the bank and then to the market. He came back, quite sheepishly saying that I would need to go to the bank and cash some of my traveler's checks. When I quizzed him for a reason, he admitted they couldn't read his signature and, so, wouldn't accept it. This was really quite funny because I had been telling him that his signature was ridiculous, i.e., he would write a "T" and then a long line. That was his signature.

One Sunday we went down to the church and it was their Sunday to have the Lord's Supper. The choir was made up of students from the boarding school and they were very good, singing from the balcony behind us. The light streamed through all of the long windows so that the interior almost glowed. I especially remember that they sang the various verses of, "Were You There When They Crucified My Lord?" I felt the Lord very close. We never heard singing like this in the Bengali churches.

Soon, it was time to go back to the plains and to the work we were doing for the Lord. I believe we were serving him in the mountains. I know we were worshiping him there, but it was always good to get home and into a regular schedule again.

One night back in Comilla, we woke up to a bad storm, and it was really windy. We were sleeping on a bed with casters and no headboard, and first thing we knew we were being scooted across the room right to the wall on the other side! That was a funny feeling. That wind actually blew the whole top off a date tree by the house. In the morning, just a tall stump stood there. Another night we awoke to see on the wall across the room from us a raging fire. Well, that caught our attention, I can tell you. It was the lumberyard burning across the street from us; we had a very long front yard so it was more like two or three house lots away but the light of the fire was shining through the French doors of our bedroom.

One day, we were on our upstairs front veranda when

one of the children called, "Come and see." Across the wall was a cow delivering a calf, or trying to anyway. Finally Abdul, our mali, who owned her came and helped her finish. That was a good science lesson.

Another time, Steve got into a rather spirited argument with our next door neighbor's daughter who saw him trying to shoot an owl. Seems she had high regard for any owl—probably some superstition from Hinduism though she was Christian. Superstitions die hard you know.

We were growing! Southern Baptist Mission Family
Dacca, East Pakistan, 1965.

Bengali Weddings

I think you might be interested in Bengali weddings. They were so, so different from ours. Let's look at it from the bride's perspective. She would have been about 14 or 15 years old. Among Christians, at meetings when the people from different churches got together for church business, in their spare time around campfires and washing at the pond, one of the important things they dealt with was marriages. The parents talked about their children and showed pictures, asked questions about schooling and such. They were always looking for a good match. The Christians tried to find a match in the Christian community; actually the Baptists tried to find a Baptist but it didn't always happen of course. There were a good many Catholics, relatively speaking. There were so many more Muslims and even Hindus than Christians that the Christian parents felt pressure to stay within their own group so their children could stay in the Christian community.

The bride's parents would contact a matchmaker to help them find a suitable groom. Sometimes they already had someone in mind, like the son of friends or a distant relative. But there was a lot to be checked out and the matchmaker did that, talking with the groom's parents, fixing the amount and type of dowry, checking on the education of the young man, his health record and that of his family, such as asking if there was any tuberculosis in the family. The matchmaker got a picture of the young man and went to the bride's parents again. This time, there were probably more than just the parents at their meeting, maybe an uncle or two and an aunt who wanted to be sure it is all done properly; some older brothers and male cousins may be involved. The parents talked with their daughter, showed her the picture and told her about the young man. It was considered wiser to marry someone whose, "home chimney's smoke she cannot see." If the girl approved, and usually she did, then the match was made and preparations begun.

The big question was the dowry. One wedding we knew of almost didn't happen because the bride's family failed to produce a bicycle, which was part of the promised dowry. Since there were no bicycles for sale in the country, with persuasion from other adults, they finally agreed to go ahead. The dowry depends, of course, on the wealth of the family. But, even the poorer families managed to get a full outfit of clothing for the groom and for the bride. Sometimes they also gave furniture and jewelry.

The actual festivities all began at the groom's house. He was bathed, that is, he went to the big pond always nearby with a group of friends and washed himself, and the friends would often throw red powder on him.

Bengali Weddings

Then he dressed for the wedding and, with his friends, went by palki (old-fashioned covered conveyance carried by men), rickshaw, car, or train to the bride's house where he met opposition at the gate. Yes, opposition. It was all in good fun, but they were very determined to get their part. The children of the area came and demanded money and sweets before they would let him in. As you can imagine, sometimes it got a bit testy. The groom always had some candy and coins, but he was nervous and didn't want to fool around or be taken advantage of.

Before he arrived, the bride had also been bathed by her friends and female family members. She came up from the pond, and walked to the house with all of the children and others with her. It was quite a party! They then rubbed her exposed body parts with a yellow paste made from turmeric to make her beautiful. After that was washed off, her skin had a golden hue. Now, you need to know that the bride was not to show any delight at this time. She was to at least act like she was very sad to leave home—and maybe scared to death too! She often didn't know the groom or his family.

When the groom's party arrived, the bride

A bride in all of her finery
Faridpur, East Pakistan, circa 1968

saw her dowry. Opening the suitcase he had brought, she found the undergarments she needed, the sari she would wear for the wedding, the makeup and jewelry she would use and possibly other saris as well. These things were purchased by the female members of his family. Oh, I should say that women and young children came inside with the bride and watched her as she dressed. There were often comments about something being cheap, not pretty, or maybe nice, very good material and so on. I don't think I mentioned that brides wear red or orange while widows wear white. Different strokes. All this time she was very somber, not smiling at all, even with her close friends. But the crowd was laughing and talking, not with her, but among themselves.

When she came out, there was great excitement. Then, she was off to the church or wherever they were to be married. The ceremony was not that different from ours, except at the end when they would

The bride & her attendant
Comilla, East Pakistan, circa 1964

sometimes tie the end of her sari to the end of his lungi. The grooms often wear lungis for a wedding even if they never do in daily life. A lungi is a tube of cloth wrapped around the waist and tied to itself. Many men may wear them around their home and poor working men wear them all of the time.

At one wedding, the bride was quite overcome by all of the excitement and though she made it to the church and was standing beside the groom, when the preacher asked her to say, "I do" she wouldn't say anything. The two preachers tried several times. Troy sent someone to our house to get a small bottle of smelling salts. They put that under her nose and she snapped right up!

After the wedding, there was a feast, and what a feast! Some of the women and girls had been working for hours to prepare the spices and cook the food. There was rice, chicken curry, vegetable curry, salad and dhoi, which is like yogurt, but so much better; not sweet but thick, creamy, and good! Then we gave the gifts to the bride and groom who were sitting before a huge tray laden with various spices and fruits, and more of the dhoi. We were to give each of them a spoonful of dhoi, feeding it to them like a baby. Of course, there was a lot of laughing and kidding.

Next, the couple traveled to the groom's home where there was another feast and partying with his family and friends. The bride was still looking sad, so she was pampered and teased and treated gently. Within a few days she would be helping with the work around his parent's home. Brides almost always moved to the groom's home. Boys were life insurance for the parents' old age. Now, when she got pregnant, and she probably would within a few months, she came home to have the first baby and stayed home for a while afterward to have the help of her mother and other female relatives.

I know of one family that had only two girls and they worked it out very well. One of the daughters married a businessman and they lived in the capital city. The other sister lived at home with her parents and her husband came to live with them. She worked in the local school. The couple in the city made much more money, so they supplied the homefolk with some of the finer things in life such as fans, a refrigerator, a radio and TV. In return, they got garden produce and such from the folks in the country. They were very happy!

Weddings were a lot of fun and most of those marriages stuck. Bangladeshis said that they marry and then fall in love. They were expecting to love each other and usually they did at least like and respect each other. This arrangement resulted in lots of happy homes; the wife usually got along well with the husband's mother and others in his family. The divorce rate, I think, had to be very low. I remember one woman who was put out by her husband because while he was gone she got involved with his brother. Her parents didn't want her to come home; they couldn't afford another mouth to feed. There were no jobs for women who were uneducated and inexperienced. Another woman, more well-to-do, told me her husband would never divorce her; he couldn't afford to. In the marriage arrangement, her family had stipulated the support he would have to give her in case of a divorce. Evidently it was very high. I heard of some abuse, forcing sex and that sort of thing, but not often and not at all among Christian women.

Men were the head of the home; some were kind and some were mean, but some women were kind and some were mean. In public, the women were careful of the way they dressed and behaved, covering their heads and that sort of thing. Muslim women walked behind their husbands or sons or whomever they are with, but that wasn't usually a problem. Once, in Chittagong, Papa and I were walking through the bazaar. It was very crowded, mostly with men as they do most of the shopping. I was behind Troy but not four paces behind. I wanted to stay close, to tell you the truth. Anyway, a man came up and gave me a shove back. He didn't hurt me at all, but it did get my attention. I didn't have my head covered and that may have bothered him too. In general, we figured, it was their culture and we should adjust, so we did. Actually, we were much more adapted to the culture than many of the other foreigners, though most made some effort.

We did take some liberties. For example, the Christian women didn't wear veils over their faces but they did keep their heads and arms covered in public. In church they covered their heads, especially during prayer and Bible readings, and we did too; at least I did. I got to like it. It was kind of a private little place with God. But, they also covered their heads whenever a man came around; I didn't try to keep up with that. And of course, they moved differently. I realized after a while, that we foreign women moved with a confidence that probably irritated some of the men. Was that good or bad? I don't know. I wanted to be humble before God. I wanted to be a good and strong partner for Troy, but I didn't feel that I had any duty to submit in any way to other men.

I have a friend, a young woman who has been working overseas and is planning to go back. She teaches the children of missionaries. They are in quite a remote area where people are not accustomed to foreigners. She and the missionary women dress as the women there do, in long skirts and veils. The rules are to keep your eyes down, don't ever make eye contact with men outside your family. That is a basic thing in many cultures that is so hard for Americans. We are just used to going at things full tilt, aren't we?

Well, this has gotten away from weddings but it is all about the role of women. I should say that the Christian women were very strong leaders of women. Some Muslim women have even gotten into politics in recent years. In the churches in Bangladesh, the women were very active in the roles assigned to them and they were very influential. The men listened to them, as they should. They saw things the men didn't.

Second Furlough

Our second furlough was spent in Winston-Salem living in the Ardmore Baptist Church missionary house. Ardmore is a very good church and we enjoyed our year with them very much. We, of course, were also near Troy's parents and sisters, June, Mary, and Mallie. Steve was in middle school. His homeroom teacher was Betsy Knott, Bill Jr.'s young wife, and he liked her a lot. It was a hard year for Steve; Troy had encouraged him to go out for football, thinking he would love it, and this was his chance to enjoy it. However, Troy went over one afternoon to watch practice and saw Steve sitting on the bench, a very miserable kid who felt very out of place. He at once let him know that he didn't have to do this, and Steve was glad to drop out. He had never played football and knew very little about it. Later, he said he never did like contact sports, but he did really get into soccer and volleyball when he was older and in Bangkok. He also lettered in cricket in Bangkok.

While writing this story, I have seen so many things differently, like here I am able to see across Steve's growing up years, and it has occurred to me that the Bengali boys were very unpredictable. His attempts at making friends were often scorned or ignored, but not always. This unpredictability may have made it even worse. He never knew if they would play with him or not. Being an MK (missionary kid) is not always easy; sometimes it is very hard. We knew it was hard for him but what could we do?

He had friends when we were in Wake Forest on furlough; we had come back for one year to Dacca and he attended the American School and had some good friends there. Then in Comilla, he was in the same situation for two years again with the Bengali boys. Finally, the year before furlough, we had arranged with the Johnsons for him to live with them in Dacca, and attend the American School. That was a pretty good year, I think.

Now this year in Winston-Salem; he was new, a young teenager at an age when it is not easy to make new friends. Gangs were already formed and he was a stranger in their midst. Even if they asked him where he came from, his answer would raise eyebrows. "What! East Pakistan. Whatcha doing there?" The girls told me their friends didn't want to hear those names of faraway places.

Becky was in the fifth grade and got along very well. Debbie, in the second grade, was chosen to go to the special school in Winston for academically gifted students the next year. However, when I explained to the lady who called that we would be returning to Bangladesh and I would be teaching her in homeschool, she was well impressed and agreed with me that Debbie would probably gain more this way, overall, than she would in the AG program. The primary school was just a couple of blocks up the street so that was very convenient.

That was the year I took Driver's Education. I had learned to drive with a friend in Fayetteville when I was pregnant with Becky, but had driven very little since. However, this seemed to be a good opportunity, so I took it and it was all right. Not sure I learned much; Troy had already taught me a lot just as we would ride along together and from my watching him. I never did drive much overseas; in Bangladesh. I drove some in Dacca but not out in the countryside. One day I was forced off the road and we decided that was enough of that. Anyway, Troy wanted to do the driving if he was in the car and he usually was. Therefore, I never had the confidence that many women my age do simply because I have not driven as much. I am now probably a more careful driver than some of them; I am sure I am well trained because I have taken the AARP courses several times and keep up on recent laws, etc.

Speaking of driving, we had a funny experience years later when we lived in Dar es Salaam, Tanzania. Troy and I went down to get our driver's licenses. We had been told it could be a challenge and it was, especially for Troy. As I told him later, I had nothing to lose, no loss of pride because I hadn't been driving that much anyway but he had a lot to lose and felt that he was losing it right there in front of God and everybody.

First, we had to take the test with the sign chart; I waited outside while Troy did his and he came out, quite crestfallen; he had failed. What? No comment. I went in and then I failed too, because when the examiner asked what did the red sign mean, I answered, "Stop." No, that was wrong. Then I asked "Could you help me please? What does the red sign mean?" "Oh," he says blithely, "that is the sign you will see when they are fixing potholes in the road. Then you are to stop." I replied, "I see, but I haven't seen any one fixing potholes in the road." Enough said! Troy whisked me out of there. He was afraid I would make the fellow mad. Actually, the guy was very nice and so was I. The young woman who came in with her driving instructor who slipped some money under the table was also very nice, and she got her permit. The funny thing about this was that we had an enormous pothole just outside our fence. I mean enormous, big enough for a car to fall into, literally. It was a little tricky to drive around, but that's what everybody did, for several years in fact.

Well, I really jumped ahead that time, didn't I? Anyway back to second furlough: That was the year we had so much snow and did we ever love it! It was so nice to have that happen the year we were home. Actually, it snowed six weeks straight on Saturday so that Troy could not keep his preaching engagement for Sunday. And what did we do? We enjoyed it! I remember Troy and I were out in front clearing the sidewalks at 10 and 11 at night. It was so beautiful. I have always loved snow, just the beauty and the crisp coldness, the feeling that most people seem to get when it snows. You know, bundle up to go out, hot chocolate when you come in. "Oh, let's get the fire going in the fireplace." All that atmosphere. Lovely! But, it couldn't last forever, and of course, it didn't.

Troy and I went to the Furloughing Missionary Conference that year in Missouri, Camp Windermere. I especially remember the trip out; we took our time and just enjoyed the scenery. We especially liked one low bridge we crossed; so low the water was running over it. Maybe you don't call that a bridge but, whatever, we stopped and walked in the water and just had a good time. Troy loved to drive and see things, and I loved doing it with him. Especially in the States, he would just come in and say, "Let's go for a ride." And off we'd go. It was so nice and I miss that.

This was the year Steve and Becky asked for baptism. I'm not sure they were really ready; they didn't talk with us that much; they talked with their teachers at church and I'm sure were encouraged to make the move. Now I wish I had encouraged them to talk more with us about it but that's long past. In Bangladesh it was never considered until a person was grown, and more often than not, when married. Personally, we both were firm believers in believer's baptism, meaning baptism as a symbol of what has already happened in a person's heart, a commitment to God made freely and willingly. Until that time, no one needs to be baptized. Enough sermon for today.

That was also the year we went with Emma Rice to a camp down in the eastern part of the state to be the missionaries in residence. The children, the older two, were lined up with the other children and that worked out okay until one night. Troy and I had gone somewhere else to speak, and they were in a meeting when the pressure came to repent, come forward, etc. Becky talked with me about that later, and I'm sorry they had to experience it. However, I guess it was just as well to know that it is part of the American culture too. It was not too pleasant, and not anything we wanted for them, but we were not to be the only influences in their lives by any means. They knew a lot of other wonderful people. In fact, I have often said, "We don't take all the credit for the good in their lives, but we don't take all the blame for the bad either." We did the best we knew how; one thing I have stressed with them is that THERE WAS NEVER ANY LACK OF LOVE. That I know for sure!

Papa and Mama Bennett came over to eat one day for lunch. Papa mentioned that he had seen in the paper an idea for older people. Since there are more women than men living longer, why not let a man have several wives, one to cook, one to nurse, one to clean, and so on. No one would have to work too hard. What did Mama think of that? "HUMPH!" He also impressed us when he recited the names of all of the presidents of the U.S.A. The early ones he knew very well; the later ones he had to stop a bit and think, but he did it.

That was the year Ray Penry, Jr. and Judy got

married. That was fun for us and the kids too. They were always fun to be with and we saw a good bit of them that year. Troy was to perform the wedding, so he talked with them about the things preachers do before a wedding, except that preachers want to talk about the marriage and the young couple, especially the bride, only wants to talk about the wedding. That can be frustrating for a preacher, but Troy usually enjoyed the weddings too. A happy time!

Also that year, I met one of Troy's old girlfriends that I had heard about but never met. I can't remember her name now, but one morning we had a call and Troy said it was this woman and her husband, in town for just a day or two and wanted to stop by to see him. Fine, so they did. She was very nice and comfortable. When she and I went to the kitchen for hot drinks, she told me she was rather shocked to see Troy's wife wearing slacks. Actually, I had just started wearing them that year, to keep warm but also I had worn them when I was a teenager and liked them. Of course in Bangladesh we often wore shalawar khameesh, which are long pants and a long top. Note that a long top meant to cover your hips. Very important! She was also shocked to see that I used makeup, well lipstick only, but she noticed.

After they left, when I told Troy what she had said, he just laughed and said, "Yeah, I guess I was pretty straitlaced back in those days." I suppose I loosened him up some. He didn't seem to think it was too much, so I didn't either.

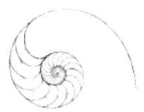

Third Term: Faridpur/Comilla

Becky's Poem
A day, suspended in the past and future.
My cheek against the cool, damp floor
While Debussey ripples with the fan's rhythm.
Long, sticky evenings of Kipling and Sarah,
And the mornings' promise of another steamy noon.
Gingersnaps and lemon iced tea
And cold papaya from the tree by the step.
We pruned the lemon tree once...
Mama wore long sleeves and attacked the thorns:
We children laughed and directed from a safe distance.

There it is. It so much revives for me a peaceful life when you still attacked the thorns of life and I was young and free to laugh and direct from a distance. And our life there was so much about temperatures: cool, hot. And music and books. Life doesn't get much better—it was a good life!

I love you! – Becky

Faridpur Baptist Church building
Faridpur, East Pakistan, circa 1967

For our third term, we returned to Faridpur for Troy to do evangelistic work and also, of course, to work with the churches in the region. We lived in a new smaller house, which was very nice. The Rythers had lived in it first and had landscaped the yard; the main addition we made was to put in some banana trees across the back. The mali (gardener) was sure they wouldn't do well in the cool season, but I convinced him to dig a trench around each tree and fill it with water once a week. Guess what? They did just fine and bore fruit like crazy. Of course, I had an advantage over him; I remembered learning in school that bananas are 85% water, so they wouldn't do well during the dry season without some help.

Carl and Jean Ryther lived in the big house as Carl was in charge of the Mission Industrial School. They had four children, Carla and Joel who were both

Faridpur Baptist Church: men on one side & women on the other
Faridpur, East Pakistan, 1967

a little older than Becky, Gary who was about Debbie's age, and Tim. The Ryther children were there the first year and that was fun; they lived in the big house just a five-minute walk from us. The last two years they went to school in West

Troy listening & learning from our friend, Mrs. Saha
Faridpur, East Pakistan, circa 1967

Pakistan and were home for breaks. Carl was quite an agriculturist; had studied and knew a lot about it so he tried all sorts of experiments. One project which we both did was to grow broccoli. It made perfect sense since the people there had grown cauliflower for years, centuries maybe. The broccoli did well and then I would go around the neighborhood and give each household a head or two and suggest they cook it just like cauliflower, which meant cut up in their curry. Of course they liked it and Carl and I kidded that we ended up buying it back from them. That wasn't true, but, the good thing about broccoli over cauliflower is that you can continue to cut it for several weeks, and that really appealed to the Bangladeshis. Our gardens were very important to us. Carl had a farm, but I just had a garden. It produced a lot of stuff which we enjoyed eating and sharing. We canned a good bit and later got a freezer and froze some things. Only trouble was that when the electric power went out, which it did on a rather regular basis, we were in trouble.

One time, the deep freezer needed to, "see a doctor" and that meant taking it to Dacca. The only problem was that Troy was out of town, but Carl was there and was planning on making that trip anyway. So, we packed the freezer and our bags in the back of the Land Rover with Debbie on the seat beside the freezer. Carl, Becky and I were in front. It was night and as we traveled along that dark road, we heard a trembly voice say, "Mama, the freezer is squishing me." The freezer had slowly shifted as we drove so we made adjustments, but we all thought it was pretty funny. Imagine Debbie squashed by that big heavy freezer!

Just in front of our house was a tank, a man-made pond, which was used by the neighbors for washing clothes, bathing, washing dishes—especially the brass pots they used. They would scrub them with sand or dirt to make them shine like new. One time, they drained that tank and our girls wanted to go with the other kids to catch fish with their hands in the mud. Well, they did, but the fish were so small. Ibrahim, our cook, a good-natured fellow and especially tolerant of anything the girls wanted, cleaned those tiny fish and cooked them. So we ate them. I think it was three fish and each made one bite apiece.

Marj with Ibrahim, our faithful friend & worker at our old house Faridpur, Bangladesh (now called), 1990

We occasionally had visitors from Europe show up and we welcomed them. They were usually traveling across the country or continents with backpacks; sometimes they would come in the house, shower and eat with us, but not always. One was a German couple. When the wife saw our piano, she sat right down and started to play. She was a concert pianist. That was a thrill for us! We never knew what a day might bring.

We also had audio tapes of the movie, *Old Yeller* and *The Sound of Music*. At rest time we would stretch out on those cool cement floors and listen to those tapes until we had them memorized. Then we could sing songs while we traveled.

Faridpur was wonderful for the girls because there was such a good group of Bengali girls near their ages. What made that time so special was the presence of all of those girls who became friends to Becky and Debbie. I ran a first aid dispensary when needed. The girls would come to our yard to play virtually every day.

Some of Becky & Debbie's friends
from Faridpur, East Pakistan, 1968

That was good, because, as I have said earlier, the boys were free to play most anywhere, but the girls had to be more modest and circumspect. The girls could come to our house and play whatever they wanted. They all learned to ride the bicycle and to roller skate. That was a sight, as often they were not wearing shoes; they just wrapped rags around their feet until they fit into the skates and then zoomed away on our concrete drive.

We started a Girl's Auxiliary (GA) mission group with those girls. They called it the Girl's Club because that went into Bengali better. We studied the *Tell* magazine and did all the activities that we could manage. I think it was primarily good because it taught them about Christians in other parts of the world. They didn't know any others and tended to think of themselves as the only minority group in the world. In Bangladesh, Christians were a very small minority. We used to say one-third of one percent of the people were Christian in name, perhaps not in practice. In this group they learned about Christians in a different country every month, and then we tried to do some of the cultural things as well. I remember especially when we studied about Brazil; I made some very strong coffee and gave them just a bit. They were not too well impressed with that taste; neither was I.

Beebha & Neebha with Beebha's baby
Dhaka, Bangladesh (now called), 1990

Also, they learned the Swahili greeting for Tanzania and Kenya, which is, "kwaheri" in English type. When we went back to visit in 1990 after having been in Africa and gone from Bangladesh for 12 years, I saw one of the girls and she greeted me with, "Kwaheri, memsahib." Can you imagine how I felt hearing those words? We were so privileged with all of our exposure to other cultures and they had so little.

Tulu, one of our girls' friends, with her family
Dhaka, Bangladesh (now called), 1990

One year we had a Halloween party. This was entirely foreign to the children and they responded with screams and giggles. I got one of the young women to be a fortune teller and she did a good job.

Another night we had a sleepover at our house. All of the girls came and slept on our living room floor, seventeen in all. It was great fun! I insisted that each bring her own pillow since I didn't have so many and they did. I must confess that one reason I did this was to try to avoid getting bedbugs or lice in our linens. It all worked out fine and everyone had fun. Not much sleep, but fun!

By the time our girls were ready to go to Bangkok for high school, a few of these girls were getting married.

Some of them attended several years in school, and one at least completed nurse's training. We loved those girls and even now when I think of them, my heart goes out to them in prayer for a good and healthy and happy life. I'm sure Debbie and Becky often have these same thoughts. They need to tell their stories someday about the girls they loved so much. There was Shobha, Beebha, Neebha, Reebha (sisters), Jooie and Jawlie (also sisters). Beejoo, Sheema, Kudu, Usha, Tulu and others. When we returned there in 1990 for a visit, we learned that Jawlie had married a businessman and lived in Dacca and helped to support the family, Jooie stayed with the parents with her husband and was teaching in the local school. This was because there were no sons to care for the parents. Jooie's husband had agreed to stay with her parents; evidently he had brothers at home to care for his parents. One of the main reasons Bengalis want to have sons is to care for the parents in their old age. There is no insurance or retirement plans.

We experienced an interesting custom one time when Beejoo became "arree" with Becky and Debbie. I don't know why. I'm not sure they did either. But it meant she would have nothing to do with them. Wouldn't even speak to them. I told them she can be "arree" with you, but you shouldn't be "arree" with her; just treat her as you always have and she should cool down eventually. She did. It's interesting, but I understand that even grown women sometimes become "arree" with one another. When they do, they hook their little fingers together to show they are "arree."

Sure enough, after a few months, Beejoo came back and all was well.

For our vacation in 1967, we went to Nepal in November. We flew to Khatmandu, Nepal. As soon as we got off the plane, the taxi drivers were crowding us to go to the hill stations. Evidently many tourists do this, but that was not in our plan. We would stay in the environs of Khatmandu, and there was a lot to see and do there. We went on to the hotel, the Snow View, which was not 5-star or even a 4-star place, but it was okay. At first we were put in the annex across the street with no heat at all. In November it was cold, especially at night. We had borrowed some winter clothes from friends and were okay on that front. Debbie remembers that her bed had four heavy wool blankets on it. She had to lift all of them up to turn over in bed. It was the same for all of us. Pretty funny!

One day we came in from a long walk and wanted to take a bath before supper. We told the bearer who said he would get us hot water. So far, we had only cold water from the spigot. But, here he came with a small gas burner, like a camp stove. He lit it and placed it under a 50-gallon drum full of cold water. "It will get hot," he said. We just stood there stupefied. Of course when he left we burst out laughing. What else could we do? There was an old-fashioned bathtub there, so evidently people had taken baths in it. Warm baths? Maybe not. We took spit baths until we moved to the hotel proper across the street and had our own bathroom with all of the amenities.

Debbie got a very bad gastrointestinal illness and we finally called the Peace Corps doctor who was in the city. He was very nice, very young, and I think very inexperienced with children. He kept telling her it wouldn't hurt, not to worry, and all the time she just wanted him to stick her and get it over with. I can't remember why he was giving her a shot, but it obviously did the trick.

Nepal is mountainous and beautiful and cool, actually cold, in November. We did enjoy our hikes and walks. We went into town and saw the Living Goddess of Nepal. We were told that she had been chosen when very young and would be the Goddess until she reached puberty. Then she would have to retire and another girl would be chosen. Meanwhile, she lived in this tall house and was cared for by special women. This was all part of their Hindu religious observance.

One day we went out to see Mt. Everest. We had hired a taxi, but when he came, he had another couple who also wanted to go. They were an American young couple. It came out that they were Jewish and had just visited Israel and now wanted to see Everest. We went to the top of

Troy with Becky & Debbie and the Himalaya Mountains in background
Nepal, 1967

another mountain where we could get a good view in the early morning. We had brought our breakfast with us, but the tea thermos had tipped over and spilled. It was cold and we wanted some hot tea, so Becky, Debbie and I plus the young Jewish woman went into the little restaurant in which there was one room with tables and chairs and a kitchen. The walls had a blackish cast over the whitewashed finish which was probably from smoke. It didn't look very clean. They invited us on back to the kitchen where they were making the tea. The fellow was hunkered down, sitting on his heels before a small burner pouring the tea through a sieve that had tea dust in it. Tea dust is the sweepings from the tea processing area. It is obviously the cheapest form of tea to be found. He would continue doing this until he thought the tea was strong enough. We were more interested in seeing that the tea was actually hot, boiling hot. But, this young woman evidently thought there was no way it could be clean. Without a word she whirled around and marched out of the little tea house. We called Troy and had a nice strong cup of tea. That tasted good!

The day I enjoyed the most I think was when we went with a Norwegian fellow and his two teenagers to a creek

Will Becky be able to get out of that crab position without getting wet?
Nepal, 1967

for a picnic and just climbing around. You can see in the picture how it was, so beautiful, and quite a challenge to move around on the rocks. I especially like the picture of Becky in the crab position on that rock.

You may have noticed that I'm not including Steve in these stories. That's because he was gone for most of the year for high school in Bangkok, Thailand. We had originally planned to send the children to Mussoorie in north India, but when the time came for him to go, relations between Pakistan and India, because of Indo-Pakistani war of 1965 over Kashmir, made that impossible. Therefore, we sent him to Bangkok where our board had a hostel for kids from outside Bangkok. Also, some kids from Vietnam came there to live and attend the International School of Bangkok. It was a good school and the hostel was good some years and better other years. It depended on the hostel parents, fellow missionaries who were asked to make this part of their assignment. Steve seemed handle the change quite well. He had lived in Dacca with the Pat Johnsons and gone to the American School there one year during the previous term, so he had been away from home before.

It was not so easy for his Mama. I can't really say for Troy. I know he missed Steve too, but he was gone a lot and actually was a more pragmatic person than I. It kinda tore something out of my heart whenever one of the children left. I got used to it as time went on, but still missed all of us being together. Of course I couldn't hold him at home, and didn't want to. He was almost 1,000 miles away with no phone, much less email or Skype. But, we were where I believed we were supposed to be and I did really want to be there. When the testing times come, that makes a big difference, that certainty of purpose.

Papa Bennett, Troy's father, died in 1967; we knew he was not well but it was a loss, especially for Troy. Then my mother died the next year, and that was sudden. She was still active. In fact, we got a letter from her after she died. It took me a while to get used to her being gone, but we were leaving on vacation that summer of 1968 to meet Steve in Thailand, so that was good. We went to Pattaya, a beautiful location with a nice beach and comfortable cottages. That gave me time to grieve.

This time in Faridpur was so full and happy for the most part. Steve was home for the summers and Christmas and Easter breaks. The girls did their homeschooling and then played with this large group of friends. Becky had learned to play the violin during our year in the US and she continued to practice and enjoy it. She even played a duet with Jane Moore on piano for the wedding of two of our missionaries. I did the best I could to teach both of the girls to play the piano, and they continued with lessons later in Bangkok.

The last year of our third term we were asked to move to Comilla. This time our move itself was very interesting and challenging! Troy was driving a pickup truck with boards on each side to build it up to about five feet so we could pack more in. It was really hard on him as he had to drive to Dacca by crossing one river by ferry, then south to Comilla with another ferry. It was an overnight trip. In Comilla he had to unload all the stuff and turn around and come back the same way. Becky had some bug that really laid her low, so Debbie and I did the packing. We had more things packed for him to take in the next load. I think he did five trips that way and then at the last, we went with him: Becky, Debbie and I, Lady the dog, Sandy the cat, Davy the parakeet in his cage and the two rabbits in their cages in the back. We were really packed into that truck. There was no back seat, so all four of us sat up front with the dog, cat, and the parakeet.

We stopped once for some reason; maybe something fell off, and we let Lady out to do her thing. Then we all piled in again and went on our way. But all of those people who had gathered and been watching our every move began to shout, "Kukur, kukur!" We stopped and looked back to see Lady running as fast as she could on her little short dachshund legs, her ears waving in the wind she made, trying to catch us. That was one time we were glad to have an audience when we stopped!

Becky would be going to Bangkok for high school, so this was a hard change for Debbie especially. She was losing Becky as well as all of those girlfriends in Faridpur. The one saving factor was that we would be much nearer to the McKinleys, who, by this time were in Feni, about an hour's drive south of Comilla. Besides the Bengalis in Comilla, there were the American Catholic nuns who taught in their school, and Father Dan, the American priest. Debbie attended a class or two there; she rode alone in a rickshaw to school. That was quite a venture, but it worked out fine. Also, there was a Danish family with two younger girls living across the tank behind our house in Comilla. We became friends, and Debbie did have some good times playing with Hannah and Tina, though they were two or three years younger.

In June 1970, we went to Thailand for Steve's graduation. We were also able to meet Amelia Roberson, his girlfriend. Later that summer we went to the US for furlough, this time in Kings Mountain, NC.

Graduation! Amelia Roberson, whom he later
married is first in the row of girls
International School Bangkok, Thailand, 1970

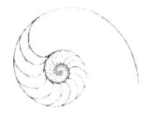

Memories of Christmas in Bangladesh

Here I am in North Carolina at Christmastime with all the beautiful lights and greenery, the trees and wreathes, the music and dramas, and I'm feeling nostalgic for the simplicity of Christmas in Bangladesh. I'm not sure the Bangladeshis would think of their Christmas observance as all that simple, but compared to this, it was simplicity itself. But then, so was the first Christmas simple—the stable, the animals, the manger, the simple man and woman, and the simple shepherds.

One of my first memories of Christmas in Dacca, the capital city, was of the young men coming to our house singing carols and dressed as some of the characters in the drama. It was really pretty grotesque, but also moving in some innocent way. Especially amusing, and yet touching, was the young man dressed as Mary with a pillow stuffed in his sari. I can't help but wonder how it was decided which of them would take that part!

The women & girls ground spices for the Love Feast. Faridpur, East Pakistan, circa 1967

Christmas Love Feast: sitting on the ground & eating with our hands!

Then later, as we moved to the town of Faridpur, we became a part of the celebration and it became a part of us. There was the Christmas party at the church on Christmas Eve for the children with the Christmas tree decorated with paper streamers, and colored tissue streamers, intricately cut, strung all over the church. They would stay there until spring to be replaced with new streamers to celebrate Easter.

And then there was Father Christmas. Speaking of grotesque! He was dressed up with a beard and had a big voice and an ho-ho-ho enough to scare the little ones. Otherwise, he was just wearing winter clothes over a very large stomach. But, he had gifts for each child and was very loving as he gave them out. We were all given a candle which we lit and took "out into the world" as we left. Going home afterward was such a joy! We could hear the children laughing and shouting and see their lights as they scattered across the compound to their homes. On some of the houses, those with a level wall along the roofline, they had placed luminarias. So beautiful in the darkness!

Of course, the next day we had the Christmas service with lots of singing and a jubilant spirit. One Christmas Day, at the end of the service one young man shouted out, "Three cheers for Jesus!" and the crowd took up the refrain. This was then followed in the early afternoon by a literal dinner on the ground. This had been prepared by the young men, supervised by adult experts, all men. Some of the girls and women, working most, if not all of the night before, had ground the spices, a very important part of the cooking process.

When the food was ready, we all gathered; up to 200 people—in an open field by the school building, and sat on the ground. Pieces of banana leaves for plates were brought and the water to wash leaves and our hands at the same time. You ate with the right hand, even if you were left-handed. Then they brought the rice, dhal – a spiced lentil sauce, curried chicken and bhajee, which is curried vegetables. Everything was eaten with our fingers. It was always delicious!

As we were eating and appreciating the taste, some young man, probably one of the cooks, would shout, "How do you like it?" and all would reply with gusto, "Good!" That was always handy! Dessert was always paiash (rice pudding), still warm from the fire and sweetened with date gur (syrup). Nothing like it! I don't like to call it rice pudding because it is so totally different from anything we see in our recipe books here. We ate that from the banana leaf too, with our fingers.

After a meal like this, we would have to have a nap. It was necessary. But, rather quickly, we needed to get up and get out visiting. We were expected to visit everyone, which was almost impossible in Faridpur. There were just too many people. One year we decided we were going to try to get to every house, but when it was getting dark and we came to one home, we found they were already asleep. They had ground the spices the night before and were exhausted. We gave up and went home.

I'm not sure we celebrated the birth of Christ any more than American churches do, but we certainly celebrated community, Christian community. We had been together virtually every waking minute from dusk Christmas Eve till dusk Christmas Day. It was good!

When in Comilla, they did things a bit differently. First, the singing and dancing group was from our own church and came into our home for an hour or two, so it was more like a party. We served goodies. I remember one of the boys got a little carried away and his father brought him back in line. This was a serious, yet joyous thing we were doing.

Another fun thing we did in Comilla was to have a party in our big backyard for all the children (40-50) a day or two before Christmas. We played games, ran races and gave out gifts. One year I took them on a Lion Hunt. Do you know that one? It's fun! I led all of the children to do what I do with their hands, and

I took them through long grass (swish, swish), then through the jungle (clear vines from your face), over a bridge (thump, thump on my chest), then the river (swim, swim), climb a tree through long grass again (swish, swish). Oh, oh, here's a swamp, splash, splash. Shhh, I heard something. Climb another tree to see what is up front. Hand over hand, hand to forehead looking right and left, then: Oh no! There's a lion. Who has a gun? Nobody! Run for it kids! And go back the same way you came, the swamp, the bridge, etc. Don't make it too complicated or you won't be able to remember when you are running back.

They were always so grateful for the gifts that the church gave them. Simple things such as pens for older boys, tiny bottles of perfume for older girls, handkerchiefs and hair ribbons, such simple things.

It was amusing and humbling on Christmas morning at church to see all of the children in a family dressed in the same cloth. Their parents had bought a large piece and had dresses and shirts made for each of their children. Several of the families did this as a practical measure. It was smart and pleasing.

One year in Comilla, we decided to have a pageant. None of the children had ever seen anything like this and just a few of the adults thought they remembered having seen it years ago. Since I had been working with the children in Sunday school, it was the perfect opportunity for them to experience something like this! It actually went quite smoothly with all of them taking it very seriously and wanting to do it right. We had the small children, my young daughter Debbie included, come in as a chorus of angels singing. That was precious! The only somewhat shocking thing was when Mary came dressed for her part in a bright orange sari. At first, I was taken aback, but quickly realized that, of course, Mary was a new bride and that's the color a bride would be wearing in Bangladesh. White is for widows. Who ever thought of blue anyway? The Virgin Mary more than likely wore brown or maybe orange. Who knows?

What can I say? All that I see here in the States is beautiful. I love the music and the colors and the atmosphere. But my heart aches for a simpler Christmas. Would it be possible to have a Christmas that was truly just the celebration of a birthday, Jesus' birthday? How could we do that? Perhaps by giving a simple gift to all the children at church and outside church as well. Maybe by ensuring that everyone had shelter for the night, food to eat, those who care for them close by. And maybe to take the story of Jesus out of the churches and all around town, young people and old, dressed up as Mary, Joseph, angels, shepherds, and kings. Simple lights shining from all the houses like stars.

The refrain going back to heaven, "Peace on earth to all men of good will."

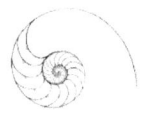

Third Furlough

Debbie, Steve, Becky & Marj on camels at the beach
Karachi, West Pakistan, 1970

The five of us together again was nice as we traveled home for our third furlough. We stopped in Karachi and rode camels on the beach. It was a bumpy ride. Harrumph, harrumph! Papa chickened out. When we came back and insisted he ride, he finally got on one of them and rode around a tiny circle.

We also had to leave a lot of things we had brought with us; we were way over our weight limit for luggage on the airplane. So we piled a bunch of stuff on a beach towel in the hallway of the hotel. We told the cleaning crew to take what they wanted. Then we went on to Zurich, Switzerland, which was lovely and cool. I remember a restaurant where we were able to get raspberries and cream! When had we last tasted raspberries? Years ago! We had a hard time getting water. All they seemed to have was mineral water. So, we drank mineral water.

We did a good bit of walking to see the city's old historical buildings and the activity on the lakeside. We also took a taxi up a mountain to see Heidi's Place, a large stone with a plaque. We drove a little way into Lichtenstein, then we rode the train to see the Baptist seminary which is now in Prague, Czechoslovakia. Then we were ready to move on to Frankfurt and Copenhagen.

We only spent one night in Frankfurt, but had to deal with a surprising development, the girls rebelled and wanted to go back home, that is, to East Pakistan. How old were they then? Becky was going into the tenth grade and Debbie, the seventh. I don't remember all of the details but if we think about it a bit, it's not hard to see what they were facing. They are going home to family they didn't remember, new school situations, a new community, and no known friends. Took a lot of courage for them to get through that. We had been offered the use of a missionary house in Kings Mountain, NC. This was not an area we were familiar with but we thought it would be a good location, especially since Steve was going to Mars Hill College in the western part of the state and not so far from us. Well, we couldn't go back to Dacca so we had to go on to the States, which as you can see by this time was not home anymore.

Another problem we had in Frankfurt was about our overweight carry-on luggage. The fellow saw that we had it in Dacca and didn't seem to understand or believe that we had left it in Karachi. Of course language was a problem. Papa was not about to pay for overweight luggage we didn't have!

In Copenhagen we were met by the Christiansen family who had been in Comilla with us. They were Danish and were so gracious to show us around. The children went with their two girls, Debbie's friends, who were much younger than she, but they had to depend on them to interpret the language; on the bus, at the zoo, getting lunch and so on. Steve and the girls were somewhat embarrassed to have to stand by while the little girls did all of the talking.

Troy and I went with the parents to see Kronborg, the castle Shakespeare used in the play Hamlet. It was huge and very imposing. We enjoyed seeing it but I can't imagine living in it. I could see Hamlet and his crowd moving around in it.

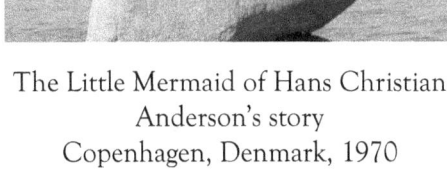

The Little Mermaid of Hans Christian Anderson's story
Copenhagen, Denmark, 1970

We all went to Tivoli

where they have a great roller coaster, right in the city. We also went to an indoor circus which was quite good. What I remember most is that we saw so many blondes, children, and adults. One day on our own, we went for a walk and found the Little Mermaid statue in the harbor. I understand it is there in memory of Hans Christian Andersen who was Danish.

It was a good stop that we all enjoyed. The only thing that went wrong was that Becky put all of her nicely folded new clothes in a bureau drawer, but we failed to take them out when we packed to leave, so she lost them.

Upon our arrival in North Carolina and the very warm reception of our family, things settled down and rather quickly we went on to a missionary house in Kings Mountain. The house was very adequate and the people of First Baptist Church couldn't have been any kinder. Kings Mountain was a very nice town for furlough, not too large, easy to find our way around. We were making new friends again and also looking forward to our Trippeer Family Reunion at Callaway Gardens in Georgia. At least Troy and I were; I suppose the children were waiting to see how things turned out.

After my Mother died two years before, some of the Trippeer sisters and brothers decided we would have a reunion when Troy and I were there. And they arranged for us to go to Callaway Gardens in Georgia; it was fantastic! Everybody was there—46 in all. Each couple had their own cabin, but of course the kids were shifting around constantly. The Florida State University circus troupe was there to provide entertainment and activities. And boy, they did! During the mornings, we would go to a craft class or do one of the circus "tricks." Of course, we always had that safety harness on us, but I climbed up the rope ladder to that tiny platform way up high from which the trapeze artists fling themselves into the air. No, I didn't fling myself! Papa tried to climb up the rope to get to the swing to be a catcher, but he couldn't quite make it.

Another day, they took the adult group to the swing, which was maybe ten feet off the ground. With their help and the harness, of course, we caught hold of that swing and "up you go." BUT, then they told us to spread our feet out all the way to catch them on the ropes suspending the swing, riiiiight; now, throw yourself backward. Yeeeah, hanging from that swing by our feet! Uncle Carl was the first to do it, and he muttered, "Whoops, I almost peed in my pants!" You can imagine, other guests started referring to us as "the family." It was great fun!

Oh, one day wasn't. Most afternoons and some nights the circus troupe would put on a regular circus show for us. One afternoon one of the fellows fell from the high-wire, and scraped the skin right down his side. By that time we had gotten to know them and it was just like one of our own being hurt. But he came back and did the stunt at the next show. That's the way to do it, I'm sure. The show must go on!

We have had other reunions since then. Carl was the

driving force to organize them and he would arrange for us to go to Myrtle Beach and stay in a hotel. One time Uncle John Trippeer came; that was great! John was Dad's younger brother. And Aunt Mary Lynn who was Dad's older sister came too. We have the story of her life that she wrote in our family records. Another time, Uncle Dick's son Trip and his wife and sister Beverly came; that was really interesting. They knew very little about us and were shocked to learn there were TEN children. Imagine that! We thought we were famous! We had one reunion at Big Lynn Lodge in Western North Carolina, one in Nashville, Tennessee, another one at Pigeon Forge and one in Roanoke at Lawrence and Marian's church.

Another time, Aunt Dorothy's daughter Cynthia came with her husband, from California I think. John's daughters came several times. For these contacts we can thank Uncle Bill, our genealogist. I do wish you all could know more of these, your cousins though, of course, we never knew ours. At present, you have cousins in California, Texas, Tennessee, Alabama, Georgia, South Carolina, Virginia, New York, not all Trippeers or Bennetts by name of course but some are.

Fourth Term – the War

"Getting to know ourselves and learning to control ourselves are the two great tasks of life. Don't make up strange and exotic penances.

Simply say no to yourself once a day and you will be on the road to sanctity for the rest of your life." In a
High Spiritual Season
– by Sister Joan Chittister

"Do not conform any longer to the pattern of this world, but be transformed by the renewing of your mind. Then you will be able to prove what God's will is—his good, pleasing and perfect will."
– Romans 12:2

Fourth term began in July 1971 when we returned to East Pakistan during a lull in the tensions between East and West Pakistan. East Pakistan had been under martial law since March 25 when the West Pakistani military seized control. The situation eventually led to a full scale war that began on December 3. Living in Dacca on Road 4, the house next to the Guest House, made this an interesting experience as many people came and went, and I was the manager of the Guest House. Becky returned to high school in Bangkok, and Steve was at Mars Hill College back in North Carolina. Debbie was still homeschooling with me. Actually, I also taught Cherie McKinley since they were in the same grade. The McKinleys and Thurmans were living in the Guest House since leaving their homes in Feni and Faridpur in the spring. All the other Baptist missionaries had evacuated out of the country in the spring, but these two families had stayed through it all. Of course, it was fun having all of those children so close.

The first night we experienced real fighting was in late August right after Becky had left. We were next door at the Guest House with the Thurmans and McKinleys to listen to a TV broadcast from Karachi, West Pakistan. The president was making a speech about the military crackdown and martial law in East Pakistan. Just as he was saying that the situation was now under control and the streets of Dacca were quiet, we suddenly heard the very loud sound of gunfire as some freedom fighters charged through a checkpoint that the military had set up just outside our gates. We had a tall wall around our yard, for whatever good that might do, since we were in a rather exposed location. Just before all the gunfire started, one of the mothers went to the door to check on the younger children playing in the yard. She saw the military checkpoint and hurriedly called the children inside. When the gunfire erupted, we all dropped to the floor. The next day, we found some bullet holes in the walls of the house. So, that was an exciting night!

I found an old newspaper clipping that you might be interested in:

"West Pakistan Surrenders to India; New Delhi Orders Cease Fire in West" December 16, 1971, *Winston-Salem Journal and Sentinel*.

Right beside that headline, but in somewhat smaller print:

"Baptist Missionary Family From Winston Live in Dacca"

Does that stir up your curiosity? It does, doesn't it? Well, the background of all of this is that after WWII, the British gave colonial India the independence they had promised if the Indian forces would fight for the Allies in the East. When they were working out the details, the Muslims of India, who were a large minority, asked for a homeland of their own led by their spokesman Muhammed Ali Jinnah. This homeland was created out of the areas where Muslims were the majority and named it Pakistan. However, these areas were split between the East and West sides of India. From this 1947 Partition, there was animosity between Pakistan and India. They fought over the country borders, especially in the Northwest, or Kashmir, a very beautiful and fertile area.

So, Bangladesh used to be East Pakistan, and Pakistan was West Pakistan, one country. However, these two Pakistans had very little in common other than Islam. They were separated by 1,000 miles of India, spoke different languages, ate different foods—rice versus bread. They had different backgrounds as well. The people of the West were large people, generally, and more aggressive; the East were more artistic and sanguine in temperament. For some reason, and I don't know why, people across the Indian subcontinent have historically tended to look down on the Bengalis which is the ethnic group of most of the people of East Pakistan. That continued with West Pakistanis taking the positions of power and control of the country. The government, as you might expect, was centered in the West side.

As tensions grew, the two Pakistanis found more and more reasons not to get along. As East Pakistanis grew and developed their own laws and systems, they began to resent the superiority of the West side. In the 1970 elections, the East Pakistani Awami League Party, led by Sheikh Mujibur Rahman, managed to mobilize enough voters to win the election. This meant they should have been allowed to control the national government. But the West Pakistanis would never allow this, and this led to demands for independence for East Pakistan. In response, the West Pakistani government brought in military forces to arrest, and even to kill, as many political opponents as they could, and to force the people of East Pakistan into submission. Millions of refugees fled into India. India recognized the new country, Bangladesh (Bengali nation), and helped the Bengali freedom fighters (Mukti Bahini) in their guerilla warfare with West Pakistan. On December 3, tensions erupted into a full scale war between Pakistan and India which lasted 13 days. So, the headline said that the West Pakistani forces in East Pakistan had surrendered, and India called a halt to any fighting on the western border with West Pakistan (now Pakistan).

The second headline might be of more personal interest to you. Who was this family from Winston-Salem in Dacca, and why didn't they get out of there when all the fighting started? Of course the family was us, Troy and Marj Bennett and their one remaining child at home, Debbie. And, why did we stay when others left? The US Consulate in Dacca notified us the day after the war began in December that a plane was coming to evacuate Americans and that we should move to the Intercontinental Hotel if we wished to evacuate. Many Americans did that, especially the American government personnel who were still there, and some missionaries from other groups. Who were those that stayed? The McKinleys, the Thurmans, the Bennetts, and Howard Teel was there part of the time, but left to join his family in Bangkok.

Some funny things happened, of course, in the midst of events that were serious and even dangerous. We had many opportunities to thank God for his protection for us and for many of our friends. In the end, we were really glad we stayed, because several Bengalis came and stayed on our property and felt safer there. We had good servant quarters, and there was room for more. But, also, after the war was over, it was so good to be able to say to our Bengali friends and others we met, "Yes, we were here during the war. We stayed." We never really thought about leaving. This was home.

Pastor Heeru & Shunu Sircar, leaders at Immanuel Baptist Church Dhaka, Bangladesh, 1971

The first night of the war, bombing began in the middle of the night, answered by anti-aircraft guns very close by that we hadn't even known were there. It was a very noisy night; wars are really noisy. Early the next morning, Kathy McKinley, in plaintive tones, called out her window to Debbie in the house next door from her, "Debbie, are you alive?" Well, of course she was alive so it struck us as funny. We fixed up a makeshift bomb shelter in the stairwell. We were in a one-story house, but it had steps going up to the roof that allowed for access to the flat roof and the possibility of a second floor at some later date. The stairs made us feel somewhat protected. We had a single bed in there, and the three of us all slept in that one bed. Now that was a sight to see! We had to call signals when one of us wanted to turn over, and of course I was in the middle and very cozy. I don't remember how many nights we slept there, but it wasn't many before we went back to one bedroom together. We had to black out any windows that might show light, put our mattresses on the floor, and move dressers and wardrobes, called elmiras, to block the windows from bullets or shrapnel. I think it was Father Tim who was at our house one night visiting, and ended up spending the night because of the curfew. He just stretched out on a mattress in the living room. Another night, Dick Phillips did the same.

A funny thing happened while we were in the blackout phase. One night, I was sitting in the bathtub in the dark bathroom and looked down at myself as I washed, but there wasn't anything there. Just blackness. My eyes were open but I couldn't see a thing. I had the feeling I was just a head suspended over the tub. Well, I got tickled and called Debbie, who failed to see the humor, and later, Troy wasn't any better, so I just had to laugh and laugh to myself. Just thinking about that small moment still makes me laugh.

We had a piano; I think it was the Moore's since they had gone home. Anyway, I knew just enough about playing the piano to teach the children the beginning steps. Fortunately, I had music books. The three girls, and also Keith and Wade, were my pupils. One day during Kathy's lesson, the airplanes kept coming over, and each time we would go to the stairwell to be safer. Anyway, they did it so often that Kathy said, "Aunt Marj, can't we just duck down behind the piano and keep going?" I thought that sounded reasonable, so that's what we did. It would have made a good picture, with Kathy hunched over the keyboard.

The declared war with India only lasted 13 days, but, of course, hostilities went on much longer, from the time of the military crackdown on March 25 until independence came on December 16. I felt so sorry for the villagers because the Mukti Bahini, the Bengali guerrilla forces, would come through and hide in their houses one night and then move on, and the next night it would be the Pakistani forces. There was lots of destruction of houses, crops, bridges and roads. It was really hard on those people, but evidently they were all in favor of independence from West Pakistan. We agreed with them that they were oppressed and subjugated by the West side, the central government, and so we supported them in their cause. Of course, we couldn't actually do anything to help, but we were sympathetic.

The day Bangladesh won their independence — thanks to help from India — they were ready to celebrate! Many had suffered great loss, but this was a day of rejoicing. You would have laughed if you could have seen the TV coverage that day. We had purchased a TV set during the time of curfews and other restrictions. One of the most interesting aftermaths of the war was shown on the TV. Soldiers came in off the street with their guns still strapped over their shoulders, but they had a poem to read or a song to sing. And girls, who normally kept their hair braided in public, were displayed with their hair flowing freely! All regular programming was kaput! At that point, no one was thinking of the work to be done to get this new nation going peacefully and efficiently. That would come in good time. Then two, maybe three weeks later, Mujibur Rahman, the East Pakistani — who had been elected to be president of Pakistan and was refused by West Pakistani forces—returned to Dacca. What a day that was as millions lined the streets of Dacca to greet him as

Fourth Term – the War

he came from the airport. We were so glad to be there, though not in that crowd.

I was especially happy because I had a real, original Bangladesh flag to wave. During the early demands for independence in the spring, people designed a flag of green with a red circle in the center and a yellow map of Bangladesh over the circle. Later, the map was withdrawn because it was too difficult to do nicely. When West Pakistani troops came in March, they started collecting all of those flags in house-to-house searches. But, when we arrived in late summer, I found a flag down in a drawer somewhere and just put it back for safekeeping. Surely didn't want to give it to you know who. Well, on the Victory Day, here we were hanging over the gate: the McKinley kids, Debbie and I with that flag just waving it to beat the band. They very quickly made lots more of the new design, but I still have the original and that image is on the cover of this book. It looks a bit battered but after all, it's been through a war.

Fourth Term - After the War

Enough of the war. Let's move on. It was good to be able to get back to work normally again, but that was a very quiet and thankful Christmas.

We had some interesting experiences with the defeat of the Pakistani Army and the resulting Indian soldiers sticking around. One, especially, became a friend of some of us and was often in our homes. He was a young fellow and very likable. He liked to visit in our homes and that was okay with us. I expect he got homesick for family and we had that.

We got our Pakistani carpets through one of these connections. We learned of some West Pakistani carpet and souvenir dealers who didn't manage to get out of the city before the Pakistani Army surrendered, and were stuck, as they were afraid to show their faces. We were able to help them sell many of their carpets to raise money, and eventually they were able to find a way to leave by airplane. It was a bit iffy right up to the last minute, but bribes can accomplish good things as well as bad.

There was another group of Naga men who got caught in the city and came to Troy for help. They were from Nagaland where the people had been struggling for independence from India for years. They had attended our Sunday services and thought we were their best hope after the war. They didn't want to slip out through the villages, which they might have done since they didn't look too different from the hill tribe people of Bangladesh. But, they were determined that if they didn't make it, they wanted it to be known. Apparently, they had been trained in Chinese military tactics. This we learned after they left. Later, we read in an Indian newspaper that they had made it out safely. We were so impressed with them. The day of their surrender to the Indian Army, which they had finally decided was the best way, they made a point to dress very nicely. They asked our servant to buy some items in the bazaar so they could dress well, and all that morning they sang hymns. Many Nagas are Christians and these men certainly behaved in a very brave and honest way.

Not too long after the war ended, we made a trip to Faridpur and asked Cherie McKinley to go with us since she and Debbie were good friends. The river was low at this time since it was the dry season, and the ferry was not able to get up to the usual place to unload passengers and vehicles. They had built a temporary ghat (landing dock) out of dirt, but then there had been very hard rain. Vehicles were slipping and sliding on the wet clay ramp and having to be pushed up to the road one-by-one. This was taking a long, long time. Since other passengers were getting off to walk, the girls and I decided to join the crowd and leave Papa to wait in the car. We walked a long way across rice fields on a temporary road. There were big cracks where the ground had been so dry, but now it was a slippery road of clay that sucked at our feet every step of the way. We got dirtier by the minute. Villagers along the way greeted us and laughed at our muddy feet and clothes. But, the funniest part of all was that just as we reached the paved road, up drove Papa and asked if we would like a ride. Of course we wanted a ride and were only too glad to go with him the rest of the way. When we had left him, we thought he might be stranded for hours, but obviously he wasn't.

Though the war was short, we remember all the trouble and violence leading up to it and the months and years afterward when the Bangladeshis were working to recover and to get their government and their society going well. There were houses and bridges to be rebuilt, and just outside Dacca, at Mirpur, was a very large refugee camp. We figured there were 150,000 to 200,000 people living there in very crowded conditions. Some of them lived three and four families in one large room. A couple with their one child lived in a very small closet. I remember once talking with an American friend and saying it seemed to be taking too long to get to some sort of peaceful situation. This friend reminded me that it took several years for the American colonies to finally form a government and get it working peacefully. I knew that was true, so it helped me to put things in perspective.

Bangladesh's problems are so huge, with the limited

land space and a very large population. Sometimes people ask why they don't do something about the population, but I tell them they do. They have been pushing family planning for years now, and many people are limiting the number of children they have. Not like China, limiting each family to one child, but to two or three.

At the time of the war, we started having the International Church, for which Troy was the pastor, meet at our house since the crowd was smaller and our home was closer to most of their homes and not so near the center of the city. This seemed wiser. We later moved out to the Catholic girls' school, to their auditorium, which was more than adequate for our growing congregation, as people returned after the war and new relief agencies came in. We had some wonderful times of fellowship, including a one-Sunday-a-month potluck coffee hour. As one young man said, this fellowship was what really drew him closer to God, since he lived by himself. The congregation was made up of a wide variety of nationalities and denominations. It was a truly international church that we all enjoyed, and where we grew in our faith.

The summer of 1972 was the year that Steve came home for the summer and Becky came from Bangkok so we had all our chicks in one nest again. Nice. We decided this was a good time to take our vacation again in Mussoorie, India. On the way we had to go to New Delhi and we went to see the Taj Mahal, which is beautiful beyond description. The white marble gleaming in the sun, and all of it reflected in the long pool in front.

Fourth Term – After the War

The Taj Mahal. So beautiful!
Agra, India, 1972

Really gorgeous!

In August, Becky and Debbie both went to Bangkok for high school. And Steve returned to Mars Hill College. So we had an empty nest.

The Mennonites came in to help with relief; also the International Red Cross and Oxfam, Mother Teresa's Missionaries of Charity, TEAR Fund, Salvation Army—so many groups came and were a huge help. The Mennonites provided funds and supplies for a medical and daycare center for this large housing project at Mirpur. We, as Southern Baptists, supplied the building and personnel, including me, and a vehicle and driver, and an ayah (nursemaid). The International Red Cross supplied medicines, and TEAR Fund provided a nurse who held clinic for people in the area, as well as tending the children in the center. The Missionaries of Charity

Marj Bennett with children at the Mirpur Center
Dhaka, Bangladesh, 1972-75

sent two sisters who did some nursing. You would have loved helping with that work. I know you would. Some of the children were so sick, malnourished; they had sores and other problems. That was when I learned firsthand that people don't starve because they have no food, but because they have to eat the wrong things. It was a constant challenge, but everyone worked together and we were glad to see some good results. We were not able to save them all, but most of them gained strength and began to smile and play. In the vehicle, we would pick up most of the children in the morning, bathe them and put clean clothes on them, feed them a nourishing breakfast with as much fortified food as we could, give vitamins and needed medicines, let them nap and later, feed them lunch. Late in the afternoon we would take them home and it was pitiful, and yet rewarding, to see how grateful those mothers were to see their little ones getting stronger. Of course, in traveling around the camp, we came across others needing medical help especially, so we often made trips to the new Sher-e-Bangla Hospital which had been opened by other relief groups since the war especially, to help the wounded, but they also treated some of the older children we brought in.

One night, I realized that I had scabies, which I had obviously picked up from all the little children I worked with during the day. We had some medicine, a kind of oil that we were to mix with water and then apply to the effected part. I think it was a half-bottle of this oil and we filled it with water. We had used it before, but this time I felt I needed it all over. I was itching like mad, so I applied it everywhere except my face and private parts. And then it started to burn, and I thought I was on fire. It must have been summer because Debbie was there and she immediately said, "Get into the shower." She turned it on and I washed and washed to get that oil off. Then I crawled between the sheets in my altogether just to get cool under the fan. I realized later that, when I had poured it out the other times to apply it, I got more water than oil, so when I used it this time, what was left was almost all oil. It wasn't diluted as it needed to be. Wheeee! You'll be glad to know that at least I did get rid of the scabies.

Another aftermath, which seems to follow any war, was the number of pregnant girls who had been raped. Holt Adoption Agency came in and tried to expedite the adoption of these babies by foreigners, but the Bangladeshi government resisted their efforts, and so they were only able to take a few. The Salvation Army from the Netherlands came in and set up a home for orphaned children. Different relief agencies from many

Joi, our first foster baby, with Troy
Dhaka, Bangladesh, 1972

countries came; it was quite an education for us to see how many agencies did come and scatter across the country to help them rebuild.

It was in the middle of all this that we were asked to take a very small baby and care for him until other arrangements were made. As it turned out, he had some sort of spinal condition that caused his head to pull back. His mother had died from hepatitis. We hired an ayah named Deedee who was wonderful; she had experience with another child who was physically challenged. This baby, Joi, was not developing normally and finally we put him in the Salvation Army home which was a very good situation for him.

Shortly after he left, a young American man appeared on our doorstep, having been sent by one of the Catholic sisters with whom we were friendly. He was looking for a home for a baby he had come upon when the mother died. The father was very old and not interested in having a baby to care for, so the mother asked this young fellow, a medical student from California who was out there short-term, to take the baby back to the US. However, he realized that he needed to go to California first and talk with his parents, who he thought would help him. He couldn't take the baby out of the country without proper papers either which could take some time.

So, we took in this little guy, two months old and cute as a button, and hired the same ayah to help since I was working every day. One problem arose. Areb, this baby, had a strange head. It was flat as a pancake on the back. Well, I thought I knew what to do about that and sure enough, after a few weeks of turning him this way and then that way, his little head rounded out just like it was supposed to be. But boy, he fought lying on his stomach. He didn't like that one little bit! We kept him for two months, and every day I loved him more. He was very responsive to music, so I would sing and play singing games with him. He began to crawl and then the fun began. Papa and I would put him on the dining room table and he would crawl from one end to the other, just laughing all the way. He was a cute little fellow, and I would have kept him had it been left to me. We never did hear from that young fellow in California, but the Holt Adoption Agency people were glad to take him with their very small group of babies, and Papa helped me to keep my perspective straight and let little Areb go, but it was hard. We went to the airport when they left, and I went on the plane and strapped him into one of the seats.

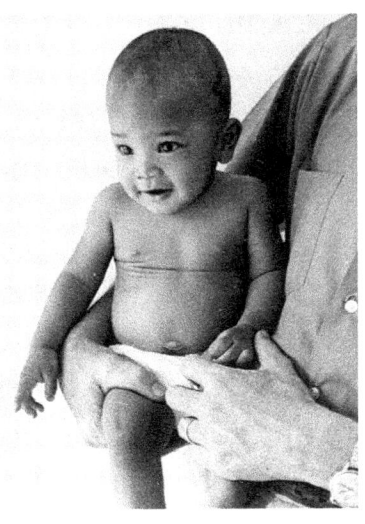

Areb, our second foster baby, was precious and very bright
Dhaka, Bangladesh, 1972

We did see him once more. When we returned to the States we stopped in Cape Cod, Massachusetts and visited him and his adoptive family for a couple of days. It was good and they really loved the little guy, so I know it was best.

Another way I was assured that it was the best decision, was an experience we had just as we were leaving the country. As we were packing up to go, a man came to our door asking for Areb. They wanted to be sure I understood that when Areb was big enough to work, they wanted him back. Well, I had to explain that he was gone to the US and would not be coming back. He was okay about it, but then I knew we had done the right thing.

After Becky graduated in 1973 from International School Bangkok, we then went on to Penang, Malaysia and also north to Chiang Mai, Thailand for some vacation. Later in the summer, Becky returned to attend Meredith College in Raleigh, NC. Debbie returned to Bangkok for her schooling. And I continued my work with the center at Mirpur and helped Troy with the Dacca International Christian Church.

Mama Bennett, who had written to us almost every week for 15 years, had a stroke in January 1972. We missed the contact with the family that we'd had through her. Then in November 1973 she died in Winston-Salem, NC.

Fourth Term
Beirut and Saudi Arabia

"Hospitality is not kindness. It is openness to the unknown, trust of what frightens us, the expenditure of self on the unfamiliar, the merging of unlikes. Hospitality binds the world together."
In a *High Spiritual Season*
– by Sister Joan Chittister

Troy was a good pastor and a fine preacher and the work in Dacca International Christian Church had gone very well. However, one day our boss, Dr. Hughey, asked us to consider a move to another country. The thought had never occurred to us, but there it was. He wanted us to move to Beirut, Lebanon for Troy to work with the international community in Saudi Arabia. Talk about a change! But, the person who had been doing the "circuit riding" in Saudi Arabia was moving on to something else, and they thought Papa was the man for the job. We had been in Bangladesh a long time, and by this time there were several new families, and maybe it was time to let them carry on the work. It was a tough move. You know, I told you this kind of change is hard for me and it was. But, as we talked and prayed, we did finally come to the point of believing it was the right thing to do. No, we didn't hear any voice from Heaven but did have a sense of oughtness which had been a good guide so far. I like to think it is God saying, "This is the way. Walk ye in it. I'll be with you." Debbie was in Bangkok in school, and it would be her junior year the next year. It would be hard to ask her to change. I went to Bangkok to talk with Debbie about it and she, as always, was a real trooper. I think she had a bit of the rambler in her, just as Troy and I did.

So, in 1974, while Becky was home for the summer we moved to Beirut. We thought this was a good opportunity for us to see Kashmir and it was fascinating. We enjoyed our trip up into the hills to stay in a mountain lodge; we rode horseback to get there and that was cool; we also went horseback riding one afternoon and Troy, the most experienced rider of the four, was dumped off his horse for some reason. That was okay; he got back on. Some of those horses could be cantankerous! One fellow kept telling us in a low mutter, "My horse name George." So finally I think Becky was the one to ride George. Another day we went on a hike and split up, Troy with Debbie and Becky with me. We left

After the bus we rode horses up to the lodge in Kashmir, India, 1974

all sorts of signs on the rocks and paths to tell where we had gone and they didn't see a one of them. Can you imagine?

It was so cold, especially at night! One day Becky thought she would just go ahead and wash her hair in the cold water available from the spigots; she almost froze her scalp! We had a Rook competition named for the places we stayed, the Srinagar Games and the Gulmarg Games. At the carpet factory where they made those beautiful handmade carpets, we saw boys starting at quite a young age, learning to tie the wool in individual knots. Then later we saw two young fellows trimming off the excess wool with long shears, just flying over that precious work. You would think they would cut the carpets but they didn't. And the wood-carved furniture; oh it was gorgeous, so tempting, but we did resist and later found we had done the right thing, as the Lebanese customs was very reluctant to let us bring any wooden furniture into the country.

We are really in the mountains, the Himalayas, highest in the world!
Kashmir, India, 1974

Through the years we had heard much about the wonders of Kashmir and we were not disappointed.

Our next stop was Tehran, Iran and the nearby city of Isfahan. What a wonderful place! We stayed in a hotel in Isfahan recommended by friends who had more money than we did. When we heard the price and saw what a posh place it was, we were shocked. In fact, Troy got sick and we teased him it was because of the high prices. The hotel was beautiful, built on the lines of a caravan serai with a huge courtyard and places to eat outside in the courtyard. At one end there was a place for performers, singers, and storytellers to be seen and heard. Again when we went out in town, we saw the workers tying the knots in the carpets, and the lovely carpets for sale. The place I remember most was a small shop to which our guide took us. Outside there were several older men sitting on the curb drinking their tea. We went inside the shop and as we looked around we realized the intricacies of the painting on these very small pitchers, plates, and cups indicated they were very valuable. Then we went to the back room, and the same men we had seen on the sidewalk were back there, their hands rough and calloused, but painting those delicate designs. It was a really humbling experience for me and another reminder that you cannot tell about people by their appearances.

We arrived in Beirut which we had visited once before, but we were in for many new experiences and exposure to remarkable people in this crossroads of the Middle East. Talk about a change from Bangladesh. This was a large, bustling international city. We moved into an apartment that had a view way above the city streets and it was a great place to watch the traffic, which in Beirut is worth watching. They have a saying that driving is like moving with a herd of cattle, just push your way through. But what they do is shout, and I think whoever shouts loudest, gets away with it. Anyway, that was entertaining. And the elevator was one of those old cage types with the stairs winding around it. Actually living in a really big, busy city was interesting and fun.

There was a fellow just down the street who had a vegetable and fruit stand. We always liked to greet him though we couldn't talk at all. We went downtown to the big suq (bazaar) and there were also many big businesses and stores nearby. Right in the middle of this busyness was an excavation, a whole block where we could see the layers they had excavated. I think we saw three layers, you know, buildings built on top of old ones. It was fascinating to us who are history nerds.

It was also great that Steve came and spent some time with us since he had just graduated from college. We got to know Wayne and Frances Fuller and their children, and they did a lot to help us appreciate the good things about Lebanon. Frances heard me say that I was disappointed in the food; I hadn't tasted anything as interesting as Indian curries. Well, she got her cook busy and we were served a fine supper with baba ganoush, tabouli, stuffed squash, hummus, and pita bread. We were hooked. Then Georgina, her helper, invited us to come to her home in the hills for a tabouli party and that was great. They showed us how to eat the tabouli salad by using lettuce as scoops. Also they served coffee, really strong, which I managed to drink. You may know I don't drink coffee, but I did this time.

I also got to keep a canary for a missionary on furlough. I put his cage on the buffet in the dining room where it caught sunlight a good part of the day. And he would sing. My, how he did sing! Prince William was his name.

Troy was going into Saudi Arabia every month. At first he went with Pete Dunn, a missionary in Lebanon who had been covering the work, but then he was on his own. The children got to go with us some; I made five trips with him so I got to know the folks there, which was great. This again, was an international and interdenominational group. He taught and visited in Ta'if, Riyadh and Jiddah for about a week each. Then he'd have one week back home before he was off again. Debbie and I had a lot of time together that year. We learned to crochet once when she stayed home sick. Officially, Troy was a Personnel Consultant, and we figured that was about as good a name as you could give him. Obviously he couldn't be a missionary in Saudi Arabia, though we were sure they knew what he was doing. As long as you do not overtly try to evangelize the Saudis, there was no problem. I think it's a little different now, maybe a lot different.

The missionaries who worked in Lebanon were so kind to us, and we did enjoy learning about their work and visiting the mountains that were just a few hours ride away from the coast where we lived. One beautiful sight was the Cedars of Lebanon and the nearby home of Kahlil Gibran. Really lovely country especially since we saw it covered with snow! Emmet Barnes took us to the beautiful old ruins at Baalbek and gave us a fine history lecture right there as we sat on some of those huge stones. It was incredible that these buildings were made with only the ancient tools of that time. When we went to Tyre and Sidon, and Damascus, Syria it was also interesting and brought many situations in the Bible more alive for me. We saw the deserts of Saudi Arabia with the trail up the mountains to Ta'if, called the escarpment. We enjoyed the beautiful coastline and mountains around Beirut, and the history that meets you everywhere.

Oh, I didn't mention this, our second war. The Palestinians and Israelis got into another war that sometimes found its way up into Lebanon. We could hear the planes overhead, and we heard about activity in Beirut, but we didn't actually see any of it. We heard firing especially at night. We heard those noisy guns again, but not so close this time. God is good and took good care of us and our loved ones. And, of course, we tried not to do anything stupid! This fighting was the beginning of what turned into several years of civil war in Lebanon, but we left that summer of 1975 to go on furlough.

That part of the world is so interesting. I hope they haven't destroyed too much of it with all the fighting, so you will have an opportunity to see it one day. You need to go out into the desert and stay until it is pitch dark—with maybe only a little light from your campfire—and lie back and study the stars. "Oh Lord my God, when I in awesome wonder consider all the worlds thy hands have made...."

"The view has not much of the beautiful in it, but it communicates a strong emotion of the divine."
– Henry David Thoreau

I think of the desert and the mountains of Saudi Arabia.

Fourth Furlough

In 1975, heading back to North Carolina we stopped at a few places on the way, the first being Jordan. We were able to go to Mt. Nebo and look across the Dead Sea and the Jordan River into Israel. We also went to Petra, and that was an amazing experience! We approached it riding on donkeys and going through a slit in the mountainside. The first thing we saw was the Treasury. It was really awesome, so beautifully carved out of the mountainside. The more we saw, the more impressed we were. As we progressed on into the ruins of the old city, we could see many caves in the mountainsides where people had lived. This was a very important trading post at one time I understand.

We didn't try to go to Israel since we were planning to return to Bangladesh, a Muslim country that was not too friendly with Israel. If our passports had evidence of visiting Israel, it might have made it difficult to get visas back into Bangladesh. We saw some great old, old buildings in Amman, Jordan and a wonderful amphitheater.

From there, we went on to England to visit Sue LeQuesne, our good friend from Bangladesh. In London, we went to Hyde Park and there was a man standing on the corner talking to anyone who would listen. Then, we toured the Tower of London, where various persons of royalty had been executed and that made it a really amazing day for us. We also visited the museum in which we saw the armor that King Henry V wore—he was not a big man at all—and the Crown Jewels among many other interesting things. When we went back to our hotel for lunch and to rest, we turned on the TV and what do you think we saw? It was a movie about two fellows who tried to steal the crown jewels. That was neat. We ended up going back to the Tower, as a friend had managed to get us tickets to see the Changing of the Keys. All in all it was a very British history day for us and we found it all fascinating; our knowledge of these things was quite limited.

Driving Sue's car, we next went to Edinburgh, Scotland, and again found ourselves challenged to remember the events celebrated there. We walked the Royal Mile and saw the castle where Queen Mary stayed to be safe. We were intrigued with the area called New Town that dated back to the 1700s. We especially noticed that, since we were going to the US which was celebrating its Bicentennial the following year. To contrast their history with ours puts some things in perspective. Those countries are really old! At the hotel where we stayed, there was a penguin zoo next door. So, we went to see them and they were really cute! At specified times in the day they go on parade; we got to see that too. They march up and down the sidewalks among all of the visitors. We kept our distance from them not knowing how people-friendly they were. But they were cute!

We then drove back to London, stopping briefly to see other British missionaries who had been in Bangladesh. We also stopped to see St. Paul's Cathedral which was awesome. We didn't go inside since they were having a service. We circled the city following a map. That was a challenge because they didn't have a beltline; we had to drive so many blocks on this street, then so many on that. But, we found the airport and flew to Jersey.

We visited Sue LeQuesne & some of her family on Jersey & in England 1975

Sue's home was actually on the island of Jersey. It was fascinating to see the pottery works there and the cows, which of course were Jersey cows, and registered accordingly. She also took us to a restaurant for cream tea which was very good. It was tea with milk of course and scones with strawberries and cream. Delicious! Her mother was shocked that I didn't drink coffee. She thought I was missing some very important nutrient. All I could think of was the little bit of milk I might use, but I didn't say so. We also saw the wall that lined her drive, about four feet high of stone. Sue told us that at one time her mother "had charged the granite wall." This was it. Why did she do it? Not on purpose of course. She was getting old and couldn't see so well.

We then stopped in Massachusetts to see Areb, our foster baby, and to meet his adoptive family. We had such a good time and were pleased to see how he had grown and developed. Of course, he didn't remember us, but we knew him. They were very happy with that adoption experience and were planning to adopt another child from India, so that was good. We went to check their lobster traps with them, and then ate the catch for supper. Very good!

We returned to the same house at First Baptist in Kings Mountain, NC that we had enjoyed the furlough before since we had friends there and knew our way around. Becky was at Meredith, Steve had gone to Korea with the Peace Corps, and Debbie would be at home with us for her senior year of high school. In the spring, Troy enrolled for a course at Southeastern Seminary in Wake Forest, NC. This was also the time that Becky decided to drop out of Meredith for a semester and stay at home to be with her family. She worked in a nursing home and that was good experience and a very challenging one. We loved the people of First Baptist Church in Kings Mountain and they were more than good to us.

It was not easy for Debbie; this was the third school during her four years of high school but she did well. She planned to go on to Wake Forest University in the fall. We would have an "empty nest." She was funny one day when she said the SAT test asked for two or three college preferences, but there was only one that she wanted, and that was Wake Forest. She did get in with a good scholarship and loved it then, and still loves it!

What else did we do that year? It was always good to see our family and friends when we were able. When Debbie graduated from high school, we took her and a friend and Becky to Washington, D.C. to see the capital of our country. And, we were properly impressed. It is truly a beautiful city, the various monuments, parks and museums. We stayed with Ray and Judy Penry who were living in Rockville, MD. That was fun!

Fifth Term – Magura

"Real religion is more than an emergency measure. It is continual. It sets the pattern of man's daily thought and practice. Like regular meals, it silently stocks the storehouse of his spirit with power. It works by the law of accumulated reserves. Tracks are laid, patterns formed, habits established. Like the continual presence of the masterworks of art, it cures the heart of second-rate satisfaction.... Above all, this continual religion gives a man a working knowledge of the ways of God. We know the ways of the world all too well. The ways of God are not so easy."
– From The Interpreter's Bible, vol. 9

At the end of the summer of 1976 we returned to Bangladesh, to live in the small town of Magura. It would be a challenge. As we traveled back, we stopped in Korea to see Steve and meet his friends and see some of his working situation. We slept on the floor in a Korean inn; that was an adventure! When we went for our breakfast with Steve, we first got some sort of orange drink, then went to another shop for some bread, and finally, went to a place upstairs to get coffee or tea. What was it about that tea? It wasn't really tea. I think that it was some sort of hot barley water. It was hot and wet. It was okay. But what do you think? In Korea, no tea?

It was good to meet other Peace Corps volunteers and also see some of our fellow Southern Baptist missionaries. Troy and I were glad to definitely have a better picture of Korea with awareness of how to pray for them. We traveled some and saw the countryside. The rice fields are so lovely!

We enjoyed most of the food. There was one day when Steve ordered for us and Troy asked him what was in it. Steve said not to ask, just eat it. That was pretty hard for him to do, but he tried. Fortunately we were moving on to Bangladesh and food we knew something about.

Our time in Magura was quite different from any other time up to that point. This was partially due to the fact that we didn't have any children at home, not even coming home from school for holidays. They each only had one trip to the field during their four years of college.

I have to confess this was extremely difficult for me, and I went through a period of depression while in Magura. It's a bit hard to explain now, but I can simply say that if I had not had a regular practice of daily devotional time with God, and if Troy had not been so wonderfully patient with me, I might have ended up having to leave the mission work. But I did, and he was, and then one thing more; we went to a retreat for missionaries from all mission groups in the country. There was one young woman there who was suffering from clinical depression. I believe mine was situational depression. Anyway, Troy and her husband got the two of us together to see if I could help her. I wasn't sure I could help anyone, but we did talk. What became of her, I don't know, but I do know that I came away thinking, "Marj, if you don't get a hold of yourself, you could end up like that young lady." She was in bad shape, and I'm sure left the field. I spent some intense time with the Heavenly Father and He healed me. It was a time of letting go—of the children in this case—and I had to deal with it. I wanted to stay on the field. I just missed them. But Jesus promised that if we left family behind, he would give us plenty more to love and care for. He did, and still is.

Our new friends and neighbors only knew us as Bennett Sahib and Bennett Memsahib. Lots of time they just called me Mashi, which means auntie, and that was fine, too. The house in Magura was very adequate for our needs, especially after Tom Thurman had made some alterations. I'm not sure what was there originally, except one door leading from room to room which Tom, with his unique humor said, "Wasn't wide enough for Marj or tall enough for Troy." Actually, what he could have said was that it wasn't tall enough for Marj nor wide enough for Troy. It was very small, but he fixed that and also put in a bathroom with a tub and shower, sink, and commode. The bathroom became one of the favorite tourist spots for women, both of the town and surrounding villages, when they came to market. I had to work on how to explain the use of things, but finally my language was adequate. They were amazed! Remember, these people had only used an outdoor squat toilet. The kitchen was transformed as well. When we arrived, it had only a sink in one corner, but we brought a kerosene stove and Troy arranged for the mistris (workmen) to build some tables and a cabinet that I used for things that needed to be locked up. Troy was really good about getting things so I could function. It had nothing to do with his appetite, I'm sure!

Otherwise, we had our bedroom, a small guest room, a living room/dining room, a study and a front veranda. Nothing fancy, but adequate and much better than the folks around us, at least from our perspective. They probably wondered about some of it. I know they never could understand why I had to stand up to do all of my kitchen work. They would just hunker down on the ground, but that didn't come to me quite so naturally as it did for them. We had a nice garden in the back, and added one other thing we had never done before—rabbits, right outside our bedroom window: one male and two females. The idea was to raise them for food. They grew well and produced young, but we finally realized the Muslims would not eat them because they didn't have the right kind of feet (Deut. 13:7). I must confess, I couldn't either, after watching them outside the window like that. We had also had rabbits earlier in Faridpur, but they were pets.

Magura was a small country town, and most of the people were very simple. We had a reading room there that was a draw, for young men especially, to come in and read the books, magazines, and newspapers. We had done this in several towns to a measured success. But, we also had church at the reading room. There were two Christian families, and they were delighted to have us living right in town. They had several children who came for Sunday school class on Sunday afternoon. We did it the Bengali way, of course, sitting on the floor. It was wonderful to go back there in 1990 and see those children grown up and active in the church, which had grown quite a bit. They also had a small, very simple church building by that time.

One lady came from a village about 15 miles from town. About once a week she would walk in to the river and then on into town. She was a convert from Hinduism and really wanted to learn and grow. At that time, she was the only Christian in her village. Her name was Mrs. Chakraborty, and she had several years earlier gone all the way to Faridpur to ask for baptism. Before we left Magura, we went to Mrs. Chakraborty's village with the worker in the reading room. We drove to the river, maybe a mile or two from town, and waited for a boat, which took us across the very small river. Then we started to walk, and we walked and we walked. We kept asking her if we could see her village yet. "Okhane," she would say with a lift of her head. That means over there. "Oi due narikel gach dekhano? Oikhane." She was pointing out two coconut palms, but we were seeing a whole line of them across the horizon so that wasn't much help. Needless to say, we were not up to Mrs. Chakraborty's endurance and by the time we reached her village we were all three pooped. Then, they gave us green coconut milk to drink which helped and we met the people who evidently had heard about us. She served a nice rice and curry meal. We rested under the shade of a tree, and then it was time to start back—on our own this time, of course. Well, we walked and we walked and finally we hailed a tanga or stagecoach. In the country, these were sometimes used for transportation, and this was the first time we had seen anything on wheels since we left our car. There were no seats, just a flat wooden floor, but it felt good to us! There were no cycle rickshaws on this side of the river evidently.

I can still remember my shower that evening. I could literally feel the water soaking through the pores of my skin. Don't think I had ever felt that particular sensation before or since. But, I remember something else much more important. Mrs. Chakraborty made that trip time after time just to sit and talk with us, actually me, or sing hymns. She loved to sing hymns, not quite on pitch, but who cares?

One day she told me how she healed a neighbor's arm which she had been told was broken. She just prayed for healing, and then she blew on it gently, all up and

Mrs. Chakraborty was a good Christian friend
Magura, Bangladesh, 1977

down her arm. Well, when she told me and showed me on my arm, I thought of breath being the same word in Greek as Spirit. I could believe God was using that good woman's faith and goodness to heal. Of course he was! Who could doubt it?

In our living room we had three cane chairs, a borrowed piano and our table for eating. But, many of the women who came really preferred to sit on the floor, and that was fine with me. This was what they were used to. In their homes, their main room was the bedroom, and we sat on the bed or floor.

Bengalis love to sing and dance and recite poetry. Often, when I went out visiting in the afternoon, several of the girls from the neighborhood went with me. They took me where they wanted me to go, where they had promised to bring me. Then they would sing and dance and invariably would ask me to sing, but not to dance. Women don't seem to dance as much as girls and young women. Anyway, I couldn't really say that I couldn't sing, but I was always at a loss as to what to sing. I sometimes sang one or two Christian songs that I like, but they would always ask for a fun song. So one day I made the mistake of singing "Old MacDonald Had a Farm." In Bengali, the animals do not make the same sounds as they do in English. So when I sang that song, with a "moo moo here" and a "moo moo there," and a "quack quack here," and a "quack quack there," they just burst out laughing, and I'm afraid asked for it over and over. I wasn't much of a witness, I'm afraid, but it was fun and they loved it. They also liked "How Great Thou Art." Most of them are a very religious people and respect any sign of our religion.

On Sunday afternoons, Troy and I would often sing through the hymn book. Some of the neighbor girls came over and were listening when one of them, Huree, began to dance. I saw that she was definitely following our rhythm and expression. That was really quite moving for us. Other times, the girls played in our front yard; actually, most afternoons they did. It was good since boys can play anywhere, on the streets and roads, but not girls. So I was glad to provide a place for them, and, of course, when I could, I went out and played with them.

I don't think they ever came over when I was playing the piano. That is interesting, and I don't know why. Maybe they understood, or their mothers did, that was a time when I wanted to be alone. That piano was such a blessing for me during that time. I missed our children so much, but still wanted to be right where we were. I would play and sing for my pleasure only; I don't play well at all but I love to try. God seemed very real to me. This really helped to sustain my faith; the words of the songs and the tunes fortified and inspired me. Missionaries need this kind of help from God as much as anyone.

The Muslims go by the lunar calendar following the phases of the moon, and every year they have one month called Ramadan when they fast from sunup until sundown. They have strict rules about how this fast is to be observed. Generally it didn't affect us, except when we were traveling. This was revealed most graphically one year when we went to a ghat (dock) to get a ferry. We had planned to eat our lunch while we waited for the ferry. However, on our arrival we noticed that all of the tea dokans (tea shops) had closed up, and no one was drinking tea. "No food or drink. Don't even swallow your own saliva." I don't remember if someone spoke to us about it, or if we just figured it out for ourselves. It was probably the latter for by this time we had been around a long time. So we just waited until we could eat without anyone seeing us. We shouldn't and didn't want to be a temptation to anyone fasting.

Another day at the ghat, following heavy rains, the Bangladeshi marketplace beside the big river was muddy and slippery. Trucks were unloading all sorts of goods for the small, crudely-built shops lined up there – cigarettes, tinned milk, biscuits (cookies and dry toast), tea, candies, soap, combs, enamel mugs and plates, anything that might be needed by travelers who had been on the road for two or three days. Other trucks were loading fresh fish, packed in boxes and covered with ice, to take to the city markets where the price would be much better.

Suddenly between the trucks and laborers carrying the heavy boxes of fish, darted two children. The older, a girl of about 7 or 8 years was wrapped in a piece of old sari cloth that barely covered her thin body. Helping her was a smaller boy, maybe 5 years old, who wore only shorts that were colorless and gray from too many washings without soap.

Between them they carried a fish, holding it above their heads. Not just a small fish, but a meal for the whole family! A large fish! Maybe six-seven pounds. The fish gleamed silvery white and sparkled as they dashed through the crowd and ducked between the shops. Their brown bodies gleamed with water and perspiration. Their faces glowed – truly glowed with joy and triumph and pride.

No one tried to stop them, to take the fish away, as if they had stolen it. No, they were allowed to dance happily through the market with their prize. In fact, many bystanders laughed with compassionate understanding, knowing their poverty. How did they get it? Had they caught it? Not likely. Did some kind-hearted person give it to them? Did they find it where it fell out of one of the packing boxes? I'll never know, but for that brief moment those two children knew unadulterated rapture!

I hope that memory has stayed with them through the many hardships they have surely faced – flood, famine, war – as it has stayed with me.

I haven't told you about when Debbie came to spend a summer with us in Magura. This was her one trip to the field during her years of college. It so happened that we also had a summer missionary with us, Steve Hooper. That was an interesting time, for of course Debbie wanted to see her old friends, especially in Faridpur. The ones who were still there were delighted to see her. Some had already married and moved away. She also made new friends among some of the older girls in Magura, and they took her out with them on their afternoon visits with school friends. One fun thing they did was to paint her hands with henna. This is something they do for brides especially, painting very elaborate and detailed pictures of plants and designs. Of course it doesn't wash off for a long time, so Debbie had that to take back to Wake Forest University with her.

Then, one day in November 1977 we got a telegram from Debbie in the States, "Becky fell up steps. Broke nose, cut forehead. Will wire if complications develop." Well, this was a wake-up call! First, because our children never sent us telegrams; we just assumed they were all right. Second, "if complications develop," didn't sound too good to Papa and me. We didn't have a good way to call, and we were due a trip out of the country for vacation but had not been able to go because we had no visas. This came at a time when all missionaries in Bangladesh were waiting and waiting for visas to leave the country for any reason at all. None had been issued for quite some time.

Well, Troy said he would try and get our visas, and so he did. It's interesting how it all turned out. The man in the office recognized him as the father of the three young people who had gone to Bangkok for high school. "And now your daughter, the tall red-haired one, she is in America alone and has been injured? Well, of course, you need to go to her. Family need to be with a loved one when they are ill or injured. Let me see your papers." Troy handed them over, and he took the one that said we had been in the country since 1957 and tore it up. Then he just used the visa that showed we had come in two years earlier from furlough; they could give visas to any who had been in the country less than three years. Why? Who knows? All we know is, we got our visas for me to leave in one week and Troy in two after he got his work caught up. None of the other missionaries could understand; well, neither could we. We were very grateful for the Bengali custom of most of the family coming to the hospital and taking care of the patient.

When I got to Raleigh and saw Becky at the airport, she was up and walking around. Although she had the scars on her face, I can't tell you how good she looked to me. It had been over a year since we had seen her, and of course, there were not that many letters, so I was relieved, pleased, delighted and tired. I had taken the 22-hour flight from Delhi to New York with no getting off the plane, and I was ready to be on land. Then Debbie came from Wake Forest, and I was content. I had the girls with me, and Troy was on his way; Steve was still in Korea at this time.

Becky was injured, not only physically but in her soul somewhere. When she looked in the mirror she didn't see the old Becky there, and that was hard to get used to. And just the trauma of a fall can make for a sense of instability and vulnerability that's hard to express. I've learned that from experience in recent years. I think she was experiencing much of that and probably much more that I had no way of knowing. I could see that it was really traumatic, not only for her but also for Debbie who had felt all of the family responsibility, though Catherine Brooks was wonderfully helpful. Troy came a week later, and then we could get ready for Christmas. Becky told me with wonder in her voice, "I never thought you would come." And I answered, "We always said, 'If you need us, you tell us and we'll come.' Of course we'll come." She hadn't really believed that before; somehow she had the idea that the work was too important to leave, no matter what we had said.

Some may think that missionaries and ministers have to put their work first and family second. Troy and I did not see it that way. I suppose I could say it was similar to our marital relationship. Troy did not want a wife to be subject to him; he wanted a partner, and that is what I tried to be. We wanted to be a team working together, using our individual gifts and training for the glory of God. In the same way, we saw our children as gifts from God for us to nurture, enjoy, teach, expose to the world and its riches, share the burdens of the needy, sing with, dance with, suffer with, feel lonely with, grow with and learn with. The list goes on and on, but it never puts them in second place. We are all in this together. I don't know what the Judgment Seat of God might look like, or if there is such a thing, but if there is or whatever there is, I hope one day we'll all stand together and thank him for our family ties. We the parents felt the call to missionary service, and these children were blessings from God given to us to care for as long as they needed us. No one else had that privilege or responsibility. Family was just as important as the ministry we were assigned to, and cannot be put in second place.

Back to our trip to see about Becky; I don't remember quite how I did it, but during that first week, I called Dr. Hughey, our boss at the Mission Board, and told him we were in the States without his permission and were planning to stay until after Christmas. He graciously approved.

Becky was living in the Baptist Student Union building across from NC State campus, serving as a resident caretaker. So, we stayed there with her and also saw some of our extended family. I can't remember any details of that visit, just how good it was to see those two girls. Without question, the hardest part of living overseas for me was being away from the children; I learned to live with it, but never really got used to it.

Fifth Term - Zambia

After two years in Magura, Troy and I felt led to work specifically in church leadership training. We asked to work with the seminary outside Dacca sponsored by several missions. However, our Southern Baptist mission in Bangladesh was focusing on village evangelism. So our area director asked us to consider leaving Magura and going to Zambia, central Africa, to help in that seminary. The missionaries who had been working there needed a furlough, and there was no one else to take over. He thought we could do it and that we needed a change. Troy had done this type of work before and I was ready and eager to teach when I could. However, it meant leaving Bangladesh again, probably for good this time. It was very hard to leave our new friends and fellow Christians in the Magura area. It was especially hard to leave our Bengali friends, our colleagues from many different countries and the place that had been our home since 1957. We did come to feel that we were doing the right thing, and that always makes a big difference, at least it did for us.

En route to Zambia, we visited Bangalore, India

to see our Baptist work there, especially the Baptist hospital. It was good to see Truman and Gwen Smith who were there training pastors to do counseling and hospital visitation, Rebecca Naylor who was the chief surgeon and a very remarkable lady, and Van and Sarah Williams. Van was a pediatrician, and he had started a really neat program. When mothers brought their babies in or when they came for delivery, he introduced them to a program of nutrition and hygiene right there at the hospital. They lived there in little huts similar to their homes for several weeks and were taught the essentials of nurturing small children and their families as well. Who can count the long-term benefits of that work?

Next, we visited Ron and Montiel Peck who were in south India at the time. Their daughters were in school at Kodi Kanal, and Ron and Montiel were living in a house nearby for their vacation. It was good to see Kodi, a cooler resort in south India, which we had heard so much about, and of course, to see the Pecks, our very good friends from Dacca.

Then we went on to Nairobi where we were to await our visas for Zambia. One serendipity was that we found old friends who were missionaries in Kenya, some

We visited our good friends,
Ron & Montiel Peck
Kodi Kanal, India, 1978

Fifth Term – Zambia

who lived in Nairobi. Ralph and Rosalind Harrell, Dale and Beulah Hooper, Zeb and Evelyn Moss were all old college friends, so we had a grand old time with old friends. Not to mention all the new friends we met there. It was great! It was a good introduction to Nairobi, which was to prove very helpful in years to come as Nairobi was the place to go for many of the provisions we wanted. The one thing I remember best is that one night the Mosses took us to a very nice Indian restaurant. It had a large window across the back of the room so that we could see right into the kitchen. We enjoyed watching the chefs making the breads, especially the naan, which are large pieces of bread, 18 inches across. They would roll them out and smooth them with their hands, pick them up and toss them into the air. I suppose they tossed them at least 2-3 feet into the air, each time the circle was a little bit bigger until they were about 18 inches across and very thin. Quite a show! They baked them in a round clay oven. They would smack them up against the inside to bake. Then we got to eat them. Deeee-licious!

After that, Zeb and Evelyn took us to an art gallery in town. The pieces were gorgeous, all of animals, like three or four giraffes in a circular interlocked position, made from the trunk of one tree. There was one of impalas with one of them leaping through the air, but actually it was attached to at least one other impala. They were all so beautiful, and of course very, very expensive. But, they didn't show them to us so we might buy them. They wanted us to see what the best artists could do. Then, when we went out looking for souvenirs we would know what to look for. Nothing so splendid as those, but it did sharpen our sense of what was good and what was bad art. Thanks to the Mosses!

One other thing the Mosses told us was that we were going to the land of heavenly singers. They were convinced that heaven's choirs would be made up mostly of Zambian singers. That was certainly something to look forward to and now we know what they meant! Zambians harmonize naturally and sing with great exuberance. There, but also in Tanzania we were to learn later, the young people come to church on Saturday afternoon and practice for hours to be ready to lead the worship the next day. Some come from quite a long way, but this is a real pleasure for them. And can they harmonize! The rich resonance of their voices, women as well as men made me feel that they were singing for the love of singing and of God. I tried to discern the difference in their singing and that of African Americans, and I decided it was the spirit with which they sang. There was nothing aggressive about their singing, just joy and harmony. I often think they must have learned that bouncing along on their mothers' backs as little ones.

We were going to teach in the seminary in Lusaka, Zambia. When I say seminary, you need to realize that most of the students were way ahead if they had any high school education. But, we were used to that. The seminary grounds themselves were very nice. We pulled into the front gate, and there before us lay the campus: four missionary houses on the left, the school itself, a quadrangle of buildings, in the center with an orchard of orange trees behind, and on the right, ten student houses, small but adequate. There were also some servant quarters farther back.

At first we lived in one missionary house and later when the Tom Smalls left for furlough, they asked us to live in their house, and they just left their furniture for us to use. That was nice since we didn't have any. So, we did that for five-six months until three new families came; then we moved into one of the student houses. That was interesting in many ways. The student houses were square with four rooms and a shower in the middle. The toilet and sink were in a room on the back porch, as well as a small storeroom. We managed fine; only time there was a problem was if one of us was in the shower, and someone was visiting in the living room. Yes, if we stepped out of the shower to go into the bedroom we were in plain view of anyone in the living room! It only happened once or twice, and we figured out how to handle it. We also decided to use a chamber pot at night rather than go outside on the porch because there were some wild critters around. We got a fire-engine-red chamber pot and had lots of fun with that! When other missionaries would come for supper or to visit they would say, "Oh honey, look, it's like that little apartment we had when we first went to seminary." It was fine for us. I could get the house-cleaning done in no time flat and then go on to more interesting activities.

And there were more interesting activities. I taught the women the Old Testament and English as a Second Language and whatever else came up. We had a wedding while we were there. Two of the students decided to marry, and we had the wedding right there at the seminary. It was fun and interesting. One thing you will notice in the pictures is that the African women stretch their legs straight out when they sit on the ground. The entire crowd was sitting and standing around the quadrangle of classrooms. Then, we took our gifts up to the bride and groom sitting at a table. One interesting thing: The bride needed a dress and I happened to have a very nice white one with some nice embroidery that would fit her. She seemed delighted. I think the brides in Africa usually wear white, though I can't say for sure.

One day in class we heard a loud boom. I said it sounded like a bomb, but one of the students assured me that it was a mine blast. She was from the northern part of the country where the copper mines are. Turns out it WAS a bomb and that was the beginning of our third war. This was the fighting between the Zimbabwean rebel forces training in Zambia and the government trying to keep control. That went on for quite a while, but didn't affect us that much. Our first two wars were in Bangladesh and in Beirut. They were very noisy, and of course, can be dangerous.

The students were also responsible for keeping up the grounds including the orchard, so one Saturday, Papa went out with them and they picked enough oranges for each family member to have one a day. The next week one of the mothers complained that her children had diarrhea. On questioning them we learned that they had eaten all of those delicious oranges in one

Fifth Term – Zambia

day! The oranges had never been divided up with the students in this way before. They didn't know how to handle this wealth of oranges.

One morning early, one of the men staff members knocked on our door and said his wife was having a baby. She needed to go to the hospital. Zambia has a very good medical service. Papa went for a vehicle, and I hustled back to see if I could help. I had for some unknown reason grabbed two towels. When I got there, I found her standing over the baby, who was lying in the middle of a puddle of water on the cold concrete floor. We quickly wrapped the baby in one towel and the placenta in the other as we heard Papa pull up with the car. Later that afternoon, she returned with the baby, all doing well. They are tough, those ladies.

I went to a Zambian women's meeting that year, and they asked me to speak. I didn't know their language; in fact, they used different languages, six were recognized as official, though English was the main one. So, I had to work through an interpreter. I really loved doing this sort of thing, going to women's meetings and seeing them so capable and taking leadership and having such a good time away from home

They tell me it's easy to carry the baby on their backs!
A student in Lusaka, Zambia, 1978

responsibilities. Early Saturday morning I was awake and thinking about what I would say later. When I went into the bathroom which I expected to be empty since it was quite early, there was a crowd of ladies laughing and teasing one another, standing in the open showers with their black skin glistening wet in the reflected light of the kerosene lanterns. It has to be one of the most beautiful sights I have ever seen. I can't explain it, but it was just so carefree and joyful and friendly. If I were an artist, I would draw a picture of it just for myself. They, of course, would be horrified for me to show such a picture to anyone else! Later that day when I was speaking, I referred to us taking God too lightly, "playing with God." I was trying to keep the thought simple. Afterward, I learned that the interpreter was at first shocked and then just didn't say what I had said; she modified it to make it proper. Seems that to say "playing with" means something very different from what I intended!

The other special memory I have of Zambia is when we went to a convention in the bush. The people had built a large corral-like enclosure with thatch walls. Around the side there was some little shelter and that is where the men sat. The ladies sat out in the middle in the full sun. We didn't have sunscreen yet. There was a lot of singing and preaching and at rest times and at night lots of visiting around the campfires. The women would occasionally form a circle and sing one of their songs with appropriate motions: "No more whiskey, no more cigarettes, no more hanging round bad places, no sir, Lord. We are God's children now.

Hallelujah." Of course, I joined in. It was a great time of fellowship and inspiration for folks who often didn't see each other from one meeting to the next unless there was a funeral or maybe a wedding.

When someone died, as one of our little newborns at the seminary did, the friends and church choirs came from all around to sing and mourn through the night. The announcement was made on the radio several times a day. They knew to listen to these broadcasts as it was the only way to get such news. So, in happy times and in sad times, times of trial and times of pleasure, God's people stick together, and it is at these times that you know that we are all one in God's family.

There's so much more to tell! I went to market with Mary Small and thinking to save bags, I told the shopkeeper that I would just put the cabbage in my basket. As we walked away, Mary said, "I hope you don't get stopped by the guards at the gate." Puzzled, I thought, "That would never occur to me in Bangladesh. They trusted foreigners there, but evidently the history is so different here that they have learned not to trust foreigners." I was still learning new stuff.

The butcher shop was interesting because they had different names for the cuts of meat. The one I liked best was "silverside" steak. Isn't that an interesting name? I suppose they got it from the British. The British ruled there for many years, and many of them have opted to stay on even with the government being all African now. I don't blame them. The weather is ideal, never too cold or too hot. We had strawberries

Victoria Falls is on the border between Zambia & Zimbabwe, 1979

all year, an everbearing kind. Very nice! Lots of advantages as long as there wasn't a war.

We went on a youth retreat at the Hubbards who lived in the country. Actually, they lived on the demonstration farm that Tom and Lucille Waddill ran, so we got to see both at the same time. One cool thing they were doing there was to bring pastors to the farm once a month for training—four Bible studies with sermons. They would learn these lessons over a two-three day period and then go back to their towns and villages, teach and preach them, and come back the next month for more. Great idea!

Oh yes, then there was our trip to see Victoria Falls. Awesome! I think it's prettier than Niagara Falls. And we were able to walk right down in front of the falls to make pictures and get soaked. Above the falls there is a wide expanse of river backed up that is very beautiful with hippos swimming here and there. Down below, way down below, the river flows on southeast.

One house we lived in had a civet cat in the attic. What's that? A large wild cat, maybe half the size of a lion. Papa and a friend decided to drive it out, which was easier said than done. They went up into the attic, which was pretty hot, and evidently smelled awful because the civet had been relieving itself on the hot water heater for quite some time. What a mess! When they tried to chase it out the hole at the end of the house where it had been entering and leaving, it decided not to go that way and came back toward them. Boy, did they scramble! A couple of us watched and laughed downstairs. We did catch the smell though. Ugh! The civet finally decided the attic wasn't such a good place for it anymore and went for a walk and was caught by some of the students and eaten for dinner. Yep, dinner. I don't know how it tasted.

I was interested one morning to see that the student wives had come over and were picking up termites under the outside lights in our yard. It had rained the night before, and there was a good crop. They also took leaves off the hibiscus plants to cook. Nothing there was wasted.

Then, another house we lived in had mice in the attic. A lot of mice! There were holes in the ceiling, especially in the dining room, and we could see them looking down at us. We saw their little beady eyes. But the interesting thing was that beside our carport, which was just outside the dining room, was a wonderful bougainvillea that had grown up on a big trellis. It had obviously been there a long time. Well, we started to notice movement in the bougainvillea that wasn't birds. We saw that there were mice trails all through it leading up to—you guessed it—the attic. So, much as we hated to do it, we cut down the bougainvillea. It would come back, but hopefully the little varmints wouldn't!

I got to drive some in Lusaka. That was liberating, since I did almost none of that in Bangladesh. Also, Mary Small had planted many of the most beautiful tea roses. The weather was ideal for them, and I really enjoyed them.

Something we really enjoyed a lot was the youth group. The Smalls had started hosting them in their home on Friday nights for supper, Bible study, and lots of fun. We took this over when they went on furlough. We had a lot of open space where they could play soccer.

We also had snakes, and it seemed almost every Friday night someone spotted a snake and Papa had to go for it. You ask why? Because these were black and green mambas, not little garden snakes. In Zambia, we took snakes seriously. One Sunday night a family came to the service telling us about their son's encounter with a puff adder. I think the most challenging snake event was when one got wrapped around the men's urinal in the classroom building. But Papa got it. He actually shot it through the window with a rifle. We also took the seminary students to a snake farm one Saturday. Creepy, but interesting.

One more great experience: Lusaka Baptist Church. The singing was heavenly, the Bible studies challenging, and the preaching always inspirational. It was an international church, and we had come to really appreciate that sort of fellowship. People were from many different language groups, ethnic groups, denominations, and countries. It seemed to us a foretaste of heaven.

That spring we were to go on furlough, so we were glad to see three new couples come to Zambia, one to be the principal of the seminary.

Fifth Furlough

After Zambia, we came to Buies Creek, NC for furlough. We stayed in the missionary house provided by Snyder Memorial Baptist Church in Fayetteville, NC which was very nice. Papa was asked to teach in the Religion Department at Campbell University. Our contacts with the students, especially for me, were very rewarding, and we found some old friends and made many new ones. There were four Iranian girls studying at Campbell trying to improve their English in order to go on to another college. I got acquainted with them and we had lots of good times, they visiting in our home and me trying to help them with their English. They spent Christmas with us and that was a special privilege for us!

This was especially true because this was the time of the hostage crisis when many American government personnel were being held as hostages in Teheran. Obviously tensions were high and the efforts at settling the crisis were not progressing very well. Finally an agreement was reached and the hostages released but since that time, relations with Iran have never been as peaceful as they were before.

Now when I hear about Iranian women or see them on TV, I often think of those girls and wonder where their lives have taken them. I pray for their safety and happiness. It was Debbie's senior year at Wake Forest and she graduated that spring; Steve and Becky were working in Raleigh.

In the spring of that year, Jerry Wallace approached Troy about us leaving the mission field and pastoring a church in the States, specifically the one where he had been interim pastor, Spilman Memorial Baptist Church in Kinston, NC. We, of course, knew nothing about the church or the area, but feeling that we should always be open to God's changing ways, we prayed about it. I could see that Papa was really interested. It is true that returning to Africa would require further language study. We had worked primarily in English at the seminary.

It was a challenging time to make a decision. Always before we had felt the same about the decisions we had made for change and moving. But this time I was torn, and it was a struggle. However, as I prayed, it seemed to me that lacking a clear sign in the sky, I needed to think about what Papa wanted as well as what I wanted. I couldn't ask him to return to the field just because I wanted it. That wasn't good and the question was, could I stay in the US because he wanted to? The more I prayed about it and waited quietly before God, the more peaceful I felt about it. And I took that as my answer. Colossians 3:15 in one translation says that

Fifth Furlough

God's Spirit acts as an umpire in our hearts to bring order out of chaos, peace out of confusion. And I felt God's Spirit was doing that in my heart, showing me the way I needed to go. I didn't tell Papa about this at the time; I just told him when I felt it was right for us to take the church in Kinston. It was several months later in a discussion with friends who asked about our decision to stay in the US that I revealed my struggle. Papa was shocked, as we did usually talk about these things and agree together about what to do, but this time was just different.

Were You Ever Afraid?

When I am asked about times I may have been afraid, there are really very few. First, I'll tell you about one right here in North Carolina.

Steve had finished his first year at Mars Hill in 1971 and we were all going to spend the weekend with the Andrews family in Wilmington. Troy and I were to pick up Bill Andrews, their son, at Campbell University in Buies Creek on the way. So, we decided to let Steve drive his car with the two girls, and we would go in our car. We would meet up in Clinton and caravan from there. We drove by Buies Creek, picked up Bill from his basketball camp and went on to Clinton. We found a place to park on the side of the road by the highway at the intersection Troy had specified, and we waited. And waited, and waited. It was at night; I don't remember if we ate supper before leaving Kings Mountain where we lived then or what, but it was dark. I don't know how long we waited, but it was a long time, an hour, two hours maybe. To say we were worried would be putting it mildly. In fact, I finally said to Troy, "If something terrible has happened and we've lost all of them, we can't complain because our life has all been so good this far."

We finally drove on to Wilmington and, once there, called the state police. Then Troy and Bob went back toward Clinton. They did meet the three kids there, and their story is actually more interesting than ours. It seems they parked in front of an ice cream stand until it closed; then they moved to a parking lot for a fast food place. As it grew later and the parking lot was emptying, Steve admitted he was getting really nervous and worried. Finally a state policeman came up to their car window and told them their parents were looking for them, and that all was well. Remember, there were no cell phones then. The explanation was so simple. There was a new bypass around Clinton since the last time we went through there, and we were on the new road and they were on the old.

Then there was the time Debbie ran across the road in Shillong when she was five years old. We were walking along a quite busy street when, for some reason, Troy got separated from us and was walking on the other side. Suddenly, I realized that Debbie had dashed across to him. Just like that – almost before we knew it. Well, it was before we knew it. So the scare was the aftershock of realizing she could have been hit by a car or truck, easily could have, but wasn't, thank God.

There was another time when we were in Mussoorie, India and we were walking back from a Sports Day of the boarding school up there, just walking along, the children and I with Aunt Montiel Peck, talking about the sporting events of the day and laughing. Suddenly Becky, eight or nine years old, who had been walking on my left side, was gone. Gone! Gone where? She had gotten a bit too close to the edge, the dirt gave way and she silently slid down the khud, the edge of the road. We had heard some real horror stories about children falling down the khud and being badly injured, even killed, so of course I was alarmed. But then I realized she was sitting on a very narrow ledge. But that ledge was 10-12 feet below the road, above a very rocky creek bed. She was way too far for me to reach to her with my umbrella which is all I had with me. But bless Montiel's quick thinking, she ran back, found one of the local porters and explained to him our problem. He came to Becky from quite a distance down the road, very carefully working down to her level. I told her he was going to get her off that ledge, just to put her arms around his neck and trust him. She did and he brought her up safely. Whew! Thank you, Lord, for the Sherpa and for Aunt Montiel. She seemed to be fine after that. I was a mess. I kept thinking, "What if?" Which of course is never a good thing to spend too much time on. In the next few days Steve enjoyed teasing me by walking on the wall above the khud and calling out, "Look, Mom, look what I can do." I must confess I couldn't take it then. Usually I would have laughed it off, but then I wasn't quite there yet. Finally, his Daddy told him that was enough of that.

The other time I can think of when I might have

been afraid was when Troy and Steve were coming home from Dacca to Comilla. Steve was in school there in seventh grade, and Troy had been there on business. The train usually took a few hours, arriving about suppertime. But this time it didn't come, and it didn't come, and it didn't come, right on through the night. Finally, I went on to sleep, feeling Troy would have some explanation when he did come. The next morning, about 9:00 or 10:00, here they came in a rickshaw. What had happened? Well, they had the bad luck to have been on a campaign train, with Mrs. Jinnah, I think, and people were stopping the train at every little junction. It was really crowded, so of course they didn't get much sleep either. Aw well, it was good to get home and into their own beds!

Another time, Troy scared me. We were in Ciskei, South Africa living in one of the missionary houses. Not long before this, another family had their house broken into, and they were roughed up. This type of thing was very common at that time, and we all knew it. Troy was at a meeting, and I decided to take a bath and go to bed. I was sitting in the tub when I heard footsteps, heavy footsteps. At least they sounded heavy to me. I called out to Troy, but there was no answer. I think I forgot all the good Bible verses I knew for times such as this. You know like, "What time I am afraid, I will trust in thee." I called out again; still no answer. Then he opened the door, and it was Troy. I was pretty mad as you can imagine and let him know that was not funny!

One more: One day we were walking in King

William's Town, South Africa. We were crossing the street when my shoe sole caught in a rough place in the street, and I fell to my knees. I called out to Troy, but he, as usual, was several paces ahead of me. But then I looked up to see a very large truck coming right at me. Well, I don't know what I prayed but it wasn't another call to Troy. He was gone on across. The truck came on and didn't slow down at all. The driver was a black man, and I can understand he might have been glad to hit a white woman. They had been treated so badly in that country. But I was just far enough across that he, driving straight ahead, just missed me. Whew! Thank you God!

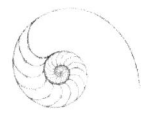

Leave of Absence – Kinston, NC

Jack & Kathryn Hankins learning to eat rice & curry with their hands!
Kinston, NC, 1982

The time in Kinston was an extremely happy interlude for us. I found plenty to do and there was no lack of challenge. And, of course, we were close to the children which I could never object to. Spilman Memorial was a good and loving church and it didn't take long to find my niche. I was teaching a great group of young couples in Sunday school who were open, ready to learn, liked to socialize and were generally lots of fun. And, they were great to bring friends so that class grew raidly. It was the sort of challenge I loved.

Other things were beginning to happen in our family. Steve was back from Korea and working in Goldsboro, NC. Later, he went to the Boys Club in Raleigh. Becky was working in Raleigh. Debbie was working in Winston-Salem the first year and then went to Louisville, KY to Southern Seminary, but was back in NC in the summers.

With the help of friends, especially Brenda Ipock and Thelma Johnson, we started Meals on Wheels which is still working today. Unlike many of these ventures, we did not ask the government for any money but got our support locally from the various churches. And the volunteers were from many different churches, so that was a good result also. We found an invaluable helper for interviewing the people who wanted Meals on Wheels delivered to them. Ora Brown knew their circumstances and was most compassionate. She and I made a good team I think. We later started an outreach ministry, called ICOR, Inter Church Out Reach, bringing churches together to cooperatively serve the needy in the community. Brenda was the financial brain behind both organizations. Thelma Johnson had prayed for this sort of thing for years and was very involved in lining up volunteers, and of course, worked many hours herself. We had great cooperation from many agencies and government services. Everyone worked together; it was really a fine experience. Kinston was a large town, not a city, but it was great for this type of ministry because we could get any place

Brenda Ipock
Kinston, NC, 1981-84

quickly for both Meals on Wheels and ICOR.

I didn't feel out of God's will at all, but I did miss the mission field, the challenges, the needs and being able to meet some of those needs, just the challenge of living in another culture, knowing those people and trying to share the goodness of God was air in my wings, light to my soul. But, I did love Kinston too. The people were so good to us and we made so many precious friends there.

One summer Troy, Debbie and I borrowed Gene and Pat Ipock's truck and camper and made a trip, stopping at campgrounds in Virginia, Tennessee and North Carolina. It was great just seeing the beauties of God's handiwork. Debbie was on her way back to seminary in Louisville, so she left us when we reached the farthest western point of our travels to go on to Louisville. Troy and I turned back east but took our time, making many stops along the way and enjoying sleeping in the outdoors. To hear the birds, the crickets and frogs and all of that symphonic music was delightful!

One other thing that we really enjoyed was deep-sea

Paul Linke & Troy after fishing
Kinston, NC, 1982

fishing. Neither of us had done much of this at all. We went with Paul Lincke, a member of the church and owner of a boat. He didn't like to eat fish, but he surely liked to pull them in and he showed us how to do it too! Many Saturdays we went with Paul, and sometimes one or two others, and spent the day. We always had a good haul, and when we brought them home Paul would even help us clean them. Lots of fun and a real change of pace for us!

One weekend Becky brought a friend home to meet us, a man friend. His name was Jesse Perry and we liked him immediately. However, I did tell her privately that she hadn't warned me that he was a bear of a man. That Christmas, 1982, they were going on to Hertford to see his parents also. So, we decided to go to Hertford the next day too. I don't remember why we were all at home, but we were and we all went to Hertford. I think the Perrys were surprised when all of us showed up, but they handled it graciously, and we were very happy to meet the parents and his brother and sister as well.

On September 24 of 1983, Becky and Jesse Perry were married in Raleigh at the Unitarian Universalist Church building. It was a happy time with family and many friends. It was a simple and very beautiful wedding. Becky had joined the Quaker meeting so that was the type of service they had. We had a gorgeous fall day; the building had two tall windows, one at each side of the front where they were seated. The golden glow from the autumn leaves filled the room with a joyful atmosphere. Different people shared favorite verses, advice, and prayers. It was very meaningful and really lovely. The reception was outside. The whole event couldn't have been any better!

Becky & Jesse Perry married in Raleigh, NC, September 24, 1983

In early spring, we were asked by Davis Saunders to consider going to Dar es Salaam, Tanzania to pastor an English-language church. Well, that got our attention! We had been at Spilman three plus years and had a wonderful response to our ministry. We loved the people, the area, proximity to the beach, oh, many things about it. But, the same call that had sounded in our hearts back in the early 50s still rang true. There are so many pastors and other church workers here in this country and so few going to other lands where so many people have never had the privilege of knowing about God's love in Christ Jesus.

Dar es Salaam has a very international population

and one of their official languages is English. However, we would need to do six months of language study before going to Dar es Salaam. That would happen in Nairobi, Kenya. Well, we talked about it and prayed about it; we were getting older as far as learning a new language was concerned. Could we do it? We went to Richmond and talked with Davis who knew the area well. The economy there was in a mess; that was not new for us, of course. We were both in good health and maybe had "sand in our shoes," which means ready to travel again. We felt as strongly as ever that the need was great and we wanted to be part of God's reaching out. So, we said yes, and that was the beginning of another adventure. We said we would go for the years remaining to us before retirement. The people at Spilman were very supportive and understanding of our decision. We had talked missions the whole time we were there, me in my Children's Time and Troy in his preaching and teaching, so it wasn't a surprise, I think.

Around this time, as we were driving up the street to our house, we saw Debbie and some young fellow walking down the street toward us. What could this mean? We had heard about Bill Reynolds but had not yet met him. He was a student at Southeastern Seminary in Wake Forest, NC and Debbie was at the Southern Seminary in Louisville, KY. So, she had come with friends to see him and to bring him to meet us before we left for the field. Bill's parents were also missionaries with Southern Baptists, but in Europe. We were delighted to meet him and liked him right away. We worked out to meet his parents as we passed through Europe on our way back overseas. That was really good. Things were happening fast!

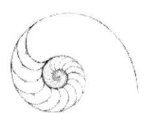

Sixth Term – Tanzania

This was something we knew how to do – pack to go overseas. So far, we had moved 25 times since 1950. We went in April of 1984 to Nairobi, Kenya. We again saw old friends including Harold and Betty Cummins, who had previously been in East Pakistan. Language study was a good experience in many ways. Swahili is not a hard language to learn since it uses the same letters as English and we found many similarities with Bengali words which had also come from Arabic.

Language school was at Limuru, a very small town outside Nairobi. Actually, the mission board had bought an old country club and converted it to language school and a center for theological education. There were small cottages for the students and staff to live in, a church, and a central building with the dining hall, meeting rooms and classrooms. There were also two missionary houses there for the ones who worked in the area. Papa and I lived in a two-room cottage: living/dining/kitchen/study room, bedroom and bath. What more did we need? Nothing.

Schoolroom where the Dar es Salaam International Church worshipped Dar es Salaam, Tanzania, 1984-88

After six months of language study there, we went to Dar es Salaam,

Tanzania where we found that a church had been started under the leadership of Harold and Rene Mitchell. Harold was not a preacher but a dentist, however he had done a good job

The children's class of our church Dar es Salaam, Tanzania, 1984-88

of bringing people together who wanted to worship in English. He and Rene also loved Bible study, so had been leading that. Dar es Salaam, which means Door of Peace is a large port city with a very old history. The old buildings reminded us of their past as a German colony until the close of World War I. Then the country, Tanganyika, was under British Mandate until 1961; now Tanzania was independent. A large part of the history of the coastal region is related to slave trading, not a pretty picture.

But, we were there to work with the International Church which was made up of many nationalities as well as denominations, very similar to the situation in Dacca. We met in one of the classrooms of the International School. We had Sunday school for the children. It was really a mixed group but we enjoyed the diversity. There was an American married to a German woman who was a concert pianist. Many others were in different businesses, with government agencies, and then there were other missionaries as well. We joined a choral group led by a German lady who was a true musician. At first, we lived in the downstairs of the Mission guest house so were able to meet and talk with many of the folks who came through the city, and there were many.

We also had a group of 42 Baptist volunteers from the US who came to help the larger mission work. Some of them had planned to be flown in our mission plane by pilot Bill Stiles to a station in the southern region. When he told them how much weight he could take on that little plane, the leader, a very large man, said he weighed almost that much by himself. They laughed, but it wasn't funny. Bill was serious; he didn't break the rules. They worked out something. One volunteer brought her guitar. Several young men were eager to learn to play it, so she was busy the whole time working with them. It was always interesting to see what they did bring; often it was things to eat like Nabs, Pop-Tarts, candy and such snacks. But, they were ready to work and we tried to find jobs to keep them busy.

We had studied Swahili and could speak some, but not very well, I'm afraid. But we knew enough to get around, and in Dar es Salaam women were able to go to the market. I liked that. I like to bargain and that was what they expected, so we had a good time! Even though there were a large percentage of people who are Muslim, it was very different from Dacca. More casual. African women are much more liberated than the Bengali women. I did learn that they say "after marriage the wife is his garden, and any fruit from that garden belongs to him, not her," if they split. I know it doesn't always happen that way, but sometimes it does. They are more relaxed about their dress and not so closely covered. I often saw Muslim women wearing the black burqas (the veil and covering over her clothes), but with their faces fully uncovered. I didn't have to be quite so strict about my dress. I could drive and I could shop.

While we were in Tanzania, we visited various game parks, often with friends. We were not in Dar es Salaam so long before we had several visitors come to see us. First, I think, was our good friend Sue LeQuesne from England. We lived close to the beach in Dar es Salaam and I remember some really nice days there. Then Brenda Ipock and Doris Powers, our good friends from Kinston, NC came for a week or so. When they came, we went to a game park and spent a night in the hotel. We got up very early to go out with a guide to see some game. We had been there on our own before and seen lots of animals, but we expected this to be much better because we had a guide. We did see several different animals coming out in the morning to waterholes. Then the car came to a dry riverbed. The guide said to drive on through it, so Troy eased the car down the bank and started up the other side, but there was a problem. The car couldn't get up the other side. The guide said he would go for help, and left with his gun. We had seen some lions in the vicinity so were a little leery of this situation, but what were we to do? After placing some mats we found in the car under the rear wheels, Troy suggested we try to push while he steered. The only gain that gave was for us to get really

Two male elephants fighting, photo by Bill Reynolds,
future son-in-law
Tsavo Game Park, Kenya, 1985

spattered with mud. Plan B? Let Brenda steer and he would help push; still no luck. About then, the guide came back with one of the trucks that belonged to the game park; they pulled out a hitch and we were quickly on top of the bank safe and sound. No lions! I tried to tell one of the men what we had tried, and that all of the women had gotten very muddy, but I should have known better than to try. For that man, and most men in that society, that was what women were supposed to do. Ah well....

In 1985, Debbie came and brought her new fiancé Bill Reynolds. Actually, he popped the question on the Eiffel Tower when they were in Paris on their way to see us. We have learned this is a typical thing for him to do. He likes to do things with class. We had met Bill, but only briefly, so this was great; they stayed about two months and worked in some of the aid groups there. Bill is a strong swimmer and one group was especially glad to have him to work with the physically challenged children in the pool. With Debbie and Bill, we made a trip to Kyela for them to do some teaching. This was Doug and Evelyn Knapp territory, but they were on furlough and Mark and Kathy Kissee were there to hold the fort. We left the young folks there and they had a good and challenging time. On the road, we stopped and tried to talk with some Maasai women since we wanted to take a picture of them. They drove a hard bargain. Troy was doing most of the talking out the window of the car. One woman came right up to the car and held his arm while talking. Later he told us her grip was like an iron vise. Those women are strong! We finally agreed to photograph just one woman. All three cost too much!

Debbie & Bill Reynolds were married in Raleigh, NC, January 4, 1986

The year 1986 was a very interesting and exciting one for the Troy Bennett family. First, Debbie and Bill Reynolds were married on January 4 at Pullen Church in Raleigh, NC. Troy and I were able to come home for the festivities. It was a beautiful wedding; of course Pullen has a beautiful sanctuary with the stained glass window behind the wedding party! And that wedding party was something else. There were 12 ordained ministers in the wedding party. Really! Afterward, someone was kidding them that if that knot didn't hold, there was no hope for them. It was lots of fun meeting more of Bill's family and Deb and Bill's friends. Our friends from Kinston did the reception for us. Such good people! They had earlier had a double shower, for Debbie's wedding and Becky's expected baby. How do you say thanks for such great generosity?

Then Becky and Jesse's first child, our first grandchild, Margaret Leigh Perry, Meg, was born on February 13, the next month, without problems. We did not travel back for that. Finally, on May 6, Steve and Susan Kirstein were married in her hometown of Marion, NC. We were able to come home for that wedding too and it was good to meet Susan especially, but also her family and other friends they had made at UNC Chapel Hill, NC. Steve had received his Master's in Social Work from UNC in 1984 and he and Susan met during that time. The rehearsal dinner was lots of fun! Bill and Catherine Brooks and their kids, who "adopted" Becky during college, were by then extended family for all our children. In the photo you'll notice that Catherine and the three girls were there. Woody and Elizabeth

Steve & Susan Kirstein were married in Marion, NC, May 6, 1986

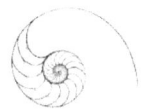

Turner whom we had known in Bangladesh came to the wedding too. What a delightful surprise that was! Several family members from the Bennetts and Trippeers showed up. Of course one of the really special ones who came was Meg Perry, just two months old. My, we were thrilled to see her, our first grandchild! It was a beautiful wedding!

Sixth Furlough: (3 Months)

From The Efficacy of Prayer by C.S. Lewis

Quoting Pascal: "God instituted prayer in order to lend to his creatures the dignity of causality."

Now you would think that would be enough travel for us, but we were scheduled to come home on short furlough in November for three months. I don't remember why, but we did, and stayed in one of the apartments at Southeastern Seminary in Wake Forest.

On the way, we stopped in Panama City, Panama to see Steve and Susan, who had gone there under her assignment with the US State Department. We were there over Thanksgiving and it was really interesting. Some local dancers performed for us after dinner. Fun! Another day, we went to see the Panama Canal, which helped us realize what an amazing feat it was to build.

When we were in the Miami Airport terminal waiting for our flight to Raleigh, NC, we heard an announcement for Troy Bennett. Our tickets had fallen out of the pocket of the bag we were carrying and someone turned them in. Thank you, God! And thank you to whoever that kind and honest person was.

It was a short furlough, but we did some interesting things. Papa decided I needed a new wedding ring since several of the very small stones in the original had fallen out. So we went shopping and found one

Sixth Furlough: (3 Months)

we both liked. Then Bill and Debbie decided to have a family wedding service, so we did. It was Christmastime and we were all at our apartment in Wake Forest. We used potted poinsettias for our flowers; somebody found a veil for me to wear over my sweatshirt; Deb and Bill had written out the ceremony they intended to use but then forgot to bring it, so did what they could remember. Steve was not there, but Becky was with Meg who was almost one year old and Jesse was best man. Deb and Bill shared the ministerial role. As you can see, it was extremely casual but meaningful, I think, for all of us since the two young couples were just embarking on their new life, and we were feeling very grateful for the 35 years we had had together. Thank you God for so many, many blessings! Afterward, we ate the wedding cake, our coconut cake for Christmas, since it was Christmastime.

"Dearly Beloved, Dear Family, we are gathered here today in the presence of God and these family members to witness and bless the joining together of this man and woman for the last 35 years and for their continuing life together in Holy Matrimony without which, of course, none of us would be here and three of us would not be here at all.

The institution of marriage is sacred and holy, ordained by God in creation and blessed by Jesus Christ's presence at the wedding in Cana of Galilee. There he turned the water into wine; today we might wish for the miracle of gray hair turning brown or stiff joints becoming young again...but don't expect it!

In marriage a man and woman are joined together in mind, body, spirit and bank account for their mutual growth, for comfort in sorrow and companionship in joy, and if it is God's will – and it was – for the procreation and enjoyment of grandchildren, and for their nurture in the knowledge and love of the Lord. And as the wise man Jack Hankins said, 'Marriage means that you will never again make a mistake without knowing about it.'"

Song: 'Do you love me?' recording from "Fiddler on the Roof."

So you, Daddy, take Mama Marjorie Ann Trippeer Bennett to be your wife. Do you promise still to live together in the covenant of marriage for better or

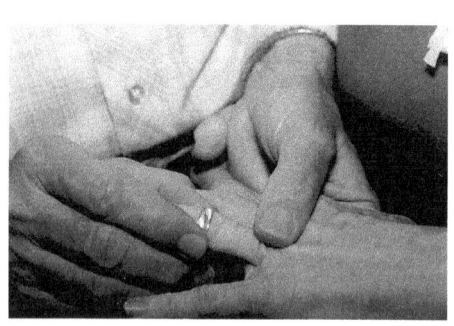

My new wedding ring
Wake Forest, NC, 1986

Troy & Marj. Do you like my corsage? Christmas Day, Wake Forest, NC, 1986

worse, for richer or poorer, in sickness and in health, for as long as you both shall live?

I do.

Do you, Mama take Daddy, Troy Carson Bennett to

be your husband?

I do.

Will all of you witnessing these vows promise to love and support them in their marriage?

We will.

Do you have the ring?

Let us pray. Bless, O Lord, this ring as a symbol of the vows remade here.

Repeat after me:

Marj, I give you this ring as a symbol of my constant love and with all that I am and all that I have, promise to be faithful to you alone as long as we both shall live.

Repeat with Marj. (Troy couldn't get the ring off his finger.)

You may kiss the wife."

Another interesting thing we did—well, the two girls and I did—was to go to a Color Analysis class. It was fun and we learned what season we were and also how to determine that for others. So, I asked the teacher if I could get swatches like she used to decide what season we were; I bought her swatches, as she was going to get a new set. So, I took them back to Dar es Salaam and had a good time working with friends to learn their season. For a couple of them it was a real eye-opener to see how much better they looked in certain colors.

I never claimed that I could tell by myself, so I did it with a group and we all together discussed it and made the decision. One friend, Christine, is a singer and had been told that she should wear black when she performs, but she did not look good in black at all. She had amazingly clear blue eyes and so sometimes wore blue, but actually her best colors were autumn colors. When she wore an orange dress, she was a knockout! And another friend, Jane, usually wore autumn colors, but after her analysis she started to wear pinks and blues, summer colors looked so much better on her. She literally looked healthier and prettier. I haven't done any of that lately, but I often find myself looking at people and thinking about what season they are.

So, we had a great three months and were very thankful for this time with our children. Then we were ready to head back to Dar es Salaam to the work that we were enjoying so much.

Seventh Term – Tanzania

We continued our work with the Dar es Salaam International Christian Church. Then, in late summer of 1988, Becky and Jesse with Meg came to Dar es Salaam to visit us and see some of the country. About a week later, Steve and Susan stopped there also, on their way to Bangladesh for Susan's State Department assignment. Before Steve and Susan arrived, we went to the Selous National Park which was a really good visit. It is always so good to see these wild animals in their

Left to right: back, Jesse, Troy, & Steve; front, Becky, Marj with Meg, & Susan at the beach near Dar es Salaam, Tanzania, 1988

natural habitat, and we saw plenty of that. We went on the train, so were able to see a different part of the countryside as well. We had a two and a half year birthday party for Meg. It was cute when she decided to help our helper in the kitchen. I know Mildred loved it.

Jesse paid the local boys to bring praying mantises to him. He kept them in our screened-in back veranda. I don't know how many he managed to take out of the country, but that was the idea; he had a permit from the museum, the NC Museum of Science where he worked. We had some good times at the beach, especially when we went to the American doctor's house, which was right on the beach. Very nice!

And, then we went on safari. After Steve and Susan got there, we borrowed Vestal Bleakley's Land Rover for the seven of us to drive through Morogoro to Arusha. We stayed at Ngorongoro National Park two or three days and had a really good guide who helped

This lion must have eaten recently. She seems very placid. Tanzania, 1988

Don't mess with the cape buffalo. The most ferocious animal in Africa! Tanzania, 1988 us to spot lots of birds as well as animals. I know these countries have these parks to attract tourists, but it also means they are protecting the animals from poachers, and that's good.

While our children were there, we told them that we had been asked to move again, this time to South Africa; or rather to one of the homelands, Ciskei, where there was a seminary for black students. Our boss in Richmond wanted us to help in the transition of the seminary from the white South African Baptist Union to the black South African Convention.

There was some pressure from the Foreign Mission Board at that time to end English language/international church work, which seems to have since been rescinded. We didn't really want to leave the very responsive work in Dar es Salaam. But, after we saw the movie, *Cry Freedom*, about Steve Biko and the situation in South Africa, we did feel a draw to see if there was any way we could help the black South Africans find their rightful place in church leadership, at least. We were to work with a missionary couple transferring from Malawi, Rue and Gwen Scott, and with a national couple, the Malois, who had already been there teaching.

Seventh Term – South Africa

"I saw the sea nibbling voraciously at the continent."
– Henry David Thoreau

So, in late fall of 1988, we arrived in Johannesburg, South Africa to be introduced to an entirely new picture of Africa. It is as modern as the US and that was new for us. We went on from there to East London, on the east coast of South Africa, a lovely city and very interesting. But, we were not to live here. We then went to King William's Town (KWT), which would be our home until we could move to the seminary. KWT would be our place for most shopping and for English-language church.

A rock formation at the Devil's Playground with two people nearby
Harare, Zimbabwe, 1988

Several miles out in the country was a very, very small town called Debe Nek just across the road from the seminary. Now, I say seminary because that was the purpose of the school, but I have to qualify that designation. The student body was made up of men and one woman, who were preparing for pastoral roles, and some of the men's wives. It was a small class, about 12 -14, as I remember. Most of the students had finished elementary school and some had done some higher work, but none obviously had done any college work. The women's backgrounds were mixed, from a limited schooling through second or third grade to graduation from elementary school. This was a very challenging situation, primarily because all of these people had come out of a non-Christian background, so we needed to teach them the basics as well as prepare them for leadership. I like to think of it as like the early Christian church. We didn't need to introduce any controversial subjects unless it might be something they would surely encounter. We moved very slowly with lots of repetition. We really enjoyed it; we had done this sort of thing before, so it wasn't new to us, but of course, the situation was different.

One of the major differences in this situation was the presence of apartheid, which means that the white people who were a small minority ruled, and the blacks and the coloreds (mixed race) were forced to live in separate homelands outside the cities. There were other restrictions as well that made it very hard for the large majority of people to live productive lives. We were working with the black people who had their own separate Baptist Convention and churches. It was our great privilege to be there when Nelson Mandela, the well-known leader of the black community, was released from prison and apartheid was ended. It was so good to share in this great liberation with our students and neighbors, and to watch with them on our TV when he walked out of the house he had been kept in as a prisoner. In Tanzania, before our arrival there, the change had already come and the African blacks were already in power in the government and other sectors.

We saw a good bit of South Africa, and it is a fascinating and beautiful place. Much of it is sparse, though there are some mountains, some quite near to us. But, many of the mountains in Africa, at least the ones I saw, just rose up out of the flat land. They didn't run in ridges or ranges. I think what interested me the most were the different flowers and trees; I had never seen most of these in all of our travels. I wonder now if Australia is the same, but I haven't been able to find out.

When Sue LeQuesne came to visit, we traveled down the coast road to Cape Town, and that was a real treat. Sue and I really enjoyed wading in the water at the southernmost point of Africa. I also picked up a few stones there. We stopped at the ostrich farm. Now that was cool. We were allowed to feed them—keep your hand straight, so they don't take a finger for lunch! And then, they invited us to sit on one. They had a v-shaped frame into which

Sitting on an ostrich was a challenging experience! South Africa, 1989

they pulled the ostrich with steps beside it that helped us to get on its back. What a strange feeling! All feathery on my thighs where I'm not used to feeling feathers. When I felt a bit unsteady, I reached for the neck to hold on; well, that didn't help much because their neck skin is very loose and slides up and down easily while the bird was moving his head backward and forward. Very interesting! His neck felt more like fur than feathers, though I suppose it surely was feathers, just very short ones.

One time, Troy and I drove from Johannesburg to Debe Nek and stayed overnight at one of the parks. We saw a great movie about lions that night. Two or three times we went to Grahamstown with friends and saw the old buildings and the great church where Andrew Murray and his son pastored. We ate in an underground restaurant that was quite exotic! And there were some amazing rock formations that we could climb on and look over the landscape. It was interesting to imagine the early Boers, the Zulu warriors and other indigenous people, and the British contending for control. There were guard stations all across that area of South Africa, a swath of territory that stretched from one coast to the other called the border area, because at one time the land was divided between the Boers and the British. And, of course, both of these were constantly trying to fend off the Zulus who were mighty warriors.

Another short trip we made was up to the Hogsback Mountain when the snow fell up there. We didn't have any snow on the lowlands where we lived, but they surely did up there. It was beautiful and a nice change. We were especially interested to see how many families with young children made a point to go and let the kids see and play in the snow.

We made several trips to Port Elizabeth for doctor's appointments—my visits for false alarms for tropical sprue—but also saw the city and environs—a lovely coast city. We also went back there with the Mass Choir at Christmastime. That was an amazing experience. I had never even wanted to be in one of those big choirs for a Billy Graham crusade or whatever, but this was something else. We started six months early, going into East London every Monday night with others from the church. Several of the Filipino young people who were contract workers in the diamond companies also went and we got to know them well. At first, we practiced in this rather small church, but then moved to another and then another and finally to the big Baptist church where we sat in sections; the tenors filled one whole section of the sanctuary, the basses another, the altos another, the sopranos another and the obbligato singers were in the balcony. WOW! The leader encouraged us to bring our friends—they didn't have to be good singers—and they could follow along with someone who knew the music well. And that's the way it was. I think of it now and my heart just swells, not with pride, but with the joy and fun and excitement we felt singing that beautiful music. And it was beautiful. We were very good. We practiced enough, that's for sure, and the director was a genius. He would be directing us and just walk up the aisle with his back to us, but we knew what he wanted. He had conveyed his deep feeling for the music to us so we felt it too. He could bring us, over 500 voices, down to a whisper in awe at the wonder of the baby in the manger. You can imagine, it was an experience of a lifetime for us. I hope you get the chance to do something like that one day.

Basically, we did more sightseeing than we had previously, and thoroughly enjoyed it, except for the apartheid. Debe Nek is an extremely small town, calling it a village is a better word for it. It has a joint post office/telephone operator/very limited general store. Maybe there was a filling station. And then, on our side of the road, way back from the road were several family dwellings. I only went across the road one time, but I often talked with the telephone operator who was very entertaining. This was especially true when I wanted to place a call to London, England. I wound up the phone and told him what I wanted. How did we wind up the telephone? Simple. There was a handle on the side of it and we just turned it around to make it ring for the operator, in this case, the guy in Debe Nek. Then we would tell him the number we wanted. We used to have this type of phone here in America. At first the operator thought I meant East London, South Africa, but when I explained I wanted London, England he got so excited. "Oh, I've never placed a call to London, England before!" But, he did it successfully and I expect, listened in to all our conversation.

We didn't have the best connections any time and sometimes it was hard to hear and understand, but it was a lot better than nothing. We didn't use it much, but the one time we were glad for it was when Katherine Fletcher Perry was born on November 19, 1989. Becky called and told us Katie had come but there were some complications. We didn't understand the seriousness of the situation until several years later. That makes me sad for I now know that Becky wanted me to come and I didn't. It's hard when you realize you have failed someone you love very much.

We did our shopping in King William's Town usually, but sometimes went into East London. Since I was trying to stay on a gluten-free diet for several months it was challenging, because in reading the labels, I found most of them in Afrikaans. Not impossible to figure out, but it took time. There were nice restaurants, steak houses, etc. and a McDonalds on the beach. One interesting thing about the stores, restaurants, offices, etc. was that there was a guard at every entrance. We had to stop and let them see what was in our bags. We got used to it, of course, but it was different.

Africa, 1988

We lived near Fort Hare University, a well-known school established for blacks from all the countries of eastern and southern Africa. Many of the present leaders in those countries were educated there, including Mandela. Several Sunday nights, Troy was asked to preach for evening service and we always looked forward to it. I remember one evening especially, when we were waiting for the crowd to gather, and some of the students started singing. Finally they got to, "Just as I am without one plea but that thy blood was shed for me, and that thou bidst me come to thee, O Lamb of God, I come, I come." And they continued to sing just the refrain, "O Lamb of God, I come, I come," over and over and over until everyone's heart was ready for worship. Such an experience of waiting before God...Wonderful!

When you spend some time in Africa, it isn't at all difficult to see why many of the Europeans came there to stay. The climate is wonderful, the land is rich, the people are gracious, the animal life is constantly amazing, and the land itself is almost telling you its story. You just have to listen. I could spend a lifetime there; that's what it would take. I really don't have words to describe it, but I fell in love with South Africa during those two years we were there, and that lives on in my heart.

We had a lot of fun with the seminary students. They seemed to enjoy the board games and cards we had, especially Uno, which a lot of people can play at one time. One of our most precious memories was at the end of the first school year during graduation. One of the students was asked to address the group in English about his experience at the school, and another was asked to speak in his own language. There was several language groups represented in the student body. The second speaker was not very fluent in English and I, at least, had not had many conversations with him. However, he made a very good effort and did well in his own language though we could not

Graduates of the Baptist International
Theological Seminary
Ciskei, South Africa, 1989

understand. Well, this day when he spoke, I noticed everyone who understood laughing and clapping. I asked what he had said, and they replied, "He says when the Americans came, we were afraid. We didn't know what they would be like and what kind of teaching they would give us. But they have been very good to us, and the best thing, they take tea with us!" We had been informed when we came that teachers took tea in the office, away from the students. Well, we knew we were not going to do that. For us it was easy, for we had come from Tanzania where black Africans were in charge, and the Scotts were from Malawi where the same was true. I don't think we ever even discussed it, we just did what we were going to do. And evidently, the students appreciated it. To us, such a small thing, but not to them!

This is a prayer that was found scrawled on a piece of wrapping paper in the Ravensbruck Concentration camp near the body of a dead child during an era of unspeakable darkness.

> O Lord. Remember not only the men and women
>
> Of good will, but also those of ill will.
>
> But do not remember all the suffering they inflicted on us.
>
> Remember the fruits we have bought, thanks to
>
> This suffering – our comradeship,
>
> Our loyalty, our humility, our courage,

Our generosity, the greatness of heart

Which has grown out of all of this, and when

They come to judgment, let all the fruits

We have borne be their forgiveness.

Barefoot in Central Park

The mission was meeting in Transkei, a homeland in South Africa, on Sunday. "Come for a small service and dinner together before we handle our business," was the invitation. Papa and I piled in the back of the van with Rue and Gwen Scott and Richard and Dee Lee. As we cruised on through the hills of eastern South Africa, from Ciskei to Grahamstown, Papa realized that he had forgotten our passports. Ciskei and Transkei were called homelands, but were treated like separate countries when you wanted to travel through them. There would be no crossing of that border without passports for the Bennetts.

We insisted, since it was too late to go back, that we could just spend the day in Grahamstown. We'd find a church and somewhere to eat lunch. No problem; so they let us out at a filling station on the south end of the main street. We began walking and it wasn't long before we found the Baptist Church. All was well. However, there was another hitch to our day, just a small hitch, but definitely a hitch. I noticed as we rode along that I had worn mismatched sandals. I had two pairs of white dress sandals and had inadvertently put on one shoe from each pair. Who needs two pairs of dress sandals? As we sat in church, I kept my feet tucked under the pew just in case someone should look at them. Doubtful, I know, but I was a bit self-conscious.

After the service, the visitors were invited to come back to the Hall for a time of fellowship, that is, to meet people. So, of course, we went and we met people including the pastor and his wife who invited us to their home for dinner. They actually seemed pleased to meet us as they had supported the seminary and were anxious to hear how things were going there since the Baptist Union had changed their relationship to it. So we had an interesting time, except I kept trying to hide my mismatched shoes.

I remember especially going to the kitchen to offer my help. I watched the lady of the house cook roasted potatoes that were so good. I have never tasted anything quite like them. First she boiled them and then dropped them into hot oil to brown and finish cooking them. Truly delicious!

After dinner they offered to give us a tour of Grahamstown, which didn't take too long. Of course, we had told them about being dropped at the filling station and our plan to meet our colleagues at 3:00 pm. As we were riding along, we knew it was nap time for all sensible people, so we insisted that they just let us out on the main street and we'd walk down to the meeting place. That is what we did, and we started walking with no reason to hurry as our meeting time was at least an hour later. We glanced into a hotel that had some very comfortable-looking chairs in the lobby, but we didn't have the nerve to crash there. Then we came to a little park in the center of town, right on that main street. Several black people were lying around taking it easy. It didn't take much for us to agree to sit down on the shady green, and not much more to take off our shoes for a pillow and stretch out for a nap. In Dar es Salaam we had learned our lesson about leaving our shoes on the side of our blanket when we stretched out for a nap on the beach. Papa's shoes were stolen and we had never heard or seen a thing.

After our little rest, we got up much refreshed and walked on down the street to the meeting place. I think we may have been a bit smug, and very amused, just thinking what the Scotts and Lees would say if they had known where we took our naps. But, of course, we weren't about to tell them!

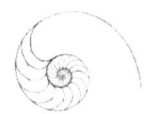

Seventh Furlough

"No ray of sunlight is ever lost, but the green which wakens into existence needs time to sprout, and it is not always granted to the sower to see the harvest. All work that is worth anything is done in faith."
– by Albert Schweitzer

We had decided in 1990 to take our furlough and then retire from the mission field. But first we had to travel back to North Carolina to enjoy that experience. I had thought it would be great if we could just

Buses are cheap, therefore crowded
Dhaka, Bangladesh, circa 1985

Rena Das, our good friend, & her baby Mou
Dhaka, Bangladesh, 1990

fly straight over to Australia, but flights don't seem to go that way. So we took the opportunity to have one more visit in Bangladesh. Steve and Susan were there, she with the US consulate and he with Asia Foundation. It was so good to see many of our old friends. There were many changes in Bangladesh: more bridges and not so many ferries. Many more people; Dacca seemed just packed with people when we went out to shop and the population had spread out much farther.

But people were the same, and that was refreshing. We saw the new retreat center north of Dacca that was being built with funds from Jim McKinley's book sales, *Death to Life: Bangladesh as Experienced by a Missionary Family*. What a blessing that is and will be for the Christians, especially the Baptists! We went to Faridpur and on to Gopalganj where the Tom Thurmans lived. I had never been there before though Troy had and it was such a blessing to see some of the results of the work the Thurmans had been doing that Troy had earlier reported. Then we went back to Faridpur, for someone had asked Troy to preach and he agreed. I would have been nervous, but he didn't seem to be. After his sermon, he asked Gloria how he did with his Bengali and she said, "Just fine except that you kept saying, 'lakini' which means 'but' " in Swahili. I expect they got the meaning of what he was trying to share with them. We were very happy to be back and worshiping with these old friends. We also went to Magura and spent a couple of days there. It was good to see what James and Guinevere Young had accomplished with the people there. There was a small, but very nice new church building there with the addition of a missionary house. They had developed an agricultural set-up for raising crops as well as livestock including goats and ducks. We were surrounded by the many reminders of God's active presence; reminded that one prepares the soil, another plants the seed, another waters and another gathers the harvest. But it is God who causes them all to grow. We were just His servants praising Him for all He had done, was doing, and would continue to do!

Dacca International Christian Church was also changing and progressing. They had called and supported their own pastor and had a place to meet. We knew almost nobody who was in the church at that time. As I have said, there is a lot of turnover, but the need was still there and other people happily served to meet that need.

We left Dhaka and went to Japan to visit Suzuki and Mayumi, who were by this time married. They had been our friends in Dar es Salaam. It was so interesting to see them in their own home, which was a blend of Japanese and Western ways. We slept on the floor on mats but sat at a table to eat. I had told Mayumi that we would like to experience the Japanese bathhouse, which we had read about. And so we did. One evening we walked two or three blocks from their home to the public bathhouse. In this one, men went one direction and the ladies another. I, of course, was watching Mayumi and her friend to get my cues as to what to do next. First, we undressed and each went to one of the spigots about a foot above the floor. We scrubbed and rinsed, and scrubbed and rinsed, and scrubbed and rinsed. I'm not sure how many times this was repeated, but they kept on doing it so I did too. Then we were ready to get into the hot tub. Oooh! That felt so good! But they were barely in it before they got out and started to dry themselves. I would have enjoyed staying longer, but evidently it wasn't done that way, so I didn't.

Another time we bathed at their house. They had a bathtub full of hot water. But first I was to scrub and rinse and scrub and rinse. Then I could get into the tub. When I came out another person went in and did the same. There was something about washing clothes with the same water. I never did get that all straight.

It was really interesting to work in the kitchen with Mayumi. I don't think I was much help, but I loved watching her prepare the rice and vegetables and such. We did have sushi one day. It was good. One day we went to Denny's, a breakfast place like in the US, except that all of the menu items were shown in pictures outside the shop and also above the order counter. I got a tofu burger or something of the sort. It was a thick slice of tofu lightly fried and then covered with soy sauce on lettuce. It was okay.

We spent several days with Suzuki and Mayumi and they took us to a street festival that was really something to see. Big crowds came out for it. All the people were laughing and shouting, waving banners and marching with the groups in the parade.

We also saw Akiko, a precious Christian friend from Dar es Salaam. She took us to an old Buddhist temple—a tourist site—with shops around it where I found some gifts for our family. Later, as we went to the airport, they stopped at a very beautiful, somewhat new temple that they wanted us to see. Of course there is so much more to see and learn about Japan, but our time was limited. We had a very fulfilling visit while there.

Then we were on our way to the USA — California to be specific. We stopped to see William and Marilyn Bennett and the main thing I remember is the noise of the dishwasher, vacuum, and washing machine, all at the same time. It sounded very noisy and overwhelming to me after the relative quiet of other cultures. We visited with their children and grandchildren and that was great fun! We also saw Janet, Troy's niece, and her family.

Phyllis, Troy's sister, had moved to North Carolina after her husband's death and we were to drive her car across country. We had looked forward to this trip because we would see many of the sites of the West and Midwest. We followed Interstate 40 with few interruptions. Our first stop was the Grand

Canyon and that was magnificent! We didn't go down into the canyon, which would have been thrilling, but just seeing it was a treat. And we did see one of those LARGE screen movies of the canyon from an airplane flying all through it. Great! We went on to Texas to see Vestal and Carol Jean Blakeley who had been in Dar es Salaam. That was so enjoyable. In Lubbock we also saw Ida Tucker and her daughter Marcia, friends from Bangladesh. Then up to Oklahoma City we went to see Badlee Mondal and Joel her son, good friends from Faridpur, Bangladesh. I was quite disappointed to learn from Badlee that no one from the local Baptist church had made an effort to get to know her and ask her to speak at their church, which she could have done since her English was very good.

Next, we stopped for two or three days in St. Louis to see Dwight and Brenda Jackson and some of their family. We saw the work they were doing with the Cooperative Baptist Fellowship: inner city work as rewarding as it was very challenging! Next, we stopped in Springfield, Missouri to see the Pecks, and that was fun of course. Ron was still working for the Assembly of God Mission board, traveling all over the world in support of missionaries working with Muslims. Our next stop was in Nashville, Tennessee to visit my sister, Mary Jean and Walt Litaker, her husband. This was great because they took us to see many of the construction jobs he had supervised. The ones we saw were all churches, I think, and they were amazing and magnificent—really beautiful! We also saw their daughter Kay and her family.

Of course the scenery we saw was just gorgeous! We have seen a lot of beautiful mountains, valleys, deserts and rivers, but none captured our hearts and souls like the Rocky Mountains out west. We were awed at the Painted, Mohave, and Sonoran deserts, the rolling hills and corn fields of the Midwest, the great Mississippi River and the Great Lakes of the north, the Smoky Mountains of the east, and the wonderful hills and valleys covered with trees and waterfalls, flowing streams, farms and orchards in Tennessee and North Carolina. This was the perfect way to come back to our home in the Eastern USA.

We lived in the Hayes Barton Baptist Church missionary house in Raleigh for that furlough year. It was close to both Becky and Debbie and their families though Debbie moved soon after to Atlanta, GA. Steve and Susan returned from Bangladesh that fall and moved to northern Virginia. Of course this was the first time we had met Katie. That Christmas we were all together which was wonderful!

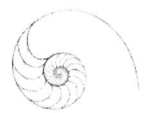

Retirement

From a sermon by Dr. Frank Tupper, speaking about
Phil. 3:7-11
Ardmore Baptist Church, Winston-Salem, NC

"...Shared suffering creates unbreakable bonds of unity. Unshared suffering cuts chasms of separation. Most intense grief is not shared – it leads to alienation.

According to Paul, to know Christ we must share his suffering.

How to share his suffering?
- not the crucifix complex
- must be his suffering, not ours

Points of entry to his suffering:
1: Scandal of the cross as a model for our lives

'Whoever saves his life will lose it and whoever loses his life for my sake will save it.'

2: Must share the real pain of real people
- common pain leads to hope without judgment, but encouragement

3: Give ourselves for the sake of the world. Jesus' suffering began during his life when he was rejected, saw evil, etc.

At the Lord's Supper we must do more than remember, we must embrace his suffering and those who suffer every day. To drink the cup is to take on his suffering and the suffering of the world and make it our own."

"The worst thing that can happen to us is never the last thing."
– John Claypool

In 1991 we retired from the foreign field to stay in the States for whatever service the Lord would make available to us. He has been very gracious in this respect. I was 63 and Papa, as the grandchildren called him, would be 63 in a few months. We had purchased a house in Winston-Salem, NC and we moved into it after our furlough time in Raleigh. Troy did interim pastoral work for several years, but then we learned he had Parkinson's disease in 1994, and his voice began failing him and he stopped preaching. This was a great disappointment since it was his gift, his passion and we had always thought he could preach and teach for many years after retirement. I was able to be involved in some good work while in Winston-Salem with the Language Missions Council. Troy also helped with this a lot. We both worked several years as volunteers at Baptist Hospital and with Crisis Control and enjoyed that service as well. We were involved in his high school reunions and we helped to start an annual meeting of missionaries in the state along with a quarterly meeting for mission folks in the Triad area in Winston-Salem.

Of course it was lots of fun to be here to get acquainted with our grandchildren. Meg was four years old when we came back and Katie was one. They spent many nights with us. Sarah Bennett Perry joined the family on April 14, 1994. We were here for her birth; actually I was at the hospital with Meg and Katie; Troy came soon thereafter. Also, we met Anna Bennett Reynolds, Debbie and Bill's first child, who was born November 27, 1994 only days after her birth. Then, on May 4, 1997 Luke Bennett Reynolds was born and we met him when he was just hours old.

I wonder what the Perry girls and Anna and Luke remember about our times together. Often we would play games, any game would do. It was always fun with Papa trying to cheat and get away with it. "Watch his eyes," I would tell them. One of our favorite games was Mastermind. Sarah and I would play while I was cooking up something in the kitchen. She foxed me every time by figuring out all of the same colors I had hidden behind the hood at the end of the game board. Seems I could

The five grandchildren in our backyard.
Left to right: Katie behind Sarah & Anna & Meg with Luke
Winston-Salem, NC, 1998

not remember that little trick of hers. As time went on, they got smarter and smarter and could beat me almost every time, even when I was concentrating. In later years we learned how to play Texas Hold'em poker and Luke would try to trick us all. Sometimes he succeeded, but we watched his eyes too and that could give him away.

We had a nice shelter in our backyard in Winston-Salem with a hammock that we all liked to swing in. It was fun to get three or four of us in there together! The Perry girls had marvelous imaginations so we played everything from Indian girls to orphans to horseback riding on the banisters of our back steps. We put a long piece of plastic on the grass and that made a great slide when it was wet—for them, not me; I'm getting too old for that sort of thing! Becky would meet us at a Hardee's in Burlington, NC to bring the girls to us or to take them back home again. One time, we had a bad storm and all of the electricity was off, including at Hardees. Katie and I walked over to the Bojangles next door to see if we could use their restroom. There was a long, very long dark hall down to the door we were seeking. We felt our way down there and then around inside the room which was pitch-black. Pretty interesting! When we groped our way back up the hall, they were very gracious and gave us a big box of fried chicken and biscuits; since it was already cooked and no customers would be coming that day. They simply shared what they had with us. So we had a picnic right in the car while waiting for Becky!

We also went with the Perrys to the Horne Creek

Farm near Christmas. That was an adventure and somewhat reminiscent of our experiences in Bangladesh! It got dark early of course, and the only light they had was a few lanterns. So we stumbled around the house looking at the furniture and seeing the way things were done in the old days. Another time we went there, I think, and they had made homemade ice cream. Now that's good eating!

We've been to the beaches in North Carolina with the Perry girls and in Georgia I went with Debbie, Anna, and Luke on a youth retreat. That was fun for me; Debbie had responsibilities on the program so I was in charge of Anna and Luke during the day. I dare say I had the better of the two jobs! Anna and Luke have not lived as close to us so we were limited in our time with them, but we had some good times visiting them when they lived in Atlanta and later in Rochester, New York.

Sometimes we went to north Georgia and met the Reynolds' at Hillcrest, the mountain home of Helen Reynold's family. It was great to walk around the roads there and go to other sites in the area. One time, my brother Bob and his wife Dot came over from their mountain home. We played poker and Bob remembered much better than I how to play.

With Anna, we went to one of the trout farms up in the mountains. Boy, that was fun! You could just drop your line in and you had a big swimming fellow coming your way. They tasted really good too. Bill and Debbie were experts with the grill. Another time we went with Debbie and the kids to the zoo in Atlanta. The lions

How many people does it take to pull in a trout? Debbie, Anna & Marj North Georgia, circa 1996

came right down to the glass enclosure where the water moat was so we got a good look at them. They were so close—just the glass between us and them. The lions also played with huge tractor tires; just tossed them around like rubber balls.

One time we were staying with Anna and Luke while Deb and Bill had gone off somewhere. When it was time for Anna to get out of school, I walked with Luke and Lady, the dog, up to the school. Anna wanted us to come inside for something so I tied Lady to a bush and she lay down. When we came out, Anna wanted to show us something on the playground and so we walked down that way with her and then on home. It was supper time before I realized someone was missing, and that someone was Lady! I quickly ran up to the school to find her lying by the bush right where I had left her. I was very relieved! She was a good dog.

When we went to Rochester, NY to see the Reynolds' after they moved there, I loved going out to the park where chickadees came down and ate birdseed right out of your hand or off the top of your head! Really tame! Also there is a very impressive gorge that we have seen in different seasons. The Finger Lakes were a great place for picnics and hiking around too.

Retirement

One time, Anna and Luke were at our house in Winston-Salem when we had a really good snow. The children down the street, CJ and Sarah Sheppard, had a nice hill right in their backyard and things to slide on. That was fun! Another time, the three younger grandchildren got painted up as Indians and while they played on our drum from Africa, they danced and cavorted all over the living room and study. What fond memories of their childhoods I have! Now they are all grown up and I am so proud of the adults they are becoming. I know their Papa would be too.

There is one sad note from this time: for many reasons Steve and Susan felt that their marriage needed to end in 1996. Troy and I went to Washington to see Steve and to help him move.

Later in 1996, we did take one rather challenging trip to Europe, and went with a tour group to Turkey to see the Seven Churches of Asia that Paul wrote letters to as we see in the book of Revelation in the Bible. We visited lots of old dear friends on the way.

Whenever we had visitors in Winston-Salem, there were two places we liked to take them. First was to see the Moravian background of Winston-Salem. Troy would take them first to Bethabara, where the first settlers came and we got the history of their struggle to begin the settlement of Salem. Then we would go to Old Salem to see everything there, the church and Salem College, and all of the shops, especially the bakery, which was our favorite. We could get sugar cake there! Meg and Katie were able to spend a week

Surviving Trippeer siblings from left to right: Nancy Trippeer, Donald, Marian Dodson, Marj, Bill, Bob, & (Mary) Jean Litaker
Knoxville, TN, circa 1998

with us in the summer and learn all about Old Salem in a camp for children.

The other place we liked to take our guests was up on the Blue Ridge Parkway to the town of Glendale Springs to see the murals painted in the church there. The main mural is of the Last Supper; the artist was very good and he had used local people for his models. Then in the basement there is a sort of shrine with other paintings. Sometimes we went on to West Jefferson to see more murals painted by the same man. Then we would drive along the Parkway, which is a beautiful drive any time of the year, a gift to the US thanks to work programs of President Franklin D. Roosevelt and the Great Depression.

I have told you about our Trippeer family reunion at Callaway Gardens in 1971 but there were others later also, at Myrtle Beach, SC, at Pigeon Forge, TN, and at the Big Lynn Lodge in Little Switzerland, NC. These were so much fun and interesting to meet all of the new members of the clan, in-laws, and their children.

Oh, there was a good one in Nashville, TN too. We stayed in a hotel but visited in Mary Jean and Walt's home and had a nice get-together at Janet and Steve's home. There was one in Roanoke at the church where Lawrence has been pastor for fifty-some-odd years.

Waco Knott, Troy's nephew, and others planned a reunion for the Bennett clan in 1995, the descendants of Romy and Beulah Bennett. It was at Tanglewood Park just outside Winston-Salem and folks came from far and wide, California and Michigan, from Oklahoma and Florida. It was great to see all of these kinfolks! Then in 2013, Cliff Rikard pulled one together near his home in Matthews, NC and we had a very good crowd there. Everybody is growing up and growing older. June and I were the remaining remnant of the original family and the in-laws—the matriarchs!

The other reunions we have enjoyed are with the Bangladesh mission crowd. Sometimes one or more of our children also have gone and that was great! This gave us a chance to catch up on some of the work being done there now as well as seeing our good friends and their children all grown up and having

Older Bennett generation
Standing, left to right: Bob & June Rikard, Marilyn Bennett, Phyllis McCammon, Muriel Bennett, Mary Knott, Mallie Penry, Marj & Troy; front: William Bennett & RO Bennett
Mocksville, NC, circa 1991

Sarah & Anna with their Papa at the Bennett
family reunion.
Winston-Salem, NC, 1995

families of their own. In 2013 it was more of a challenge since I am now on oxygen 24/7, but Becky and Debbie wanted to go and very kindly wanted to help me attend. So we went by car to Jackson, Mississippi. It was a real challenge for them, but we did enjoy our time together and the time at the reunion. Each time we go, we feel this may be the last time for one or more of us to see one another, and that makes the time even more precious.

We did not try to go to any of the Africa mission get-togethers. The International Mission Board has had an emeritus week at Ridgecrest every five years and those have been fantastic, a chance to see so many of our missionary colleagues from all of the countries where we served!

I haven't mentioned Steve and Amelia's wedding in 1999. Amelia Roberson was his girlfriend from high school in Bangkok, Thailand and they reconnected after his divorce. The ceremony was in Washington, D.C. in their church at the time, the Seekers Church. It was a beautiful wedding, very simple but just what they wanted. And we were able to meet many of her family and their friends which was great fun! The rehearsal dinner was at a Vietnamese restaurant—Amelia's background—and it was very good. Then for the reception they had ordered Indonesian satay that arrived late, so when we went to their apartment after the wedding, we had a grand feast!

In 2001, Troy and I celebrated our 50th wedding anniversary. The children arranged a very nice party at Ardmore Baptist Church in Winston-Salem which was our church. We saw lots of old friends. It was really nice; even though Troy's Parkinson's was getting worse by then. Even so, we enjoyed seeing so many old

Bangladesh reunion: so good to see folks we love!
Tennessee, circa 2005

Steve & Amelia Roberson were married in
Washington, DC, October 9, 1999

friends and family, not only from Winston, but also from Kinston and Roanoke and others. The grandchildren decorated our car, so we just left it on there for a time to let folks know we were celebrating! In the next few days the people in several cars passing on the street cheered us.

As Troy's Parkinson's Disease took more and more of his independence, and we saw through his sister Phyllis's experience of moving from nursing home to hospital to another nursing home repeatedly, we knew that we needed to make other arrangements for ourselves. This was partly because, in my family, some of us had just died without any warning. If this should happen, none of our children were in a position to take Troy in. So we started the search for appropriate housing. We didn't find anything in Winston-Salem that seemed

50th wedding anniversary, left to right: Troy, Katie, Meg,
Sarah, Anna, Luke & Marj at Ardmore Baptist Church
Winston-Salem, NC, 2001

right for us, and then we heard through Debbie that John and Alice Tumblin were saying we should look at Twin Lakes Community in Burlington, NC, so one day we did. As we drove in, I was impressed with the "neighborhood feel" of the place and when we went into the Tumblin's house, Troy commented, "I could live here." So we began the process rather quickly and were accepted and financial arrangements were worked out for us to move in late May 2003.

When we moved to Burlington, we came to a place where we knew almost nobody, but it wasn't long until we had made friends here at Twin Lakes and at our church, First Baptist of Burlington. I worked with the small children in Sunday school and Mission Friends. Both of us enjoyed especially working with the international students, first in Winston-Salem and later here at Elon University.

Troy continued declining in health during the next few years and was suffering some cognitive failure.

The hat says, "I'm their leader. Where did they go?" Winston-Salem, NC, circa 1996

Parkinson's can be so cruel and affect any and every muscle in the body. It was hard for him, but he never lost his sense of humor. "If I can't preach I can at least make people laugh." And he did. He came up with some doozies. I never knew what he might say. But folks just laughed. And he loved to tell stories and our new friends in Burlington loved to listen to them. As I said later, those stories were not exactly true, but they were good stories and that was what counted.

He was active to the last. He died in February 2007 after a fall due to his Parkinson's. The day he fell, we had been to church for a senior luncheon and then he walked to the mailbox, turned around and his feet got tangled up. The fall caused a massive bleed in his cranial cavity. He died peacefully and the three children and I were with him most of the time the last week.

A Pilgrim at Tinker Creek
– by Annie Dillard

"To experience the present purely is being emptied and hollow; you catch grace as one fills a cup under a waterfall."

After Troy died, I went to Rochester by train. That was an adventure. I stopped in Washington, D.C. first to visit Steve and Amelia, then on to Philadelphia to spend some time with Meg who was a student at Swarthmore College, then to Harrisburg, PA to visit the Tegenes, our friends from Winston-Salem. That was memorable for me as we worshiped at their Orthodox church. Very meaningful! Then I traveled on to New York City to visit our good friend Ursula and her husband. She had been a student at Wake Forest when we were in Winston-Salem. I went on to Rochester to be met by Debbie. Between New York City and Rochester the train rode right along beside the Hudson River. It was wintertime so it was not particularly beautiful, but very interesting. And of course, the other people on the train were entertaining to talk with and study. Another really special thing I did while with the Reynolds': I went to see Niagara Falls for the second time. Troy and Steve and I had gone there before in 1954.

Maple Crunch Cake

Grease loaf pan or angel food cake pan

Mix well these 5 ingredients: 1 c. flour, 3/8 c. sugar (1/4c. +2 T), 3/8 c. brown sugar, 3/8 c. brown sugar, ½ t. salt, 1 ½ t. baking powder.

Make a well in the center and add in order: ¼ c. oil, 3 unbeaten egg yolks, 3/8 c. water, 1 t. maple flavoring.

Beat till smooth.

Combine ½ c. egg white in bowl with 1 t. cream of tartar, beat till stiff. Fold in 1/2 c. chopped pecans or other nuts.

Bake for 50-55 min at 325 degrees F.

Browned Butter Icing

¼ c. butter on low heat till golden brown

Add: 1 c. sifted powdered sugar, 2 T. cream (evaporated milk will do), 1 t. oil, 1 ½ t. vanilla, 1 T. hot water

Mix until cool. Spread on cool cake.

I suppose I could close this with my 80th birthday celebration. I turned eighty on August 8, 2008, which we thought was pretty magical. So we planned to all get together at my church's house at Ridgecrest in Black Mountain, NC. There was plenty of room for everybody and different things to do for all of our varied interests. We had a grand time. Meg and Katie took over the baking of my favorite cake, Maple Crunch Cake, which is so delicious. We told stories and played games and did puzzles. But I had told Becky once that one thing I had never done that would be on my bucket list, if I had a bucket list, was to go skinny-dipping. I had never been skinny-dipping and thought I might have missed out on something really cool. Sooooo, Becky talks with a friend up there in the mountains, not far from Ridgecrest, who said there was a perfect place for skinny-dipping up beyond her small hotel and that we could use that. So, we girls, me, Amelia, Becky, Debbie, Meg and Katie all went skinny-dipping. The two younger girls opted out. It was a very nice spot, very secluded—or so we thought—a small pond near an old home place. We could see the old chimney still standing there. So we went in and my only problem was that I could have used some of those rubberized shoes. The bottom of that pond was all very soft mud and rocks.

Retirement

Then we lay on the bank in our altogether and dried like turtles in the sun. Lovely! Then we decided since it was girls day, we would get dressed and find some place cool to eat lunch, which we did. Just as we walked away, a couple of fellows came from the other direction with their dogs, looking for a drink. How long they had been in the neighborhood we didn't even talk about; didn't want to know. We found a great place for lunch in Asheville and went back to the cottage. Not too many complaints when we got home. We were asked, "Where have you been? What did you do?" No comment.

Left to right: Amelia & Steve Bennett & "Evie" Evaline Noah Alexandria, VA, 2014

About this time I started writing this book and now I am going to stop.

– Love you all, Gram

Her Name is Tad

"Oh, that's a pretty dog. Is that a wiener dog?"
"Yes, some people call them that, but they're really called dachshunds."
"Can my little girl pet her?"
"Oh yes, she's very friendly."
"What's her name?"
"Her name is Tad. You know, just a little bit of a thing."
"Is she a boy or a girl?"
"She is a female."

Many times I would meet people and they would ask me these questions and many more. Here at Twin Lakes Community, people sometimes asked if they had seen me around. "Well," I would say, "have you seen the lady walking the little

Tad, our dog from 2002-2014
A really good dog!
Winston-Salem & Burlington, NC

black dachshund? Well, that was me."

We got Tad at the little crossroads town of Bailey, NC. She was the last of the litter. The people had the mother, and Tad looks like her. I asked if I could see the father, but when the owner brought him in, he never put him down on the floor. He was not at all friendly, not pretty and had a really rough coat. The mother was very pretty and had a silky, satiny coat like Tad's. They had kept her in the house with the puppies. Our three granddaughters went with us to pick her out, and all three wanted to hold her riding back to Raleigh.

In the past we had many dachshunds, and they were good little housedogs. They belonged to the whole family and we never really trained them much except for the necessary commands. With this one, I learned after about six weeks that my husband Troy, was purposely not having anything to do with the training. He said she was my dog. I was the only one who really worked with her to teach her to sit and stay. I had a couple of books on dog training I read that gave me some ideas which I tried to use.

Shortly after we got her, we had visitors with small children. She was running around with the children and I thought one of them might get hurt tripping over each other. I was talking and said a strong NO—not to her but in my conversation—and she came to a dead stop. That's when I realized I could really train this dog. I taught her basic commands and how to walk on a leash. But it was six or seven years before I really taught her tricks like sit, roll over, play dead, and more.

I did not teach her to stand on her hind legs because dachshunds can have back trouble.

I did not give her extra treats for tricks, because dachshunds can get too fat. One person said to me one time, "Oh, that's what they are supposed to look like! I've always seen them round." I made trick time her meal time in the evening. She proved to me you can teach an old dog new tricks. I taught her to roll over, to stay, and to wait with a treat right in front of her nose until I said, "Come."

She was a good dog. She never got on my bed because I don't like animals on my bed. When there was a thunderstorm, she would pull her bed over right next to my bed because she was afraid. She really wanted me to get out of bed and go lie down on the couch where I would let her lie down with me. Then she would go back to sleep. Once during a storm, I gave her a homeopathic medicine my daughter had for anxiety. When I gave it to her it did help. She calmed down. So I used it when she was really afraid.

As we got older, we both were having physical problems. Tad was having more accidents. I was now on oxygen full-time and had been for over a year, and with my problems with breathing I couldn't do for her what she needed. She got so she couldn't jump up on the chair or couch, and I couldn't pick her up without getting short of breath. She needed a good walk every day, and I just couldn't provide what she needed. Because of my health, I decided she needed a new home. My daughter, Becky, took her to Raleigh for two to three weeks while we did some searching. We heard about this lady who takes in dachshunds who need a home and we decided that was the perfect place for Tad. She had other dachshunds to play with, she had this woman to love her, and she had a doggie door to go in and out easily to a fenced-in backyard; she even had a ramp to go up and down to the yard without having to climb steps.

A few months later, we heard from this lady that Tad was sick. When she took her to the vet, they found that she had a large mass on her bladder and liver. So we determined the merciful thing to do was to have her put to sleep. She was cremated and her ashes will be distributed with mine when my time comes.

Conclusion

I have come to see living in Bangladesh, in Africa, and in Lebanon where we got to know refugees torn from their homelands and often their families as well, as a very special blessing.

When I read my Bible and see how Jesus loves the marginalized people; those who are poor and needy, those who are so very aware of their need of God's help whether it comes from an aid agency, a government, or a mission, my mind is flooded with images of faces. I can see men, women and children; on the streets, on the ferries, on the ferry ghats, working in the fields and in their homes to make the little they have stretch to feed all in the house. I learned that people don't starve because they do not have any food, but the food they can get is not the right kind and not enough – not nutritious, many times not fresh, too often what others throw away. So why do I see living there as a blessing? Because I have had the opportunity and privilege of doing a little bit to help these people, and it was just a little bit. And I have also learned from them that nice houses and fine cars, all this stuff, is not necessary to have a happy and rich life and loving family, to serve God.

I hope God in my life doesn't sound presumptuous. It is not intended that way at all. As I read the New Testament, my understanding is that God is in the lives of all of us who believe in him and are earnestly trying to follow the Way of Jesus. And that's me and that's many of you as well. I remember coming home for furlough and then finally for retirement thinking and saying, "If it were not for all of you who have given, and prayed and supported us all these years, we could never have done what we believed God had called us to do." Truly those who hold the ropes are absolutely as essential as those who go out to serve. God needs each of us, doing different work and in different places. I am simply sharing the glory of my life, supported by you. I love to hear your stories also; you may think them uneventful, but you have also known many funny, wonderful, strange people and experiences in your life. I often remember the words of Psalm 115:1

> "Not to us, O Lord, not to us, but to your name be the glory
> For your great love and faithfulness."

Since I gave my life to Him those many years ago, He has never failed to guide me, comfort me, strengthen me, and console me. He knows that I have tried to live my life each day following Him. Of course I have not always succeeded, but He is, if anything, patient and has continued to work in me through others and through my quiet times with Him, through reading His

Conclusion

Word and singing His praises. I can honestly say that I am the richest person I know in everything that is important as I understand it. But of course I don't know all of your stories yet!

We all were tiny babies at one time. But as we grew we needed more space and we found that there was more space, more wonders, more fascinating people, many more interesting sights and foods and smells and music. There was so much more that we were challenged to open our hearts and minds, to embrace and make part of our own lives. Yes, sometimes it is a bit scary and some people may think we are foolish, but we make the choice and we have the fun and the adventure! I made my choice to go where I believed God was leading me. Now it's your turn. Just remember, if you let him, God will be with you. As the Irish say, "God before you, God behind you, God beside you, God within you."

For many years now, my motto has been, as Oliver Wendell Holmes Sr. so richly states it in *The Chambered Nautilus*:

Build thee more stately mansions, O my soul,

As the swift seasons roll!

Leave thy low-vaulted past!

Let each new temple, nobler than the last,

Shut thee from heaven with a dome more vast,

Till thou at length art free,

Leaving thine outgrown shell by life's unresting sea!

Mother's Story

Leona Mary Edwards Trippeer,

    daughter of Gertrude Gaeb Edwards,

        daughter of Paulina Moore Gaeb,

            daughter-in-law of Anna Kreuer Gaeb

My mother, Leona Mary Edwards, was born March 17, 1901 in Chagrin Falls, Cuyahoga County, Ohio. She was the oldest of the four daughters of William Arthur (Art) Edwards and Gertrude Gaeb Edwards. Art had been born and reared in Chagrin Falls, the youngest of the three children of William and Ann Jones Edwards. His older brother Henry was the firstborn and Ida Ann, the second. It seems to me important to go back to this generation to have a more complete picture of my mother's life.

In his obituary, William Edwards is described as an industrious and successful citizen of Chagrin Falls. His business was digging cellars, etc. and because he did good work, he prospered. But also, quoting his obituary, "He had no patience with pretense. In his nature there was no compromise. In him there were but two paths, the right and the wrong. With all the sweet influences of nature, we loved our friend forever." I'm not sure what this last sentence is supposed to mean, but evidently his work was always well done and he was respected for his honesty and integrity. He must have been hard to live with at times, especially for a son who may not have been of the same type.

William was born in Shropshire, England in December 1837. He came to America at the age of 35, and stayed two years before returning home to marry Ann Jones at the St. Nicholas Church in Liverpool, and bringing her back to Ohio. They settled in Chagrin Falls where it is said there were a considerable number of British immigrants, especially from the Shropshire and Devonshire areas. This community surely made the adjustment for the newlyweds much easier.

Ann Jones, born September 11, 1845 at Shropshire, was the daughter of Thomas Jones. In her picture, she appears to be a woman of good health, smiling easily and with a pleasant face. According to her obituary, she was known as, "A most kind and devoted mother. She was generous-hearted, quiet in disposition, and it has been said by those who have known her for years, that they never heard her say a harsh word against anyone." Interestingly, my father many years later made the same assessment of my mother. What a wonderful legacy to leave!

Mother's Story

William Edwards was able to buy a plot of land (1.64 acres) on the corner of Bentleyville Road and Orange Street, which for a time was known as Edwards Hill. There he built three houses, one for himself and Ann, one in which Art lived with his family and one for Ida Ann and her husband, Harry Frost. Henry, the oldest son, was to live in the house his parents had used, but he never did. Subsequently, Art and his family moved to another house in Chagrin Falls on Cottage Street. Later, Art's second daughter Marian and her husband Obe Hawkins and son Danny lived in the corner house on Bentleyville Road until they died. Art and his daughter Gladys lived in their Cottage Street house until they died.

I like to think of Mother as a girl with her three sisters, Marian, Gladys and Dorothy, living so near to this paternal grandmother who was of such a kind and gentle nature. Their grandmother lived until 1920, which would have been when my mother was 19 years old. William died in 1910. It surely had a positive impact on the girls to have a loving and generous grandmother living nearby.

Very little is known about Gertrude Gaeb, my maternal grandmother, except that her father came from Niederheckenbach, Rheinland, Prussia to Ohio and married her mother, Paulina Moore on June 28, 1881. They had at least four children: Gertrude, Joseph, Kathryn, and John. Gertrude was born in June 1882 in Avon, Ohio. She married Art Edwards about 1900 in Chagrin Falls, Ohio and died May 21, 1918. Quoting from her obituary: "Another family has suffered irreparable loss in the death of a young mother and loving wife when Mrs. A.W. Edwards passed away at her home on Orange Road at 2:30 am Sunday after a week's illness. Inflammation of the brain is given as the cause of demise. She had been sick but one week. A particularly sad feature is the fact that four children, all girls, are left motherless...She was 36 years of age. The daughters are Leona, Marian, Dorothy and Gladys...Funeral service was conducted by U.R. Bell and the Lady Maccabees of which Mrs. Edwards was a member."

Mother told us children that her mother died of spinal meningitis, and evidently it was something of that nature. While her mother was sick, they had to move her bed into the kitchen to keep her warm. After her death, it was necessary to burn all of her clothing and the bedclothes to prevent spread of the infection. At this time Leona was 17 years old; Marian, 15; Gladys, 10; and Dorothy, 8.

My Mother cared for her mother and then for the younger three children after her mother's death. In order to do so she had to drop out of high school. This must have been very hard for her as she was a very active teenager. She did graduate two years later in 1920, listed as:

Nickname "Leon"

Commercial Course

Girls Glee Club, '17,'18, '19,'20

Basketball, '17,'19,'20

Orchestra, '17, '18, '19, '20. She played the harp.

Also graduating that year was her younger sister, Marian.

Mother (on left) with her sister Marian Hawkins in later years
Chagrin Falls, OH, circa 1940

I suppose this is the place to tell a bit more about the sisters. Mother's sister Marian, with whom she was understandably very close, married Obe Hawkins and remained in Chagrin Falls all her life. Obe was a toolmaker; they had one son, Danny. Gladys, the third daughter of Art and Gertrude, loved horses. I remember seeing her right before we left Ohio, and at that time she was wearing men's pants, which was unusual for that time, but would have been more suitable for the work she did. The youngest sister, Dorothy, married Dave Hall and also stayed in the area. They had four children, some of whom have been contacted for this information by my brother Bill.

After finishing high school, Leona also attended Kent Normal School in the summers, while teaching during the winter. I understand that Normal Schools were for teacher training. I remember her telling me some interesting anecdotes about this teaching experience. It seems that she was teaching in a school mostly made up of Italian immigrants and several young male

Mother attended Kent State Normal School, now Kent State University Kent, OH, circa 1922

students were larger than she. Evidently they could be quite intimidating and if she had not developed her ability to control young people with her manner and presence before this time, she surely would have needed to in this situation. She had to exert her authority often. She also told how they drank vinegar instead of water, and that the children would sew one dress or shirt on top of another as the weather got colder and then reverse the procedure in the spring. Evidently the school facilities were very primitive and children of all ages were together. Quite a challenge!

Leona's return to her own education and vocation was made possible because of one special woman, her Aunt Ida, Art's sister. Ida and her husband, Harry Frost did not have any children; she tried to adopt a girl who lived with her, Marie Simmons, but Marie's mother would not sign the papers. Marie did continue to live with the Frosts and took Frost as her surname. The Frosts later divorced but Marie stayed with Ida throughout her youth.

What would Leona and the other girls have done without Aunt Ida? Leona was able to cook and care for the house but there are so many things a girl of 17 doesn't know yet, especially about rearing other girls quite close to her in age. Here we have to deal with the inadequacies of Art. It seems that his interest was in gardening and harness racing. According to the records, if he ever got a job he didn't stay with it long. And he had no interest, or at least inclination, to have much contact with the girls. I suppose this wasn't too unusual in the days when men did the outside work and women were expected to handle home and family. However, in this case, the girls needed help. And their guardian angel was there in the person of Aunt Ida.

After a couple of years, Art was able to hire a live-in housekeeper Mae Ferrell. What a relief that must have been for the girls and Aunt Ida! Within two more years, in 1921, Art married Mae and they began their own family. This arrangement, plus the help of Aunt Ida, made it possible for Mother to go to work teaching and to get teacher training in the summers. I suppose it also brought some income into the house!

However, the story of Art and Mae is not a happy one either. She bore two children William Robert "Billy" and Ida Ann, both born in 1922; Billy in January and Ida Ann in December. By this time the four girls of Gertrude were from 12 to 21 years of age. This was quite a load for Mae who succumbed to tuberculosis or some form of consumption. She was taken to a sanitarium and was there most of the time until 1928 when she returned home. However, in the next two years she had two more children and again had to return to the sanitarium and stayed there until her death in 1934. Thus Aunt Ida was almost exclusively mother to the four younger children.

In reading about Chagrin Falls, I find that there was a special emphasis put on educational opportunities from the earliest days. Also, Chagrin Falls was the educational center for that area with many children coming from other towns for their high school education. By the time Mother would have been in high school, they had a new building very adequate for that day, with many opportunities including the Commercial Course, which she took. I find this very interesting since I never knew her to mention having any knowledge of commercial subjects or interest in them. She did work in a department store as department manager for several years while I was in elementary and junior high school. Also, she had taught in a kindergarten when her younger children were at that level.

The original land for the first settlement for Chagrin Falls was bought by Noah Graves and his friend Seth Henderson for a total of $4100 for 420 acres near the Falls. The people of Chagrin Falls from very early in their history showed a concern for the ecology of the area. The town is located on the Chagrin River and there was great concern about the pollution that threatened to kill the fish in the river. One of the first industries to be started was the milling of bags for commercial products. The town is named for the Falls which are located on the Chagrin River. There is some disagreement about where the name Chagrin came from, but it seems to be either from an early explorer and settler or from one of the Iroquois Indian words. Leona and her friends could easily have found shards and other reminders of the Iroquois presence in this area in the past. In the mid-1800s there was a huge flock of pigeons that flew over and was talked about for long afterward.

About 1900, horse racing was introduced to the area. A racing ring was built in the town with stables, wooden grandstands, and an exhibit hall. The instigators used some very exciting publicity to attract the many tourists who usually came from Cleveland to enjoy a day at the Falls. This seems to have been actual horse racing and also harness racing. This of course was what appealed to Art Edwards who was a harness racing jockey. The more conservative citizens were greatly concerned that this would encourage drinking and gambling. When after a few years this proved to be true, the racing was stopped. But while it lasted, it was big and much publicized, as shown in the history of Chagrin Falls.

Also about 1900, a bicycle craze started and many men and boys were seen on their cycles. However, one young lady is quoted as saying, "I am having cycle fever but dread the gaze and comments which the first woman rider will have." Since Mother was very athletic, it is entirely possible she took her turn a few years later, although I doubt they would have had money to buy one.

I find it intriguing to try and understand Grandpa Edwards (Art). I must say that I never heard Mother say anything negative about him, but then she didn't about anyone. But why was he not able and willing to work and support his family? He evidently did have a good garden and that's something, though the girls probably did a share of that work too. Mother later showed she knew how to garden well in her victory garden during World War II.

I can't help but wonder what Art's childhood was like. With a father like William Edwards; strong, successful, industrious, virtuous, rigid, and uncompromising and a mother like Ann Jones Edwards who was loving, quiet and generous, what sort of home would that be? She was also several years younger than he. Was Art a sensitive child—frightened of his father and perhaps for that reason spoiled by his mother? Did he see himself as not able to measure up to his father's expectations, and therefore didn't try? The history shows that harness racing was the thing in Chagrin Falls about that time, and it would have been exciting and something he could do for he was rather small. I wonder if his father was a big impressive man. And what was his brother Henry like? Just like his father maybe? Or did he also not measure up and so disappeared from the scene when he was old enough? It is interesting that Art stayed right in Chagrin Falls all of his life. I wonder if one reason Aunt Ida helped out was because she understood Art and realized he couldn't or wouldn't do any better. The grandparents were gone by 1920 and she was the only family there.

I can remember Mother talking about Aunt Ida since she didn't call her Aunt Ida Ann. I wish I could remember the things she said, but from what I now know, Aunt Ida was the mother to all of the children and so she was the one to teach the girls how to cook and clean, how to dress and behave with nice manners. She must have encouraged them to think big because Mother certainly took on many challenges as a teenager in high school, even with the responsibilities at home. I think Ida must have had a heart something like her mother, Ann Jones Edwards, "who never said a harsh word about anyone." When I think how those two women must have grieved and worried about Art and his neglect of his family, and about Gertrude who even in earlier pictures doesn't look very healthy, I can see the beginnings of my Mother's courage and her calmness in the face of adversity and financial stress. Where would they be without Aunt Ida? I think it's hard to exaggerate her importance in the rearing and training of this family. Art never did develop a sense of responsibility toward the children and the younger children especially have nothing good to say about him. We don't know enough about Gertrude to know what traits she may have instilled in her girls, but we do know something about Mother's paternal grandmother who lived next door for at least a few years and we know what Aunt Ida did. And what she did tells us much of who she was. In her obituary we find: "Although she was actually their aunt, Mrs. Frost reared and was mother to...Marie and the children of Art and Mae...and grandmother to their 12 children." I realize now that one reason Mother made her trips back to Chagrin Falls from Roanoke, Virginia when we couldn't all go was to see Aunt Ida who was living in a convalescent home until she died in 1957 at 79 years of age. I wish I could have known her!

It is interesting that the second child of Art and Mae, Ida Ann, is not listed as one of Aunt Ida's children in the genealogy that Bill later did. She is listed as their child, her marriages are recorded, and after her second marriage ended in divorce, she moved to Chagrin Falls to live with Grandpa Edwards and Gladys in the house at 35 Cottage Street. She stayed after their deaths until 1991 when the house was sold. Mother used to often mention Billy Edwards, Art's only son, and Ida Ann as well as Aunt Ida. I would like to know more of Ida Ann's story!

So Mother's mother died in May 1918, but 1918 was also the year remembered by the old folks as the year of the Flu Epidemic. Evidently it was terrible and many young adults were taken by it. Once when I was a teenager and regretting what I considered my excess weight, Mother expressed strong feeling against any kind of dieting. She said at the time of the Flu Epidemic many young women were trying to be very thin, and thus did not have the resistance to fight off the flu and died as a result.

Of course 1918 was also the year that World War I was over and the boys finally came back. Chagrin

Mother's Story

Falls had a spontaneous celebration with a parade and flags. The cannon was pulled to the top of Grove Hill and fired. Speeches were made in Triangle Park in the center of town and Kaiser Wilhelm's effigy was burnt publicly. During the war there had been much anti-German feeling, which would not have been easy for those of German descent.

We can imagine the joy and relief of parents and other family members when the war ended, as well as the young women who had been through some lean years. The town itself had grown during the war, new stores had been opened and progress had been made in the town's economy. Chagrin Falls was being recognized more and more as the center for Cuyahoga and Geauga counties. One touch was recognized as needed to dress up the town and that was to pave the streets and sidewalks. So far they had only stone sidewalks and boards stretched across dirt roads for crossing. Sometimes those boards tilted with disastrous results.

A.G. Trippeer was one of the answers to this challenge. He had a paving company and had moved with his family from Peru, Indiana in 1919. Now this might be only a footnote in our Chagrin Falls history except for the oldest son of the Trippeers. Ben Trippeer, like so many other young men, had just returned from France, luckily with no serious injuries. He was working with his father and getting to know the new home community. I don't know how long it took him to find Leona, but find her he did!

When I once asked her where they met, she said it

was out on a country road. Now I can picture Leona and a friend sloshing along on a muddy road coming back from their teaching duties at school, and along came young Ben with a friend or two in a car. As gallant young men do, they offered them a ride. The girls accepted and that was the beginning of the story. The rest is history! Being the son of a strong mother, he may have recognized the value of Leona's strong character and sense of humor. She also had an uncanny ability of meeting people and eliciting a friendly response; people respected her.

I can imagine she was quite taken with him for he was a charmer, good looking with a ready smile and a very cheerful disposition. He had some fun stories to tell from his war days and I'm sure those held her rapt attention. He also was something of a rebel and was not beyond doing some cutting up with his friends. His upbringing had been very strict since his mother at least had come from a very religious home. Daddy said the most exciting thing they were ever allowed to do on Sundays was play croquet. After the war, Daddy came home with a new freedom from those restraints; I expect this was true of the society in general.

During this time Leona was busy with her own responsibilities, teaching at Mayfield School and also attending Kent Normal School. In the Chagrin Falls Exponent of December 22, 1921 there is a note that Miss Leona Edwards entertained her Sunday school class in the parlors of the Congregational Church. I expect Ben and Leona took advantage of the various opportunities for fun and courting: the new movie theater, making maple sugar in the winter, ice skating and sledding, the roller skating rink, the circus when it came to town, walking the lanes and across the Stone Bridge which now allowed two lanes of traffic. And if they needed to know what time it was, they could see the clock in the steeple of the First Congregational Church.

Leona after she met Ben
Chagrin Falls, OH, circa 1922

We do not know the date of the auspicious meeting between Leona and Ben but they married March 18, 1923 at the home of the Trippeers. It was a small, quiet wedding. Her father Art was not there. "Both are highly esteemed young people and have the best wishes of their many friends," quoting the *Exponent*.

One thing I find amusing and intriguing is that I have recently learned that the newly married couple lived with his parents in a basement apartment for 14 months until they were able to find their own place. That could not have been easy for anyone. I'm not sure that Granny Trippeer approved of their marriage but she knew her son and he was just back from the war. Also during this time the first child Ben was born at the end of October 1923. John, Dad's younger brother, was still at home and not long ago said simply, "I never could figure out why Ben and Leona stayed at the parent's house so long." Now this was an old man reminiscing, and that was all he would say. Hmmm. A few months later Daddy was able to buy a house to which they moved to in July before Mary Jean was born in November 1924.

At birth Mary Jean had a brain tumor between her eyes just at the top of her nose. Ben and Leona were warned to be cautious that she did not bump this exposed area which appeared to be a large swelling in which Mother said you could see each beat of her heart. Because of this, Mary Jean learned from the beginning to scream for what she wanted and she got it. This condition of course required surgery so they were sent to famous brain surgeon, Dr. Danny, at Johns Hopkins Hospital in Baltimore. How very frightening it must have been for the two young parents! She was in the hospital two months; Mother stayed with her all the time and Daddy came for the surgery and for two weeks after, and later for one week and to bring them home on the train. As Bill commented in his genealogy, "She recovered rapidly, probably faster than the parents!" It must be remembered that Mother was also pregnant with Bob. Following the surgery, which many children did not even survive, Mary Jean's incision healed quickly but surely this whole experience was very traumatic for the young Mary Jean and left its mark on her life.

After Mother's return to Chagrin Falls, Bob was born in September of that same year. Bill was born in

August 1927. And then, of course, Marjorie in August 1928. Now return to "Early Life, Ohio" for the rest of the story!

Written by Marjorie Ann Trippeer Bennett, daughter of Leona Mary Edwards Trippeer, granddaughter of Gertrude Gaeb Edwards, great granddaughter of Paulina Moore Gaeb and Ann Jones Edwards.

I am deeply indebted to my brother Bill (William Mowbray Trippeer) for his extensive work on the genealogy of our family. Also I am very grateful to Mrs. Meriel Wilkinson for the Chagrin Falls History published by the Chagrin Falls Historical Society, 2005.

Daddy's Story

I remember my Daddy telling this story when I was just a kid. I'm sure he liked to tell it partly because it is a great story of courage and endurance, but also because my Dad was named after his grandfather Benjamin Trippeer, the hero. He had grown up working the farm in Indiana with his father and other family members, wresting a living out of forested land. It was a real pioneer existence. They lived in a log cabin and the other outbuildings were all of the same. But as Benjamin grew up he and his brothers saw many improvements in farming machinery and more modern buildings.

Later, after his marriage to Lucy Lynn, he settled in town and began a lime business. He went into construction and had a threshing machine to be rented out across the county. All in all, he became a successful businessman and influential in Miami County, so named because of the Indian tribe who had occupied it earlier. Unfortunately, Lucy died after 19 years of marriage and giving birth to 7 or so children, the last two of whom died in infancy. Fourteen years later Benjamin married Rachel Townsend Rader, a widow lady. Benjamin lived with his second wife Rachel in the house he had built on River Street in Peru, Miami County, Indiana.

Now the story I have to tell took place in March 1913 when my Dad, his namesake, was 14 years old. The Wabash River ran right through the town of Peru and from the name of the street, the Trippeers lived right next to the river. The weather was still cold when the rain began and it rained and it rained and it rained. And of course, the river began to rise. First it breached its banks and then began creeping up the hill toward the house. Benjamin and Rachel were busily toting the most valuable things they had to the upstairs just hoping the house would stand. They had some nice furniture they had managed to buy, but some of it was just too big and heavy to move. They took pictures off the walls, the family Bible from the top of the bookcase where it always stayed, and some of Rachel's favorite dishes. But the water was coming up the steps and into the house now. They could hear the shouts of neighbors calling for help, cows bawling, dogs barking. And still it rained like it would never stop.

Rachel began to shiver and shake. She had been sick with consumption for the past few weeks and still had a hacking cough. She pulled her shawl closer around her and began to murmur, "Please God, please God...." She thought of the children and grandchildren. What was happening to them? Finally she said to Benjamin, "We need to go upstairs. It's coming in." They could see other houses and outbuildings floating by like toy boats little children played with. The river was full of debris from houses upstream from them. Would their house withstand this torrent?

She wondered, what could Benjamin do? He had always been so resourceful to get them and others out of trouble, like the little boy who was almost drowned in the river and the little girl who fell into a well. He had saved them both, but he was no match for the river when it was like this, like a vicious animal just eating its way over the land.

Finally, Benjamin seemed to break free from a trance of thinking that this could not be happening to this good strong house, and now saw that it was happening and they needed to act and act fast. Quickly, he helped Rachel up the stairs and through the bedroom to the window that opened out onto the front porch roof. Rachel grabbed a couple of quilts off the beds as they passed through and followed him. It made her heart ache to see the bedrooms all nicely made up. What would happen to all this?

Climbing through the window with her long wet skirts wasn't so easy but he helped her and soon they were hunched up against the outside wall of the house and looking for a rescue boat. But they saw no one, and eventually Ben decided they should climb into the big tree right beside the house and tie themselves in which they did. Along about evening time, at last there came a boat being steered by one of their neighbors. He stopped and they could see the boat was already crowded, but Benjamin insisted they had to find room for Rachel and get her to some place warm. He would wait for the next boat.

"Now Benjamin, that may not be 'til mornin, you know, it's getting dark now."

"Well, I'll hope for the best. Y'all get goin," he said as he checked Rachel to be sure she was tucked in real good with the quilt.

And then began his long vigil, through the night, still raining, cold even with the quilt, and hungry. He hadn't eaten in hours. Benjamin began to talk with God about this predicament. "You know, Lord, we've been in some terrible messes before, but I do believe this is the worst one yet. And I just might be gettin' a mite too old for this sort of thing. I do hope you'll watch out for Rachel. That cough sounded really bad. You've been mighty good to me all these years, two good wives, seven good children and now those fine grandchildren. I've had good health and friends. Naw, if I was to go tonight I couldn't complain, for life has been mighty good to me." And he dozed off to sleep, not good sleep but little

My dad, Ben, (on the left) with two other boys
Indiana, circa 1914

catnaps that helped.

And then came morning and with it came the sun and no more rain! Made Benjamin want to stand up and shout, "Hallelujah!" And it wasn't too long until another boat came along, bringing hot coffee to boot. He rather carefully untied himself and climbed into the boat, stretched his legs and his back and neck and declared it was a good day to be alive. Then he had some hot coffee!

There is a bit more to this story because Benjamin made the headlines: "70-year-old man endures night in the tree," and he was the pride of Peru and the hero of the Wabash River flood. And of course, young Ben Trippeer was the proudest one of all for that was HIS granddad.

The Wabash River flood
Indiana/Illinois, March, 1913

Nancy's Story

What is it like to be the youngest of 10 children, and all so close together, the oldest just 11 years old when you were born?

Nancy Lynn Trippeer was born in Willoughby, Ohio on January 26, 1934. She was the last of 10 children of Benjamin and Leona Trippeer. She started life the hard way. Oh, her birth was simple enough I think. This is relatively speaking of course, as she was born in a friend's house with maybe a midwife; I don't know. She was also rich (or cursed!) with big sisters: Mary Jean, Margie, and Marian. At the time, I was only five years old, but what I do remember clearly is when Nancy was six months old she had pneumonia. My memory is of Mother sitting next to the crib in the living room, holding a bottle of Spirits of Camphor to baby Nancy's tiny nose, never leaving her side for two weeks. Daddy was away at the time so we other children, though young, had to take care of ourselves. Ben, as the oldest, carried a heavy load of responsibility with the help of an older woman who came in. Nancy pulled through but was very tiny for several years, though not sickly.

In 1936, we moved from Willoughby, Ohio to Roanoke, Virginia. Nancy was only two years old when we moved. Being so tiny and with her curly hair, we older kids thought our baby was the prettiest one around. She did take a place in the queen's court in the Mardi Gras parade for the city of Roanoke. She was also by far the smallest of the girls in the doll show/parade. Fortunately she did not suffer any long-term problems with her health and actually managed to become very tough and could hold her own with the boys in sports. Thus, sports became the focus of her life and she excelled!

When Carl went into first grade, Mom took a job helping with a home-based preschool and kindergarten. This was great for Jim and Nancy as they were ready for this first step in schooling. Later, they went to Virginia Heights Elementary School. The school commanded a fine view, situated on a hill overlooking the junction of Grandin Road and Virginia Avenue with all of the activity in the neighborhood business district there.

Nancy & Jimmy on the tricycle
Roanoke, VA, circa 1939

Going to Virginia Heights School involved a walk of six long blocks, which we walked twice a day since we went home for lunch. Actually, we enjoyed the walk as other friends were going that way too. There was a cherry tree that we sometimes raided. Once, Nancy broke a branch climbing into the tree and got a good scolding. There were two main shortcuts we took to shorten the walk, one from Virginia Avenue to Northumberland and another from Maiden Lane to Windsor.

One of Nancy's most vivid memories of Virginia Heights was the old enclosed circular fire escape by the Little Building. It was fun to have fire drills. The children on the second floor were marched to a door at the end of the hall which led into the fire escape. Each child was given a burlap sack to sit on to make the sliding go easier. It was very dark in that tube so when one reached the bottom, she burst out into the sunlight of the schoolyard. Great fun!

In our "Trippeer Box of Memories" there is a book Nancy put together at some time about England. She was not an outstanding student but this book she took great care to make nicely. She paid much attention to detail especially about the royal family. Don't know what grade she got for that. When she was young, she was diagnosed as dyslexic, but later said she was not.

From Virginia Heights Elementary we all then went to Woodrow Wilson Junior High School. It was situated on a hill right behind our house. We could almost wait to hear the bell and run up the hill without being late. Right beside Woodrow Wilson was a very large expanse of land that was used for athletic games at the school. At the time we attended, the building was not quite finished. It was shaped like a giant "U" with a space in the center back that had a poured concrete floor. It was a perfect place to practice our tennis serves and returns. It even had a line at about the level of the net. There were also basketball goal posts behind the school, which we used to good advantage.

Nancy had a good friend all of the way through school. This was Virginia Lee Cox. They got into all kinds of mischief together; evidently they sparked each other to devilment. But the interesting thing is that somebody else in our family was also friendly with Virginia Lee, and that was Jimmy. In fact, he was so friendly they finally got married and she has been part of our family now for many, many years and we all love her like a sister. Of course when we got together she and Nancy would remember some of their high jinks and have a good laugh, which sometimes they would tell us about and sometimes they wouldn't.

Nancy was very active in sports when she got to junior high school. She was justifiably proud of the letter she got for most total points scored in sports participation. She was only the second person to earn 1,000 points and that was an achievement! Later at Jefferson Senior High she was elected Best Female Athlete.

Nancy said, "I remember one teacher used a ruler to hit our hands when we made any trouble. I only did that once. Another time Virginia Lee and I kicked a ball over the fence and down the hill into the traffic on Grandin Road, a very busy intersection. Don't remember any punishment for that—they must not have known who did it, and we weren't telling!"

But what was it like being the youngest of all that crowd? "Well, I think I got my own way more, but I was obedient. At school, some of the teachers let me know they expected me to do as well as one or another of the older siblings. Especially Miss Dorothy Payne who taught journalism. She tried to persuade me to work on the paper 'like Margie did.' Well, that was not my interest and I told her so. Actually, I remember her being quite mean to me, but the worst was Miss Cooper. She said I was insolent—I probably was—and sent me to detention in the auditorium. That wasn't too bad because Mr. Harper was in charge and he liked me and questioned, 'Why are you here?' "

When Nancy finished high school in 1952 she was asked to play on a softball team in Washington, D.C. for the summer. The deal was that she would be a park worker during the day and then play ball at night. Then they would travel on weekends to play. It was quite a liberating experience for her and she enjoyed it immensely. She remembered the long walks to the park from the boarding house where she stayed. There was a bus strike on, so no help there, but she did ride the streetcar some. Washington, D.C. was a very different place from Roanoke, VA.

Around that time, Dad, Mom and Nancy moved into an apartment in Harrisonburg, VA because Dad's business—selling Diversey chemical products for the food industry—was growing and he wanted to concentrate in the Harrisonburg area where there are a lot of chicken farms. This was an interesting flashback to his past, for at one time his father had tried to breed and raise chickens and Daddy had learned something about that work. At this point, he talked about retiring with a small poultry business. Nancy enrolled at Madison College as a day student.

After Daddy died, Nancy came back to Roanoke and took a job at Shenandoah Life Insurance Company. I suppose she enjoyed it well enough since she was a very sociable person, but I'm sure office work was not her first choice. She worked there several years but tired "of punching keys and all the noise." This had been her first introduction to computers.

Then Nancy went to work with the Baptist Children's Home in Salem, VA. At first she was a housemother in a boy's cottage, but later was moved to a special cottage which had been built for junior and senior students getting ready to finish high school and go out into the work world. These were teenagers in the orphanage system that needed to learn skills for living independently, shopping, laundry, cooking, and such. They lived in a house together instead of at home or on campus. Nancy was uniquely fitted for this because she kept up with all of the sports news and knew as much, if not more, than the teenagers did about their teams. Also, she made them do their chores and wouldn't let them get away with anything they shouldn't be doing. This was challenging as some of these students had an attitude, but Nancy could handle that. She could be quite fierce at times and she expected obedience. It was called the Step Away program; she worked with another woman on a three-day rotation schedule. One young fellow did give her such a hard time that they finally moved him to another cottage, but after that he came to visit Nancy every week just to see if she was doing okay. Obviously something got through to him. She also mentioned two boys from Africa who had been sent to relatives here in the US. She said they were well-behaved, smart and spoke English very well. She worked with the Home for 17 years and it was good for her and for at least some of those young people.

About this time she had a boyfriend named Billy, quite a serious boyfriend. When asked about him, she simply said, "Yeah, sometimes I wonder what happened to him. What might have been." She said he told her she would never marry as long as Mom was alive, so I asked her if that were true. After thinking a few minutes, she said, "Well, I didn't want Mom to be alone." Mom and Nancy lived together for 13 years and became very close. They had so many mutual interests, the family, sports, etc. Both of them worked and so had their own interests as well.

Nancy sold the house after Mom died in 1968 and used some of the money to go to Hawaii with a couple of her friends. Then she rented an apartment, but she was not made to live alone. As she said herself, she had a couple of bad years then. The other family members could see she needed help. Fortunately Carl and Rita offered her the attic of their house, which they had finished off for their girls; she accepted and that was her home until she died.

Actually, when Carl died quite suddenly, Nancy came back from Myrtle Beach where she had gone that summer to work for her friend who had a small hotel. I asked her what she would do now, and she answered without hesitation, "Well, I'll stay with Rita, of course." She didn't want her to live alone either. And she wouldn't have wanted to live alone herself. She had many health issues, which increasingly limited her ability to function. She always loved the grandchildren and great-grandchildren but was closer to Carl and Rita's and especially Cassie, one of Carl and Rita's grandchildren. She died on October 28, 2010. The day we knew she would die, Marion and I were there with Rita, Virginia Lee, a number of Nancy's nieces and her grandniece, Cassie. We gathered to be with her – singing old hymns and sharing memories.

Nancy as an adult
Roanoke, VA, circa 1955

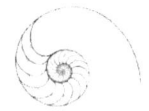

Lou's Memories

Some of the best memories that Lou, my brother Bill's wife, shared with me were about Nancy. Seems they had some experiences with her that none of the rest of us had. When Nancy was in high school, she went to Texas to spend two weeks with Bill, Lou, and the two children. However, while she was there, she complained of a severe belly ache, which was determined to be appendicitis. Her response was to try to get the next plane back to Roanoke, but the doctor nixed that. So then she suggested she should get on the train for Roanoke. I don't know how that was to help as it would take longer. The doctor said, "Okay, but they'll be taking you off somewhere in central Louisiana to bury you. So...."

"Lou" Dameron Trippeer

She had the surgery and got along fine, but of course had to stay on for several weeks to let the incision heal. Lou said at one point she noticed Nancy ducking into the bathroom about every hour. Finally she called through the door, "Okay, Nancy, what's going on?" To which Nancy replied, "Well, I may as well tell you since you have run out of Band-Aids." It seems her incision had come open and she was trying to repair the damage with Band-Aids! Of course that entailed another trip to the emergency room and a little longer at Bill and Lou's house.

Evidently she didn't wear out her welcome, for a year or two later they invited her to go with them on a camping trip out West. Lou said she was great for entertaining the kids. But she ended up entertaining other folks too.

When they got to the Grand Canyon and were approaching the drop-off, Nancy began to protest that she was terrified of heights. Evidently she was quite vocal and ended up giving all the onlookers a good laugh. But she would not go down that trail once she realized that if they passed a mule or donkey train, the beasts get the inside track, that is, the safer side. I wonder if they left her there and went on their own adventure.

Later, they were in Yellowstone National Park and were preparing to ride horses to some distant point across a very large meadow. Then it was made known with loud protestations that she had never ridden a horse either. And evidently she wasn't ready to ride one then. One of the grooms, seeing a chance for good sport, encouraged her mount to rear up and put on a show. That did it.

Finally when everyone had mounted, Nancy was still standing on her two feet. They had one more horse, very old and swaybacked. They attached this horse with a long rope to the guide's horse so it wouldn't go wandering off—with Nancy on it of course.

Seems Bill had never ridden a horse either, and when his horse thought a shortcut across the meadow to the barn was a good idea, it went and took Bill with it. Bill tried valiantly, "Whoa, horse!" but to no avail. It was quite a sight since Bill's feet had come out of the stirrups and he went flying across the meadow with his legs flopping as he went. I expect he and Nancy both were glad to get down on good solid earth again.

On that road trip, the family and Nancy went all the way to California and to Disneyland. Bill and Lou have two children: Ann and Bob, and three grandsons: Andy, Michael and Richard. Lou said Nancy was really great with the boys because she knew so much about sports and understood their interests.

Another memory of Lou's was when their son Bob was born; Ann came down with a 105-degree fever and had to be in the hospital and needed one adult with her. Lou brought Bob home at three days old. When Ann's fever broke after six days, she came home but was still very weak, so Bill called Mom to come and help. She arrived by plane dressed in wool because Virginia was cold, but Texas was hot. Anyway, Ann took a dislike to Grandma and started eating paper, wallpaper off the wall, covers of magazines, etc. What to do? Grandma would have to leave. It was a very strange and sad situation for everyone. But as Lou says now, it was understandable from Ann's perspective: there was a new baby in the house, she had been very sick and had to go to hospital, and then she came home to this new person telling her what to do. Also, Bob couldn't drink milk, so they had all that to deal with until they got him on soy formula.

It was interesting to hear from Lou about the strong bond between their grandson Michael and our Aunt Mary Lynn. I'm sure she told me, and I don't remember how this got started, but it was very special to Aunt Mary Lynn, our father's sister. Bill and Lou had many opportunities to know Mary Lynn. They had lived in Massachusetts and been with Mary Lynn and her family when their boys were still at home. But later when Bill and Lou lived in Lakeland, FL, Mary Lynn was in the Carpenters Retirement Community there. They lived close to her and took good advantage of the opportunity to be family to her. It was really great to hear stories of the early life of the Trippeer family. Daddy was oldest, Mary Lynn next and then Dick, Dorothy, and John.

Bill and Lou also saw Aunt Clara when she came to Florida to a retirement community. Aunt Clara was my dad's aunt, Grandpa Trippeer's sister-in-law, married to Uncle Will Trippeer. Evidently she was quite a character, she once went to a concert and fell going up the steps to the hall. Blamed God and never went to church again. Lou tells me that she and Bill saw her several times. In Florida, she would call and tell them she was taking them out to lunch. Then she would come and get Bill, Lou, and their two children, Ann and Bob, and take them to a very nice restaurant/bar. There was a rotating bar which she and the children enjoyed tremendously; they rode it all the way around. She had done this so often the fellows working there knew her by name. After the free ride, she would usually get sand dollars for each of the children.

Lou said she was lots of fun and loved children. She was always stirring up something, then she would laugh uproariously. She drove a big car, probably a Buick, which she had to give up when she started to run up on curbs and knock over fire hydrants. Aunt Mary Lynn called Uncle Dick who was Clara's sponsor where she lived, and he told her she had to give up her car. I think she said she was 80 at the time.

When they were all younger, she and Mother were preparing a splendid luncheon for Granny and Grandpa Trippeer's anniversary. Of course there were several guests. They were busy in the kitchen and when the roast was ready one of them brought the good china platter from the dining room. After they had plopped the roast on the platter, they realized that the platter was quite dusty. They dusted carefully around the roast and served it in fine style!

One last story about Aunt Clara: She did a really neat thing when she died. Having no children of their own, she left some money to Mother, but stipulated in her will that if Mother were already dead, the money was to be divided up evenly between us 10 children. I remember when we were notified of this gift. We were in Bangladesh and were both surprised and very pleased that we were remembered in this way.

Assorted Treasures

I hope you like poetry as much as I do. I don't like all of it but I do love some special poems and wanted to share them with you and also some favorite quotes.

"Gratefulness"
– by George Herbert

Thou that hast given so much to me,
Give one thing more, a grateful heart.
See how thy beggar works on thee
By art.
He makes thy gifts occasion more,
And says, If he in this be crossed,
All thou hast given him heretofore
Is lost.
But thou didst reckon, when at first
Thy word our hearts and hands did crave,
What it would come to at the worst
To save.
Perpetual knockings at thy door,
Tears sullying thy transparent rooms,
Gift upon gift, much would have more,
And comes.
This notwithstanding, thou wenst on,
And didst allow us all our noise:
Nay thou hast made a sigh and groan
Thy joys.

Not that thou hast not still above
Much better tunes, than groans can make;
But that these country-airs thy love
Did take.
Wherefore I cry, and cry again;
And in no quiet canst thou be,
Till I a thankful heart obtain
Of thee:
Not thankful, when it pleaseth me;
As if thy blessings had spare days:
But such a heart, whose pulse may be
Thy praise.

Christmas Day, On the *President Cleveland*

"My Eternal King"
– From 17th Century Latin, translated by Rev. Edward Caswall; set to music by Jane Marshall

"My God, I love Thee;
not because I hope for heav'n thereby,
Nor yet because who love Thee not
Must die eternally.

Thou, O my Jesus, Thou didst me
Upon the cross embrace;
For me didst bear the nails, the nails and spear,
And manifold disgrace.

Why, then why, O blessed Jesus Christ,
Should I not love Thee well?
Not for the hope of winning heav'n,
Or of escaping hell;

Not with the hope of gaining aught,
Not seeking a reward;
But as Thyself hast loved me,
O ever-loving Lord!

E'en so I love Thee, and will love,
And in Thy praise will sing;
Solely because Thou art my God,
And my Eternal King."

"The Celestial Surgeon"
– by Robert Louis Stevenson

If I have faltered more or less
In my great task of happiness;
If I have moved among my race
And shown no glorious morning face;
If beams from happy human eyes
Have moved me not; if morning skies,
Books, and my food, and summer rain
Knocked on my sullen heart in vain,
Lord, thy most pointed pleasure take

And stab my spirit broad awake;
Or, Lord, if too obdurate I,
Choose thou, before that spirit die,
A piercing pain, a killing sin,
And to my dead heart run them in!

Virginia, Roanoke College

"Indwelling"
– by T.E.Brown

If thou couldst empty all thyself of self,
Like to a shell dishabited,
Then might He find thee on the Ocean shelf,
And say— "This is not dead,"—
And fill thee with Himself instead.
But thou art all replete with very thou,
And hast such shrewd activity,
That, when He comes, He says:— "This is enow
Unto itself—" Twere better let it be:
It is so small and full, there is no room for Me.

"The Chambered Nautilus"
– by Oliver Wendell Holmes Sr.

This is the ship of pearl, which, poets feign,
  Sails the unshadowed main,—
  The venturous bark that flings
On the sweet summer wind its purpled wings

In gulfs enchanted, where the Siren sings,
   And coral reefs lie bare,
Where the cold sea-maids rise to sun their streaming hair.

Its webs of living gauze no more unfurl;
   Wrecked is the ship of pearl!
   And every chambered cell,
Where its dim dreaming life was wont to dwell,
As the frail tenant shaped his growing shell,
   Before thee lies revealed,—
Its irised ceiling rent, its sunless crypt unsealed!

Year after year beheld the silent toil
   That spread his lustrous coil;
   Still, as the spiral grew,
He left the past year's dwelling for the new,
Stole with soft step its shining archway through,
   Built up its idle door,
Stretched in his last-found home, and knew the old no more.

Thanks for the heavenly message brought by thee,
   Child of the wandering sea,
   Cast from her lap, forlorn!
From thy dead lips a clearer note is born
Than ever Triton blew from wreathèd horn!

While on mine ear it rings,
Through the deep caves of thought I hear a voice that sings.

Build thee more stately mansions, O my soul,
　As the swift seasons roll!
　Leave thy low-vaulted past!
Let each new temple, nobler than the last,
Shut thee from heaven with a dome more vast,
　Till thou at length art free,
Leaving thine outgrown shell by life's unresting sea!

On original sin: "We are not sinners because we commit sinful acts; rather we commit sinful acts because we are sinners...original sin...the sin at the heart of all sin is a refusal to believe, a lack of faith. From this fundamental lack and estrangement from God flow all of the warped and distorted actions we call sin."
Romans 8:19-21; 2 Peter 3:10-13; Revelation 21:1
– Prayer by Richard Foster

"A Monastery Almanac"
– by Joan Chittister

September has a strange and wonderful feeling. It is the best part of the summer and the hardest part of the summer. Just when summer gets perfect—fresh nights, soft sun, casual breezes, crushingly full and quietly cooling trees, empty beaches and free weekends—it ends.

Life is like that, too. Just when we get it right, it starts to change. The job gets easy and we know just how to do it and they tell us we're retired. The children grow up and get reasonable and they leave home just when it's nice to have them around. The days get less full of work but we're older now and too stiff to play. The money we never had enough of to spend on clothes abounds after the mortgage is paid off, but the body has lost the shape for style.

We celebrate the autumn equinox this month—one of only two days of the year in which daytime and nighttime are of exactly equal length. From now on daytime will begin to wane. But there is nothing to fear from this diminishment of the kind of life associated with sunlight. The night times of life have their beauty and their lessons, too.

That's life on the edge of autumn. And that's beautiful. If we have the humility for it. Humility is a natural virtue. It's one of those things that everybody has to get eventually or else die in misery. Diminishment, for instance, is one of the facts of life that breeds humility and diminishment is part of every experience. We get to practice it all our lives. Humility is the survival mechanism of life.

At the end of the War in Bangladesh and in South Africa.
– by St. Francis of Assisi

Lord, make me an instrument of your peace.
Where there is hatred, let me sow love;
Where there is injury, pardon;
Where there is doubt, faith;
Where there is darkness, light;
Where there is sadness, joy.
O Divine Master, grant that I may not
So much seek to be consoled as to console;
To be understood as to understand;
To be loved as to love,
For it is giving that we receive;
It is in pardoning that we are pardoned;
And it is in dying that we are born to eternal life.

At Troy's death
"I'll Walk with God"
– Music by Nicholas Brodzky, lyrics by Paul Francis Webster, 1954

I'll walk with God from this day on
His helping hand I'll lean upon.
This is my prayer, my humble plea,
May the Lord be ever with me.
There is no death tho' eyes grow dim;

There is no fear when I'm near to him.
I'll lean on him forever, and he'll forsake me never.
He will not fail me as long as my faith is strong,
Whatever road I may walk along.
I'll walk with God, I'll take his hand,
I'll talk with God, he'll understand;
I'll pray to him, each day to him
And he'll hear the words that I say.
His grace reveals the paths I've trod;
Now I'll never walk alone while I walk with God.

Two-Part Invention: "The Story of a Marriage"
– by Madeline L'Engle

"Our brokenness can be an instrument for change. Pain received rightly has the power to transform our lives. I look back at my mother's life and I see suffering deepening and strengthening it. In some people I have also seen it destroy. Pain is not always creative; received wrongly, it can lead to alcoholism and madness and suicide. Nevertheless, without it we do not grow."

Gandhi's Seven Deadly Social Sins:

Politics without principle
Wealth without work
Commerce without morality
Pleasure without conscience
Education without character

Science without humanity

Worship without sacrifice

– Proverbs 30:7-9

"Three things I ask of you, O Lord; Do not refuse me before I die.

Keep falsehood and lies far from me; Give me neither poverty nor riches,

But give me only my daily bread. Otherwise I may have too much and disown you and say 'Who is the Lord?'

Or I may become poor and steal, and so dishonor the name of my God."

Ardmore Baptist Church, Winston-Salem, NC
From a sermon by Dr. Frank Tupper, speaking about Phil.3:7-11

"...Shared suffering creates unbreakable bonds of unity. Unshared suffering cuts chasms of separation. Most intense grief is not shared – it leads to alienation.

According to Paul, to know Christ we must share his suffering.

How to share his suffering?

- not the crucifix complex

- must be his suffering, not ours

Points of entry to his suffering:

1: Scandal of the cross as a model for our lives

'Whoever saves his life will lose it and whoever loses his life for my sake will save it.'

2: Must share the real pain of real people

- common pain leads to hope without judgment, but encouragement

3: Give ourselves for the sake of the world

Jesus' suffering began during his life when he was rejected, saw evil, etc.

At the Lord's Supper we must do more than remember, we must embrace his suffering and those who suffer every day. To drink the cup is to take on his suffering and the suffering of the world and make it our own."

"In a High Spiritual Season"
– Sister Joan Chittister

"In the deep of winter we find ourselves face to face with the fragility of life, true, but to leave 'a wild swans footprints' behind us is to leave a memory of beauty, once present and never to be duplicated again."

From Bob Hair

For 2008 when I saw the pictures from the Hubble spacecraft.

When asked how he, a scientist, could explain his

faith in God, his reply was, "I believe God created the world and everything in it. Science just explains how he did it."

Humor:

"The Wise Men were truly wise men. Unlike most men, they stopped to ask for directions."
– an anonymous wife

A man was visiting a nursing home when a lady in a wheelchair spoke to him, "You look like my third husband." He responded, "How many husbands have you had?" She replied, "Two."

"Kiss a toad first thing every morning. Then you can know that nothing worse can happen to you for the rest of the day."
– Twitter

Moving (the emotional aspects)
1- Accept the idea that you are going to move

2- Begin to think about the new place in terms that will affect you, such as: housing, friends, church, schooling, distance from family members, etc.

3- Sort things around the house – throw away old papers and magazines, coupons, ragged cloths that won't make a good dust cloth or packing materials.

4- Sort letters you intended to answer and haven't; those you will, keep and those you won't, throw away.

5- Clean that drawer in the kitchen with odd jar lids, rubber bands, broken measuring spoons, measuring cups from soap and milk cartons and all broken pencils and crayons. Do not let yourself be tempted to keep any of this junk! There will be more where you are going.

6- Have a good cry, preferably with a friend whom you're going to miss most. It wouldn't hurt to visit each of your favorite places, such as a special tree and views not to be equaled in the new location. Feel really bad for about 30 minutes or so.

7- Now you're ready to begin packing – unless you're able to afford those door-to-door movers – in which case you can just enjoy yourself in your old place one last time. You will be tempted to watch them pack to be sure they don't break that crystal bowl from Aunt Ellie or punch a hole in the upholstery. You can do that, but be warned: the packers will act as if you're not there and would be much happier, and maybe more careful, if you weren't. May as well go for a walk.

8- Leave with the sure knowledge that you have been happy in this place, you can be happy in the next. It all depends on you.

(These are words of experience – after 34 moves since we married) - Gram/Marj

www.ingramcontent.com/pod-product-compliance
Lightning Source LLC
Chambersburg PA
CBHW071950110526
44592CB00012B/1046